Design and Visual Communication

I0112903

Bruno Munari

Design
and Visual Communication

contribution to an educational method

INVENTORY PRESS

Originally published by Editori Laterza in 1968 as
Design e comunicazione visiva
contributo a una metodologia didattica

This book originated as a set of roughly fifty lessons on Visual Communication presented at the Carpenter Center for the Visual Arts at Harvard University in Cambridge, Massachusetts, between the beginning of February and the end of May 1967.

The lessons allowed me to experiment with some innovative methods for teaching the building blocks of design and visual language in an ideal setting. The time available was too limited to allow for coverage of every topic within the framework of a single course. But it was adequate to try out a new pedagogical method built not upon antiquated notions of what is beautiful or ugly, but instead upon what is right or wrong according to a shaping concept.[1]

The students in the course were of varied backgrounds and what was perceived as beautiful by a Brazilian wasn't necessarily so by a Chinese peer. Adopting a common "shaping concept," however, it became possible to examine and confirm whether a given solution was correct or incorrect. The notion of beauty was superseded by that of formal coherence.

Another innovation was our use of the most up-to-date instruments: tools that contemporary technology now makes available to visual communicators, so that they no longer need to create manually what can be done better and with greater precision mechanically.

The present book begins with a series of dispatches published in the Milanese newspaper Il giorno, *describing for readers the academic setting within which the course took place. The second half of the book consists in a structured and annotated corpus of illustrative materials that constitute a relatively complete course on visual design. The resulting volume doesn't pretend to be*

5

the definitive treatise on the teaching of visual design. It aims instead to provide a field-tested contribution to the development of a comprehensive course that will, in turn, need further testing and revision.

B.M.

The Carpenter Center for the Visual Arts in Cambridge, USA.

part one LETTERS FROM HARVARD

When it comes to the notion of research on visual communication, Italian art teachers snicker away smugly under their moustaches (which some apparently grow just for that purpose). That's because they already know *everything* about art: they have always known what art is and isn't . . . with absolute certainty. There's little point in arguing with them because that certainty is inborn. In their classrooms they continue to teach the art of the past, no matter how remote, sticking fast to the conveniences of tradition, to keeping their noses clean, to wasting as little time as possible.

What do Italian art school students study? What do they think? They are forced to learn fresco technique. When they graduate (or, better still, even while enrolled), they become aware that the outside world bears little resemblance to art school, that the international art scene is changing in ways that Italian art schools neglect. So, they ditch fresco painting in favor of kinetic art and other contemporary modes of visual communication. In order to inhabit the present century, they have little choice but to become autodidacts thanks to the retrograde approach to teaching.

What good is a model of arts education incapable of training individuals to bring the most advanced technical tools to bear on shaping the world of the near future? Why not teach these new tools and techniques—I take it as a given that art can't simply be "taught"—instead of those of the past? The past never comes back, and even when it is revived (as in the case of Art Nouveau), it becomes the object of play. Accordingly, a model of arts education centered only on the art of the past is useless for a visual practitioner whose job is to operate in the near future.[3] The past can only serve as a source of cultural information anchored in its own era. Otherwise, it becomes illegible.

Today, after two days of polar winds, a light blanket of snow has descended upon the icy streets with some rays of sunlight suddenly breaking through to illuminate my typewriter. I lean out the window and spot a leafless tree profiled against a brick wall. Out another window I observe large groups of students moving between university buildings along white pathways. Some have their coats unbuttoned; others are overly bundled up, wearing balaclavas and odd headgear. Young men and women from all over the world, from warm and cold countries (colder even than this one). They all made their way to this university precisely because here they are entirely free to select a course of study and the teaching is provided by individuals with genuine area expertise. If I had to propose a comparison with Italian institutions, night, craft, and trade schools come to mind: schools where students graduate with solid technical expertise. Because it's not art but technique alone—the latest techniques—that can be taught. Art is either present or absent. Trying to explain art is like trying to explain Zen.

I read the statements submitted by applicants to my course. Without exception, they talk about experimenting with novel forms of visual communication. "I'm interested in unfamiliar expressive means"; "I've played around with light and am intrigued by new methods"; "I want to get to know contemporary technology"; "I went to see *The Projected Image* show at the Boston Institute of Contemporary Art and am convinced that much more can be done";[4] "I think today's artists can make use of computers"; "visual communication interests me—not so much a specific medium as multiple ways of communicating visually. Munari's ideas strike me as different from the ones I've studied and I see value in exploring new approaches"; "I'd like to apply these experiments to my own artistic work involving less the creation of objects than environments"; "I'm interested in current technology"; "I believe that this course will expand my awareness of modes of visual expression"; "I'm a physicist rooted in the scientific disciplines but, at the same time, am interested in the visual arts; I'm taking a course in computer graphics, which I love and would like to explore its artistic potential"; "I've experimented with lights and shifting colors"; "My interests and Mr. Munari's have a lot in common: I want to familiarize myself with new—new to me at least—means of visual communication"; "I want to take this course because I love the playful, experimental character of Italian design, about which I'd like to learn more. I need to design a theater set this spring and believe that this course will be helpful"; "Participating in a large enrollment course, rather than a studio with two or three students, would be great"; "I love working in groups."

This is what young people say and write because they see studio training as the best way to learn the tools of their future trades.[5] They don't envisage art school as a place to cultivate painting or sculpture as a hobby. The methods of visual communication of epochs past often prove inadequate, static, and slow by the standards of today. No one would bother to draw a circle by hand after the invention of the compass: that is, unless they were trying to win a bet or to show off. So, given the tools that are currently available, I don't believe it's necessary to learn to draw what can better be photographed.[6]

SHAPING STUDY PLANS
AROUND INDIVIDUALS
(NOT THE OTHER WAY AROUND)[7]

There are two ways to structure a course of study in an art school: the static and the dynamic.

The first forces individuals to adapt to fixed schemes that are almost always outdated or soon-to-become outdated due to everyday practicalities. The second implies a constantly shifting approach, suited to the needs of individuals and the present challenges they encounter.

Static approaches, with their restrictive, inflexible study plans, prompt a sense of unease and even open rebellion among students. Some students become so persuaded that it's useless to fight for coursework better suited to their actual needs that they soldier on apathetically or even abandon art school. Dynamic approaches are built around a state-of-the-art core program that is modifiable as a function of interests that emerge in the classroom itself. Only at the conclusion of a semester does the shape and evolution of a course assume its definitive form.

Core programs must be developed considering both the principal components of the course and its objectives. The instructor must demonstrate flexibility and responsiveness, shaping each session as a function of the needs that emerge in class and the individuals involved, with the goal of involving everyone in the task of formulating questions on the given topic: in this case, the topic of visual communication.

Visual communication is a vast subject area that encompasses drawing, photography, three-dimensional modeling, and film; abstract and realistic forms, static and moving images, simple and complex ones as well. It extends to questions of visual perception rooted in psychology such as the relationship between figure and ground, camouflage, moiré patterns, optical illusions, illusory motion, mirages, the persistence of vision, and afterimages. It includes every aspect of graphics, from the design of typographical fonts to newspaper page layouts, from exploration of the limits of word legibility to the techniques that facilitate the reading of texts.

All these facets of visual communication share something in common that informs my teaching here: objectivity. Unless an image employed to convey a message is objective, it's unlikely to succeed as an act of visual communication. An image needs to be legible to all and for all in the same key. Otherwise, no visual communication occurs or, for that matter, communication. There's only visual confusion.

Suddenly, small clouds flit across the sky, projecting their shade on everything and constantly altering the intensity of the light. I'm in the campus office I was assigned in Emerson Hall (which houses Physiology, Psychology, and Sociology), and as I write, the light in the room shifts as if someone were entertaining themselves by opening and closing the window.[8] It's time to turn the lights on. The building is completely covered in ivy, so it must be pleasurable to plumb its green geometries in summertime, leaving behind the blinding light.

The opening session of my Visual Studies course was built around an exercise in free-form collage working with materials from a varied set of magazines.[9] The collages helped me gain some insight into each student so that I could address them subsequently in an individualized manner. Without this insight, it would have been impossible to establish a mutual understanding. I then went on to examine the collages and soon arrived at the conclusion that the group was exceptionally heterogenous. Some were struggling with fitting in socially, or with racial challenges; some didn't know quite what to do or were childish; some were already mature from the standpoint of graphics and self-expression. Some of the students worked in groups; others sought out tables in the most distant corners of the room so they could work in isolation. Some worked purposefully and finished up quickly; others used up the full three hours of each class session without overcoming their doubts.

The resulting works varied in genre and format, encompassing everything from pictorial to narrative compositions; some were compact, others scattered and made up of disconnected components.[10] These differences aside, everyone believed that they made some kind of statement.

During the second session students will be asked to present their work with classmates invited to comment on what they see and to reflect on how the images speak to them. By means of these collective deliberations, students' intentions will be put to the test: if the composition is confusing or the presentation is unclear will become evident during a free discussion of the images. I will limit my own role to helping address problems as they arise and to explaining why some solutions are (naturally?) intelligible while others aren't, as well as what is meant by "visual communication" and "objective images." A consensus will emerge around certain images. My task will be to explain how it is that an external image meets up with the mass of images that we carry within us. Each of us is a warehouse of images that derive from our world of experience: a warehouse shaped and accumulated during the entire course of our existences. The images in question are both conscious and unconscious. Some are distant, belonging to our infancy, some proximate. All are tightly bound to, freighted with, emotions.

Objective images, images shared by many, necessarily dialogue with our personal image repositories and the subjective sensations with which such images are associated. This dialogue is the basis upon which one determines which images, forms, and colors to select when communicating information to a given audience.

Much of this visual language is well known but it's important to stay up to date and to rely upon the lessons that individual experimentation provides. As you can well understand, there's no space here for the artist who asserts that "this is the way I see things; if others don't get it, so be it: it's their problem, not mine." An artist's personal image of the world has value only if the act of visual communication, the image's support, is endowed with objective value. Otherwise, we are drawn into a world of more or less secret codes in which messages are exclusively understood by a small circle of individuals: insiders already "in the know."

Everyone knows that when a skilled printer first picks up a new book, they inspect the front and back, run their fingers over the fold of the cover, study the typeface, the layout, and font (is it original or furnished by a secondary supplier?). They critically examine the paper stock, the binding, whether the spine is rounded or squared off, where the text begins on the page, how the margins have been set, paragraph breaks, the numbering system, and so many other details. An ordinary reader, unfamiliar with the complexities of printing, simply scans a book's title and price tag, and then buys and reads it. If you ask them about the book's typeface, they have no insight or interest. There are no points of contact with items absent from their private world of images. Distinctions between typefaces are invisible to them.

To get to know the images that surround us is to expand our potential points of contact with the world. It implies seeing more and understanding more. It's very interesting, for example, to examine the structure of objects, even the structures that make up their surfaces: their so-called texture, which is to say the natural or artificial physicality of a surface established by marks that don't compromise its uniformity. A white sheet of paper is of little interest when smooth. It's of greater interest when rough and even greater interest when this irregularity assumes a structurally recognizable form akin to that, for instance, of the pores of the skin, thereby visually communicating the idea of skin. Cases in point are the skins of animals (from lizards to crocodiles), tree bark, plaster walls, or rusticated cement. Everything that the eye sees has a surface structure of its own and every surface pattern, grain, or pebbling is endowed with a distinct meaning: so much so that a crocodile-textured water glass would be judged anomalous. This principle of animating a surface is well known in the textile industry, where fabrics are said to possess a "hand" —that's the technical term—meaning a particular tactile effect associated with their visually communicative properties. In men's fashion in particular there are many ways to render surfaces interesting by means of uniform weaves.

One of the foundational exercises in any core program in Visual Design is the study of surfaces for the obvious reason that every image that a visual designer sets out to develop for purposes of communication will require a support. I say this because it's not just form that one must study but also . . . appearance. The point is worth underscoring.

Apologies in advance for another digression on American life but I have something funny to share with you. Here in Cambridge, I'm living in a room on the top floor of a three-story building that serves as the Faculty Club. My room is small but warm and comfortable. Above me, between the ceiling and the slate-covered roof, resides a

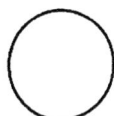

ORANGE

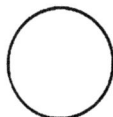

APPLE

BALL

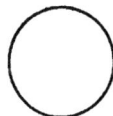

MOON

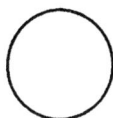

WOODEN SPHERE

squirrel whom I've never actually met but whose gnawing can be overheard, especially at night. If you've been in the United States, you know that fresh fruit is never served in restaurants; (at most, one encounters fruit salads, not always of the freshest sort). But I wanted some fresh fruit, so I headed over to a supermarket where I bought some lovely apples. Only two of us were in residence at the Faculty Club at the time because it was a holiday and even the security guard was absent. It was just me and the squirrel, each of us nibbling on fruit: me, seated in an armchair with my apple, the squirrel perched somewhere. I could hear but couldn't see him.

To enhance their awareness of the communicative power of surfaces students were invited to transform an ordinary, inert blank sheet of paper by every means and with every creative tool at their disposal.[12] In so doing they were asked to modify the surface while respecting its uniformity, which is to say, without creating artistic compositions. Why? Because it's devilishly difficult to delimit a problem. To gain true understanding it's necessary to more deeply probe precisely those questions that youthful enthusiasm will initially dismiss as readily surmountable. Large numbers of exercises need to be carried out to tackle the most narrowly framed questions. Students, on the contrary, always want to rush into developing full-blown projects, just as they want to drive a car or play an instrument right off the bat. In our initial collage exercise, everyone

ORANGE

APPLE

BALL

MOON

WOODEN
SPHERE

immediately set about cutting up magazines and pasting them into mysterious
assemblages: assemblages in which some
students, despite being unsure about
what they wanted to say, ended up
communicating their mood. This time
things were different. The effort to
develop an awareness of a surface's
properties without expressing anything in particular proved disorienting.
Solutions included covering the surface
with dots or signs, scraping the paper
on the ground, wetting it down, applying fingerprints or varied rubber stamps,
folding the sheet into recurring patterns, and making black markings with
sponges. Some students just looked on
and seemed puzzled. After some initial
experiments, a few simply departed.

TEXTURES[13]

The students enrolled in my Visual
Studies class filled many sheets of
paper with textures, which is to say,
they rendered a plane surface expressive while respecting its uniformity.
Each student approached the exercise
with their own distinctive sensibility.
Some made use of tiny pencil marks,
others of broad strokes executed with
pastels. Some roughed up the surface with sandpaper to render it more
absorbent and then applied a coat of
black dust; others created lattices with
subtle, uniform folds using white, gray,
or black sheets of paper.

No longer anonymous because of
their enhanced materiality, these uniform surfaces can be further animated

by condensing or extending the resulting textures, even to the point of giving rise to recognizable figures. A physical phenomenon exists that aptly demonstrates this passage from a uniform surface to a surface pulsing with figures: the way in which iron filings respond to sound waves. If you scatter iron filings evenly over a square plate of sheet metal of about thirty centimeters per side and run the bow of a violin along one edge as if you were playing the violin (in effect, rubbing the edge like strings), the iron filings arrange themselves into geometries that are determined by the acoustical vibrations. As it becomes denser, the material of the texture begins to form images while what we perceive as the backdrop becomes ever more rarified.

In short, by adding density to various textures one can begin to develop figures that, though initially indefinite in character, take on well-defined contours to the point of becoming precise geometric figures. Adopting this approach, every student was asked to draw what they wished so that they could experience in person how an image gradually emerges out of the fog and assumes precise contours. For those familiar with geometrical textures, a case in point is how the repeated insertion of intermediary one-millimeter points within a grid originally formed by one-millimeter points separated by one-centimeter decreases the gaps, eventually giving rise to a dense black mass made up of points.

The same procedure can be extended to linear surfaces by means

of the repeated addition of lines each inscribed into the target locations of an existing grid.

Exploring the degree of a figure's visibility as a function of the distance between eye and image is one of the most interesting experiments available to us. This is something that deeply engaged the attention of Divisionist painters whose figures often become visible only at a certain distance, whereas viewed from close up their paintings appear as little more than scatterings of formless marks.[14] Likewise there are certain drawings by [Saul] Steinberg executed on graph paper (in other words, on a surface that a graphic intervention has already rendered expressive) in which some adroitly drawn additions lead us to perceive the grid as a cage containing a bird. Such cases will be dealt with later when we grapple with the question of double images, not to mention figure-ground relations, relations within figures themselves, and the like.

Since we are talking points and lines, which is to say *connections*, a black mark on these specialized modes of training is the disconnect between students who graduate knowing everything about visual communication and employers unaware that such a subject matter even exists. As students enter the real world and interact with industry leaders and managers, they sometimes face an insuperable hurdle. If we autodidacts who have developed a knowledge of visual communication by means of sustained thought and study, teach such skills to students, then there's also a

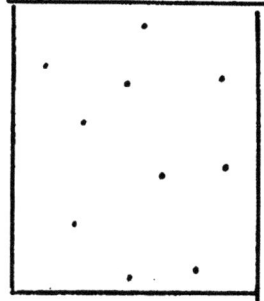

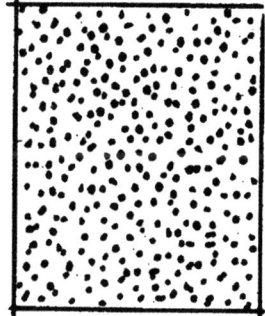

need to establish schools for employers to insure a meeting of minds. Many industrialists establish in-house consultancies on visual communication which they confuse with advertising, public relations, image management, and hostesses. When they themselves were students, such a domain of study simply didn't exist (any more than did psychology which many confuse with psychoanalysis). Now they are well-established figures and can't be retrained. They already know everything they need to know and consider the rest nonsense. This helps to explain why so many forms of visual communication today are so poorly executed: from street signs and advertisements to the page layouts of periodicals and the design of objects. Because it's so hard to obtain solid statistics on the success or failure of public relations campaigns, everything is ultimately all the same. Vietnam, the latest battle in the war between miniskirts and longhairs, a hit single: these are the highs and lows that characterize today's distractable world of visual communications.

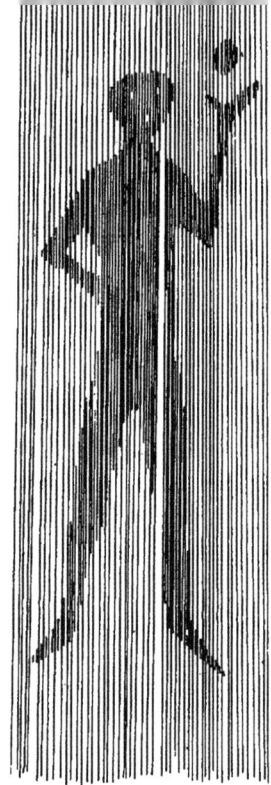

OPTICAL ILLUSIONS[15]

The United States is truly an advanced country: the entire US—not just New York as I once believed. By comparison, we Italians are a bunch of simpletons who address problems in a rudimentary manner and prove clueless when immersed in a more advanced civilization. What do we do when we are hot, for example?

We open the window. Such a primitive solution! Here in America, one *never* opens windows. The window in my room is painted shut precisely because it was never opened to begin with. Every now and then, it is repainted white to ensure that it can no longer move up or down. My room is heated with an old-school heater. But when it's too hot—as I noted earlier, the weather changes often and we've had some lovely days recently— all you have to do is to turn on the air conditioning and set it to the proper temperature. Without ever opening a window, the temperature cools in an instant. I asked a local and it appears that it is just as hot here during the summer as it is cold during the winter, which explains the presence of air conditioning in my room. Perhaps you have noticed that the air produced by air conditioners has a distinctive odor: it smells of motors, lubricants, dry metals. It's the same smell as automotive heating systems which, after a while, becomes intolerable. Up in the transom over my door, however, there's another device: an electric fan that serves as an air exchanger. All you have to do is push a nearby button and the affected air goes away. The rumbling of the air conditioner is just about masked by that of the big electric fan. The radiator is silent. One has the feeling of being in an airplane close to the engines. The room is small, as already noted, but filled with amenities. I can turn the bathtub on to create a new soundtrack that also provides some additional humidity. Or I can wet down the heavy

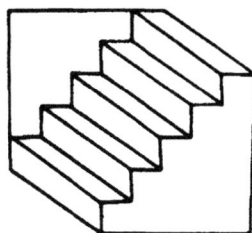

Stairway or cupboard under the stairway?

terry cloth bathmat and hang it on the edge of the tub to further increase the amount of evaporation. I can even dip a towel in water and hang it off the towel rack on the side of the sink. Outside in the streets firetrucks are forever going to and fro, while in the skies I hear the occasional rumble of jet engines. I shut down all the machinery and head out to breathe some real air.

At the Carpenter Center, the students in my Visual Studies course are experimenting with figure-ground relationships: with the correlation that often exists between a geometrical or non-geometrical figure and the background against which it appears.[16] You can gain an understanding of this problem by calling to mind a noted illustration of how our perceptual system processes two equivalent images: one consists in a white vase viewed against a black backdrop; the other in two human profiles, facing one another against a white background.[17] In this example, the background can either serve as the figure, or the figures as a background. It's black in one case, white in the other.

This fact is of considerable importance to the study of visual communication because designers must always develop images as a function of the settings within which they appear. They need to know that the figures they devise aren't open to alternative interpretations. Or, on the contrary, they may decide to deliberately exploit ambivalence such that the negative of an image—to use a photographic analogy—makes the decisive contribution

Negative-positives

to an act of visual communication.[18] In such cases, it's easy to fall into the trap of commonplace notions like the assumption that all figures stand out against their backgrounds. But this isn't always the case. Be that as it may, one works best when one has an adequate understanding of a question.

Figure-ground effects are underscored in certain works of abstract art precisely because optical ambiguity gives greater weight to the pictorial work.[19] Most, if not all, works of Op art rely upon precisely this effect: a surface with white and black lines has no background or, rather, alternates between white and black, thereby giving rise to a distinctive optical vibration. The earliest abstract paintings (by Kandinsky, for example) consist in still lives of unrecognizable objects floating in a nebulous atmosphere that serves as a backdrop. Here color performs a static role: there are colors in front and colors in back, each fixed in their location. When figure-ground effects come into play instead, colors (or white and black) shuttle back and forth between the object and the viewer, giving rise to a novel effect.

This exercise can be completed by exploring the negative zones that surround any image. The student places a transparency over an illustration and starts covering over all the negative areas such that, removing the transparency, they capture precisely what was behind the figure. The same operation can be executed with a camera but, when done manually, it has even greater value given that students are able to

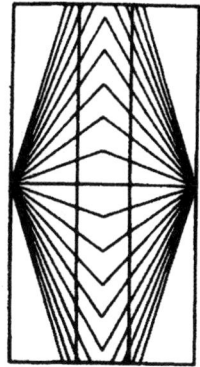

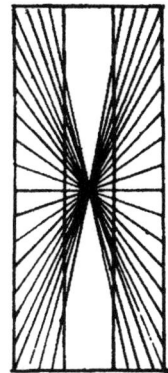

The vertical lines above are parallel

produce something in black and white that is endowed with the same value as a positive or negative. In a second phase they can even rework their treatments to either increase or decrease this visual effect.

I called a carpenter to unstick the window of my room. It only opens ten centimeters but makes no noise.

REAR-GUARD AVANT-GARDE RESEARCH[20]

Let's talk a bit more about Advanced Explorations in Visual Communication. As the course title suggests, my seminar is dedicated to considering advancements in visual communication.[21] The term "advanced" here doesn't refer to items left over from past explorations. Rather it refers to ones that lie ahead: that are "avant-garde" (even though that's a label that no longer makes any sense). I was invited to Harvard to teach this specific course.

So, it's probably a good time to clear up the matter of "avant-gardism." In Italy avant-garde art is frequently spoken about with the understanding that avant-garde refers to art derived from aesthetic principles that sets out to revolutionize everything that came before. Artistic avant-gardes made good sense in the 1930s. To speak of avant-gardes today, especially in a subjective sense, makes little sense except, perhaps, for a small circle of initiates. The ways of thinking and acting that were characteristic of the historical avant-gardes are useless today. The phrase itself, with its

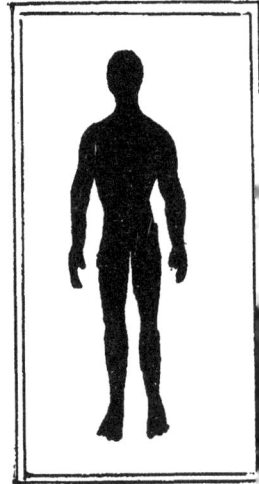

MAN

Rear guard

26

futurist-fascist resonances, summons up romantic heroics.

Today, on the contrary, we pursue research: *visual research*, to be precise. The difference between avant-gardism and research is that the former is subjective in inspiration and the latter propelled forward by technical considerations. The latter's point of departure is the pursuit of expressive efficacy from the standpoint of visual communication irrespective of informational content or aesthetic canons, whether past or future.

I should add that the sort of research into cinematic language currently underway at the Monte Olimpino film studio, though neglected in Italy (as is so often the case), can here be appreciated in its proper light.[22] In all my travels I've encountered no equivalent: an organization that pursues visual research with rigorous methods, firmly grounded in all the constituent parts of a visual language—in this case, that of the cinema. Today one encounters all the conventional expressions of avant-gardism, but few of this kind. The pattern has become familiar: anything born in Italy is dismissed as imitative of work in other countries where smarter people reside. It's as if we Italians were still living the era of the great Capitals of Art (cities that have long had little to offer). Another case in point is the *Programmed Art* exhibition organized by Olivetti in 1962, which subsequently toured American university campuses. It made a big splash everywhere except Italy. Barely a mention in the press despite

MAN

Avant-garde

drawing nearly seventy thousand visitors.[23] Eventually, the major national venues became interested, but belatedly (and not without skepticism).

One of the primary materials we are exploring in my seminar is artificial light: in particular, the ways in which, in the process of interacting with artificial light, materials can transform ordinary light into a complex means of visual communication.[24] Artificial lighting has made it possible for human beings to inhabit a second world and expand their potential range of knowledge. Artificial lighting accounts for half of our existences today. Visual information reaches us via television sets in our homes. Enormous luminous billboards light the major avenues of cities. Even in Italy, street signs are now increasingly illuminated both day and night. It's light that allows for the exploration of the worlds opened up by microscopes. The cinema and many forms of contemporary art come alive thanks to lighting.

Light comes from multiple sources, from incandescent to fluorescent to neon to sodium vapor lamps to black lights. How can this medium be used for purposes of visual communication? What are the physical characteristics of various types of light? What are their uses? How do they interact with different plastics in different settings?

At present, the electric signage that abounds in major cities was entrusted to electricians or technicians without the needed cultural training with only rare exceptions. They craft trite figures with electric signage completely unaware of the power of the medium in which they are working.

Our initial experiments conducted in the classroom involved the study of how materials can render light beams expressive. The students engaged in these experiments with genuine gusto: experiments that allowed them to view the results of their work right away on any scale. Three projectors were pointed at the walls of a white room with little natural light so that a continuous parade of enlarged projections could be seen in the three luminous zones. The projections documented student experiments involving the manipulation and animation of transparent colored plastic materials cut up into small pieces. They also involved chemical or physical processes that explore the degree to which these materials can serve as effective tools for visual communication.

In and of itself, colored light—a green or red light, for instance—isn't useful for purposes of visual communication. The eye won't linger over a flat surface illuminated with colored light. The manipulation of transparent colored plastic materials animates such surfaces not unlike the manner in which Seurat's pointillist techniques animate the surface of a canvas. What were once referred to as "pictorial materials" but are here referred to as "textures," can be explored in all their variety by studying the transformations that light beams undergo as they traverse these media, these transmutations of plastic. When they reach the screen (or white wall), they abound in details that alter the light itself (not unlike the way that the skin's pores elicit visual interest whereas the skins of shop window mannequins don't).

"If you don't like the weather, wait five minutes." That's how they reassure you around here that more congenial weather is just around the corner. In the mean-time, the snow from a few days ago is melting into pools of water and rivulets are coursing down city streets. Ambling about is like finding oneself inside a giant dish of melting ice cream, with large chunks of snow that had remained attached to tree branches thanks to the chill of night falling around you. Care is required because there are lots of trees and one of these missiles could easily land on your neck. I headed over to the Harvard Coop where I bought an umbrella that turned out to be "made in Italy." In the meantime, the temperature rose and, even though the Charles River remains covered in ice, the sun is hot. Boston is at the same latitude as Rome.

The students in my Visual Studies course are learning about elementary structures. After becoming familiar with textures, which is to say with black-and-white and color surfaces, they are now going to study how such tex-tures relate to structures. Everything in the world we inhabit is (or appears to be) governed by structures. The structures in question are actually four-dimensional given that the forms that things assume are always undergoing constant change. Think of the seed of a plant and its cyclical transformation into a tree that flowers and bears fruit, thereby producing seeds. Everything transforms itself: sometimes visibly, as in the case of plants; sometimes over centuries, as in the case of minerals; sometimes in an instant, as in the case of an electrical spark. For present purposes, we are leaving aside this fourth dimension to concentrate instead on the three dimensions of width, length, and height. We will begin with two dimensional structures that can be drawn on sheets of paper: structures that are best thought of as the visible surface of three-dimensional structures.

Some will object that not all things in nature possess a structure and that chance agglomerations and assemblages exist as well. I would respond by citing from memory Einstein's dictum that "chance is how we describe phenomena whose laws we don't currently understand."[26] The microscope has shown us how many features of the world that once seemed random (because they were invisible to the naked eye) are instead highly structured. Likewise, electronic microscopes have transported us ever deeper into the world of matter, exposing more structures still. That's because structures—such is my conviction—embody an equilibrium of forces. As an ancient Chinese saying puts it, because everything in nature is an equilibrium of forces, everything is structured.[27] Under a microscope, even a mass of snow that, at first glance, looks like amorphous mush, reveals the beautiful and varied hexagonal crystals of which it is composed.

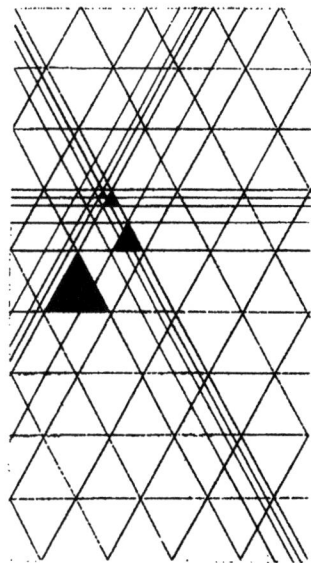

Modules and submodules

Accordingly, we can't necessarily trust what we see with our eyes. The eye is an imperfect instrument that provides a limited understanding of the natural world. What are the students in my Visual Studies course doing in the meantime? They are drawing grids on sheets of paper into which they will subsequently insert three separate geometrical shapes. Tracing grids on a flat surface is the simplest, most basic way to generate structures. It divides a two-dimensional space into equal parts, allowing that space to accommodate a multitude of forms built upon the lines that compose the grid. Whereas it's always difficult to establish the boundaries of a shape in the absence of a grid, a gridded surface provides a firm feeling for the overall surface and, as a result, inspires greater confidence when it comes to positioning and understanding the relationships between different elements on a page.

An analogy with music comes to mind. Music might seem like the freest of the arts. But it's reliant on rigid temporal modules that in no way limit its expressivity. As was demonstrated in the student work from our prior class meeting, shapes emerge in the process of densifying textures. For the moment, let's limit ourselves to the three most elementary shapes: the circle, square, and triangle. The design of our visual experiments reflects the fact that, as is widely known, all other shapes derive from these three.

We start by inscribing right-angled shapes into a rectangular grid. Next, we work with triangular shapes. Round shapes have been excluded because they don't truly exist: it's a given that the maximum packing of spheres assumes the form of a tetrahedron and the maximum accumulation of disks on a single plane tangent to a circle assumes the form of a triangle.[28] Therefore, the two shapes from which all others derive are the square and triangle, as regards two dimensions, and the cube and tetrahedron, as regards three.[29]

At the end of the last class meeting, I told my students that their homework assignment was to draw 50 four-centimeter black squares, 100 two-centimeter squares, and 200 one-centimeter squares. They complained about the workload. Once I explained that it would have taken far longer to draw the squares one by one and then color them in, they understood that our process was an unconventional one. This made me realize that we hadn't yet made use of paint brushes. Instead of drawing and painting a shape, it's far simpler to cut out a shape and move it around a surface, particularly when a one-centimeter adjustment would require completely redrawing and repainting it. This method of composing by shifting components around until a visual equilibrium is achieved and the compositional materials can be affixed to a support is well known to graphic designers.

A female student protested: "we've never done experiments of this sort before. I'm not sure I really understand what we're up to . . . but I love the course."

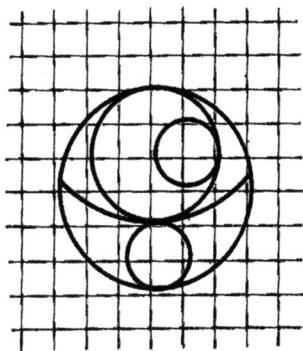

Circles traced within a grid

I stopped in at the Harvard Square newsstand and bought five nice red apples (on the heels of my discovery that, for reasons that continue to elude me, fresh fruit is eaten not in restaurants but in seclusion).[31] Walking by the pharmacy on my way back, I remembered that I needed to buy some postcards. So, I went in and bought postcards and a roll of film for my camera. There I spotted an attractive alarm clock which I bought as well. If you need an excellent wool scarf—it's still cold outside—you can find one at a store on Brattle Street whose window display showcases plastic buckets and hardware, but where you can also purchase stamps for picture postcards.

Just because in Italy one purchases apples from a fruit vendor (who, at most, will wrap them up in newspaper) and alarm clocks at a watchmaker's shop, doesn't mean this is true elsewhere in the world. One needs to adopt a flexible mindset, quickly adapting to every setting in which one resides for any extended period. Soon enough, everything begins to feel normal and one could even end up marveling at the fact that the ticket booth for the Cambridge-Boston subway doesn't also sell hippopotamuses.

Designers particularly need to cultivate such mental flexibility (I have graphic designers in mind). What's the proper tool to shape a particular kind of visual communication? Some might jump to the conclusion that drawing = pencils. Or magic markers or pastels or chalk or charcoal (like that used in traditional art schools to the point that, at the end of every day, a bath was required to remove all the charcoal residue from one's body).[32]

A point of clarification: the kind of drawing we are talking about here doesn't involve the realistic or non-realistic representation of recognizable objects. Every drawing is composed of signs and it is these signs that endow a drawing with expressivity.[33] We possess signs to write and signs to draw. The signs we employ for purposes of writing in our native tongue don't necessarily have communicative value. You can write with a ballpoint pen, a typewriter, a pencil or a house painter's paintbrush, or a can of spray paint. What's important is the legibility of written words.

Painters, draftsmen, anyone and everyone involved in visual communication by means of drawings, is concerned with the expressive powers of signs. Rendering signs expressive means endowing them with visible graphic attributes, dematerializing standard usage in order to imbue the altered sign with its own distinctive personality. As a case in point consider the contrast between a wool thread and a steel wire as graphical elements. Fundamentally different in their materiality and structure, they yield divergent visual messages as a function of their divergent natures.

So how do you render a sign expressive? Making use of different tools on paper or other supports. A sign made with a drawing pen is cold and mechanical, less so when drawn by hand with a ballpoint pen. Switch to a calligrapher's pen and the line becomes increasingly varied and even more expressive if the chosen support is textured paper. Drawn in pastels on a rough paper surface it's even more expressive. And so on and so forth.

Designers are entirely free to select the right materials and tools in their pursuit of expressivity. They can develop a wide array of solutions for adoption in the proper context. Without excluding other means and materials, they can mark up a sheet of transparent plastic and photograph it. They can etch signs into a black film-strip and print them as negatives. They can trace forms with a light beam on a photographic plate. They can generate a humdrum sign and then transmute it on a Xerox machine. With a range of tools extending from pencils to sponges, they can manually gener-ate variegated marks, either directly on paper or indirectly via carbon copies and the like. Think of Rouault's dark, ponderous marks; the fluidity of Matisse; the nervous vibrancy of Ben Shahn; the marks generated by means of the alternation of thick and thin emulsions in some Miró lithographs; the marks of a Grosz; Pollock's swirls of dripped color; the variety of marks characteristic of Klee; the luminous signs found in kinetic and programmed artworks;[34] the tracings of light found in Wood;[35] Boriani's phosphorescent surfaces;[36] the contrails left by jets in the skies . . . By means of this exercise, graphic designers can become aware of all the possible variations of a given sign and of how to select the right solution for the right context. Another useful exercise is to group these solutions into loose but well-defined clusters on the basis of their shared graphical attributes: to find, in other words, a way to build up blocks of images that have been freely structured according to a given sign.

Once they overcame their initial burst of enthusiasm and desire to try, do, and learn everything all at once, the students in my advanced research course on visual communication have worked hard. They have done so both successfully and methodically.

The pursuit of expressive artistic and visual effects via the use of the colored plastic materials selected as a function of their transparency continues to yield interesting outcomes. The projected colors that result from the handling of these materials and the resulting textures possess an optical vibrancy that reflects the methods employed. Unlike the case of lighting gels in the theater, here the light itself undergoes transformation; it becomes a sort of "light-material."[38] In many "avant-garde" kinetic art works that make use of light, light is exclusively understood as a physical phenomenon, not as a visual language. The same approach characterizes the Museum of Science and Technology where, once again, it's the physics alone that is communicated.[39] Now that this sort of kinetic art is becoming better known in America as well, the situation remains the same. Few are the objects that go beyond demonstrations of the physics of light that engaged the artist's interest. Admittedly, it's difficult for art critics to stay up to date on these developments or to distinguish meaningful work from mere illustrations: that's because there's no connection here to traditional forms of art or craft and technical knowledge is required in order to judge when an act of visual communication transcends the mere physics of projection. Most art critics stay mum on the subject for this very reason.

After this exercise using transparent materials to render light-materials communicative, my students have dedicated themselves to a methodical study of the available effects with the aim of amassing a catalog of possibilities. Each student has their own box filled with slides prepared with varying techniques and experimental methods; each is developing a visual language in concert with these tools.[40]

The Polaroid Corporation, a company headquartered in Cambridge, sent us an expert, Mr. John McCann, to lecture the students on the nature of polarized light.[41] Only by understanding its physics can students achieve good results. He explained in what it consists, the nature of light itself, how light waves are filtered by Polaroids, the varieties of plastics that can be employed to alter light, principles of reflection, and all those additional attributes of light that I can't go into here but are summed up in any good encyclopedia.[42]

After the lecture, students learned how to generate the full spectrum of colors by sandwiching colorless, transparent plastic materials in between polaroids.[43] Let me explain this experiment for the benefit of readers. Polaroids are a form of thin plastic sheeting normally used in the manufacture of sunglasses. Usually medium gray, the variant used in sunglasses is olive colored. Applications in industry, research, and science are many. Polaroids can be employed to make transparent plastic models that allow for the study of the internal stresses that an object will endure because, when overlaid, they reveal inner tension lines. Polaroids replace the old Nichols prisms once used to study crystals and in optics labs.[44] They eliminate reflections when placed before camera lenses.

If you sandwich a pane of cellophane from a pack of cigarettes between two Polaroid disks and look at it against the light, the once clear cellophane appears in a variety of colors. If you slowly rotate one of the two disks, the colors shift until they become complementaries. Such is the elementary physical phenomenon under study. Some questions arise: how many colorless plastics are capable of generating colors? Which colors do they produce? How can they be employed? How does the color vary? Is it possible to generate color gradients or geometrical effects? What's the proper angle at which to hold a plastic sheet to obtain the desired color? How can all of this become integrated into information-rich or expressive forms of visual communication? How can these materials be manipulated to render light communicative? What textures can be created? What happens to the color? Does the material behave the same when melted down?

Once again, given that this is the first time that this medium is being used for purposes of visual communication, competent use presupposes a complete and precise understanding. What applications might this sort of medium have for purposes of visual communication? It goes without saying that every means of visual communication must be employed in accordance with its characteristics and affordances. It's a mistake to approach literary works as if they were oil paintings, philosophical treatises as if they were sculptures, plays as if they were films, visual artworks as if they were works of literature, and so on and so forth. Such operations aren't impossible: you can till a field by dragging a plough behind a gold Cadillac sedan but there's a mismatch. I remain persuaded that it's better to use tools that are well suited to a given application. So, what sorts of opportunities does the medium of polarized light offer us?

First and foremost, the ability to explore colors in their natural state, colors extracted from white light itself, and variations on these very colors. No other medium allows me to so effortlessly generate a composition—let's refer to it as such—that visibly changes colors and encompasses the full range of color including complementary colors. The same effect can be achieved by means of an animated film or a cartoon, but with so much more effort and so much less precision!

ACTING WITHOUT THINKING[45]

Harvard students have their own distinctive mode of dress. The commonalities become apparent when one studies groups of students exiting various schools and strolling along the campus's tree- and snowbank-lined footpaths. Despite the variability of tastes in fashion, individual whims, the randomness of what was ready at hand when each student woke up that morning, and an overall lack of fashion consciousness, one item is frequent: white pants.

White pants on both men and women, generally so tight as to form pleats behind the knee. How do you tell the men from the women? The women generally fill out the pants more fully, particularly in the upper portions.

Not everyone is wearing white pants. Some are wearing blue; others sport fabrics so faded that the color is elusive. In all cases the pocket area is distended due to the fact that whatever you stuff into the pockets of a tight pair of pants will necessarily stick out.

Their shoes are either snow boots or, sometimes, tennis shoes. Tennis shoes are so ubiquitous that Jannacci's famous song *He Wore Tennis Shoes* (*El portava i scarp del tennis*) wouldn't make sense.[46] Some wear black or colored rubber boots with buckles of the sort found on suitcases which they leave unbuckled, thereby emitting rattling sounds as they walk, not unlike those of the bell collars worn by horses pulling stagecoaches. Their socks are either white or black, but always matched. It seems that the absolute freedom they enjoy disallows mismatched socks.

Wool sweaters or pullovers are worn under a shirt. And the shirt—tartan patterned, with giant flowers, white or colored and striped—is worn over the pants, never tucked in. Some also don ties. But those who do carry them in a hand, throw them around their necks like scarves, or stuff them into a pocket. Ties are "worn" but it doesn't quite matter how.

When the temperatures drop one encounters other garments: shearling sheepskin coats, heavy overcoats of the sort worn by Hungarian soldiers, peacoats, bearskin overcoats (mostly worn by women), oversize low-hanging brightly colored pullovers, black scarves long enough to wind around an entire person, plaid blankets, windbreakers and ski jackets, etcetera. The headwear includes wool berets, nothing at all, gray top hats, bowler hats, cyclist caps, motorcycle helmets, and military berets.

The occasional student committed to pursuing originality at all costs shows up in class dressed in gray, wearing a tucked-in white shirt, a proper tie, a standard overcoat, and a felt cap.

Everyone dresses as they please. They are free to choose from the clothes they have at their disposal in their dorm rooms. Individualism is respected and, as a matter of fact, one never feels ill at ease among individuals dressed in this manner.

The students in my course on Visual Studies, each expressing his or her personality, tackled the assignment at hand: a free composition involving a space modulated by means of square modules. They brought their black cardboard squares with them and are now distributing them within the compositional space. I told them not to start with an "idea" for the composition but to act first and think later. This is something I repeat often. Preconceived ideas get you into trouble. Let's imagine that you are determined to create a form that simply doesn't fit within a rectangular grid. You will end up expending an enormous effort with a dubious outcome. There's no point in shackling yourself to an idea, in approaching a project as if it were the drawing of a city square or thematic painting. On the contrary, it's essential to explore the possibilities of a modulated space, to see what sorts of shapes arise within square modules and how they interconnect. Acting first and thinking later means relying upon intuition instead of reason. It means allowing oneself to randomly distribute shapes, form groupings, to divide them up, alter them, cluster them, make new juxtapositions, alter them anew, regroup them, move them around, rotate them, turn the sheet over, alter it again . . . until the combined forms that have gradually emerged themselves dictate how the composition is best completed.

Only as such can one truly understand quadrilateral grids and what they offer, always keeping in mind the well-established principle that every tool is endowed with its own optimal, spontaneous, natural powers; powers that give rise to logical forms that satisfy us in ways that only simple and natural things, things that haven't been laboriously contrived, can. Even though rectangular grids tend to dominate and the only options available were two submodules and diagonals, every student created an original piece of work. Some relied on symmetries, others on gradations in value; some developed rhythmic compositions, others played with the balance between white and black squares. Other solutions hinged on the interplay between negatives and positives: both the black and white shapes were treated alike and made capable of serving alternately as figure or ground.

During our three-hour class, students are always welcome to get up and have a look at what their peers are doing. The experience of learning is collective and the resulting images prompt the creation of other images still. There's no place for worrying about plagiarism here. There's no need for cries of "He copied me!" in a setting in which everyone is free to act according to their temperament which, as observed in the case of dress, varies from person to person.

UNINVITED GUESTS[47]

There's always a secret visitor or two infiltrating my classes on light as a medium of visual communication. Sometimes students bring along their friends to share what they are studying. Given that everything appears simple, some guests ask to try out the lighting effects. I let them do so. Likewise, the apparent simplicity of certain visual effects initially excited my students' imaginations but now they are seriously committed to gaining an in-depth understanding how one can achieve more than random effects.

Two visitors showed up at my last class and observed everything with great interest. The lights in the room were dimmed. Four projectors were pointed at walls on which individual students projected their slides. Two of the projectors displayed images sized at about one square meter each on a white wall. Another vastly enlarged the image of a slide with fixed colors on an oversized screen while, via a fourth projector, a dynamic slide with moving colors and polarized light was superimposed onto the dark areas. The aim was to amalgamate two images: the complementary fixed colors of the static slide with the mobile colors of the dynamic slide. The projections came and went quickly but were sustained long enough to control the resulting effects. The projectionists alternated just as quickly as did the images. There was a great deal of animation in the room.

My two uninvited guests studied the effects carefully, noting down how they were being achieved. The later asked to speak to the "professor." They were the organizers of an event for young people to be held in Boston in a locale known as the Discotheque, a place not unlike what is known in Italy as a Piper Club.[48]

They wished to invite me and my students to visit their facility. Given that the décor was entirely based upon projectors, they even offered to have my students, if so inclined, exhibit their slides at the venue.

A few evenings later we stopped in.

The hall was an enormous space, roughly twenty by twenty meters. Crisscrossed by beams, the ten-meter-high ceiling was black; the floors were wooden and the walls white. At one end of the room there was a seating area for members of the audience who wanted to watch the performance; at the other end there was a meter-high stage for the musicians. Hundreds of young people gathered in between. The club was in an abandoned synagogue in an outlying Boston neighborhood.[49] The band played loudly, the young people came alive, ten projectors projected images on the walls that alternated quickly. A movie camera played a film loop in slow motion over and over (loops are sequences that have been arbitrarily selected, scratched up, and recut). Another film was projected at random onto ever shifting surfaces; it contained advertising clips from the movies and television which appeared ludicrous in this setting. Two large spotlights mounted on the walls were connected to the drum kit; they flickered on and off to the tempo of the music, alongside the projections. Stroboscopic lights were pointed at the dancers, transforming their movements into a multitude of discrete film sequences. Blue, red, and yellow lights on random timers flashed on and off behind a semi opaque curtain hanging from the ceiling.[50]

Above this array of lights, a high-powered projector cast a fifty-centimeter beam of light around the room and across the dancers at the whim of an audience member.

Taken together, layered one on top of the next, moving about the walls, all these effects, including the powerful projector that sometimes followed the beat of the music, still left the venue dark enough that, if you lit a match, it would have been noticed. The combination of light and sound, the looseness of the mix, the overall effect, in short, proved quite monotonous: so much so that one was led to reflect on how difficult it is to vary an overall effect that, being the sum total of every possible effect, breeds uniformity. An observation: young people are clearly seeking something different when it comes to these sorts of environments. Once upon a time, temporary wall decorations in the form of theater flats were employed (as I believe they still are when dances are staged at the Press Club in Rho).[51] Likewise clubs and societies adopted a classical or modern style, opting for all dark-polished wood, rough wood, or cloth interiors. The resulting premises, however, became static once they have been completed. The embrace of mutable decorations allows instead for constant scene changes at greatly reduced cost and effort. The venue, thus, needs to be neutral and the décor consists exclusively in projections. As is the case with all new phenomena, once discovered, they tend to be employed indiscriminately and in a random manner instead of prompting patient, in-depth exploration.

For the moment it's clear that a deeper knowledge of how to animate these sorts of spaces isn't considered urgent.

STRUCTURES[52]

As everyone in Italy knows, tetrahedra are filled with milk.[53] They consist in packages made from plasticized or paraffin-covered cardboard in the shape of a pyramid whose base is an equilateral triangle. Four equilateral triangles joined together compose the overall form. The resulting object is hard to carry, all the more so given that, when you grab one by its vertex, it feels like you are grabbing something by the ear. This said, there's no way to tip it over (just like the cube and the sphere, unless the instructions suggest otherwise). Every side of a tetrahedron can, in fact, serve as its base.

What is surprising about this object made from four equilateral triangles is that it's fabricated from a tube.[54] This suggests that, for technical and industrial reasons, tetrahedral shapes are one of the ideal ways to package liquids. Everything can be done mechanically and only two welds are required to complete the object. This packaging solution has required, in turn, the development of custom containers that can accommodate the packing together of large numbers of tetrahedra in ways that respect their geometry. Such containers have a complex hexagonal form as perhaps you have yourself observed when milk crates are delivered.

A designer may be commissioned to develop packages of all kinds. Accordingly, he or she needs to know how their shapes, the machines and materials that are used today, and how three-dimensional forms can be combined for purposes of packing the maximum of objects into the minimum amount of space. In my Visual Studies course, we are currently examining structures and their uses, modules, and combinations. Given that humans are accustomed to living in cubical spaces, surrounded by right-angled walls, quadrilateral grids are among the simplest for us to imagine. But tetrahedral structures are far more complicated; we aren't so well acquainted with them. Sure, an artist whose dream is to design a cathedral's doors may well balk when it comes to designing an everyday object that isn't cast in bronze like a milk container. Such individuals typically scorn what they don't know how to do. They ignore the fact that triangular structures aren't only integral to milk containers but also, for example, to the design of the United States pavilion at the Montreal World's Fair: an immense construction of metal and plastic that would barely fit into Milan's Piazza del Duomo.[55] The building system is that devised by R. Buckminster Fuller and has been undergoing testing in various parts of the world. A similar structure, twenty meters in height and made in cardboard, was on exhibit at the Milan Triennale.[56]

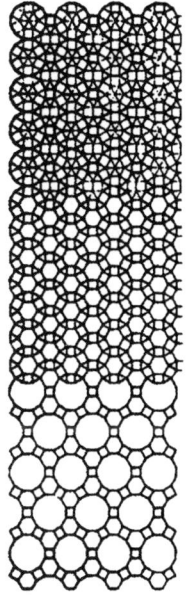

Connections between different structures

When you join the sides of a large number of equilateral triangles edge to edge you end up with a flat surface that appears to be made out of hexagons. The result is not a sphere but a two-dimensional flat structure. So how does Mr. Fuller create his spheres? Every now and then, at predetermined intervals, he inserts a pentagon made up of equilateral triangles

Ordinarily it's hexagons, not pentagons, that are composed of equilateral triangles.) The resulting pentagons composed of equilateral triangles assume the form of low-profile pyramids with pentagonal bases allowing for the entire system to produce the curvature required by spherical structures.

No doubt you have watched many soccer games on television. I rarely do so because I know so little about soccer. When I did, however, I couldn't help but notice that the ball is made from black and white hexagons.[57] Just like a Fuller dome. Do I know who won the game? Not a clue. Who was playing? I don't recall.

Take a close look at the ball next time you are watching a game: you will see the same structural principles at work that shape the Montreal dome. The landscape extends into the interior of the dome; there are trees and flowers as if in an enormous greenhouse. The interior space can thus unfold freely without any need for external walls as a means of shelter from the elements. That's the job of the dome, a portion of which is equipped with triangular shutters, six per hexagon. Actuated by photoelectric cells and electronic systems, these furl and unfurl as a function of the light, regulating its intensity in the process.

The final shape these objects assume feels no less natural than the products of nature itself. This is how the notion of "imitating" nature is understood in my course: the imitation of systems of construction rather than of finalized shapes (because the latter induce neglect of the structures that determine them).

SIMULTANEOUS PROJECTIONS[58]

Shifting color images appear sharp on a screen. Suddenly, sections slide away and are replaced by images in other colors and with other forms of animation. The entire screen begins to slowly alter. The vertical stripes of which it is made up rotate. Images fade and slip away, only to return abruptly. All the while, the colors of the images themselves continue to fluctuate. Sometimes it's a single image that changes while the others remain stable . . .

In my research seminar on light, we are experimenting with the effect of multiple projections on plastic screens. The images in question might well be described as abstract. They are experimental in character, capable of undergoing infinite transformations, from abstract to photorealistic. The aim of these experiments is to understand their potential as a mode of visual communication. The qualitative and informational value of a given image will be assessed at the time when these experiments are put into practice.

In the Carpenter Center's lab, I had a model built of a projection system consisting in three vertical screens on rollers large enough to allow for multiple projections on their inside surfaces. My students, working with the materials they prepared, have been testing out the capabilities of this tool. The composite image can be the sum total of three simultaneous, non-overlapping projections. The rotational speed of the screens is adjustable—slow for present purposes—and the projections can either include or cover over single images on the screen. Three information streams can thus be served up simultaneously. Each of the three streams needs to be distinctive.

Let's imagine that one of the vertical screens is filled with red and green diagonals. We overlay this projection with a series of opaque vertical lines. As a result, the red and green diagonals now appear intercepted by vertical cuts, dark areas where there's no projection visible. Into these gaps we project a blurred full-color image which we also intercut with vertical bars and, into these additional gaps, we project yet a third image: a black and white halftone screen. The rotation of the vertical screens will cause the images to fluctuate continuously. The variations can be accentuated by altering the projected images themselves, swapping out the slides in the projectors, or projecting three appropriately edited film strips using all three film projectors.

Let's now return to earth or, better, let's return to the highway. There we are accustomed to viewing the landscape unfurling before us like a promotional travel film with a second film embedded within it: the inverted version of the same landscape that appears in the rearview mirror. What's so odd about this? These days, all of us have become used to simultaneous images and, as I have often insisted, static individual images interest us far less. A television playing in a bar introduces moving images into a setting already filled with moving images. The simultaneity of images and sounds is (perhaps regrettably) a world that we can no longer escape: a world in which it is perfectly normal to attend a live soccer match while listening to another match on a portable radio. The venerable illusion of an infinitely receding space once experienced in barber shops thanks to opposing mirrored walls belongs to the past, not unlike the anamorphic paintings of famous men once composed of vertical strips wedged into enclosures such that different faces appear when the viewer is positioned to the right, the left, or the center (where the image was painted onto the strips' edges). All are simultaneous yet static effects.[59]

What are the opportunities today in a world characterized by proliferation and simultaneity? Are we to shed tears for a past that will never return much like elders who lament their long-lost youths? Or are we to intervene and collaborate with the aim of bringing some order to the chaos? My answer is the latter. After all, what did the artists of the past do when they developed their work? They sought to render an order—understood as the "aesthetic"—visible in the midst of nature's chaos: an order governed by laws concerning the harmonic relationship between parts and wholes. They sought to transmit aesthetic information in visual form in an objective manner so as to enable everyone to share their discoveries. Even ordinary people could thus achieve a partial understanding of a chaotic world.

By immersing ourselves in our environment and deepening our understanding of contemporary media we too are exploring whether it's feasible to bring order to the imagistic chaos of our times. The chaos in question is the product of the constant and simultaneous use of every medium at our disposal whether due to haste or ignorance: a "haste" inspired by the desire to preempt others from beating us to the punch and assuming ownership, by any means available, of a medium of communication; an "ignorance" of the legion of opportunities available to us engendered by excessive haste.

The constant and simultaneous exposure to every medium possible breeds a monotonous psychopathology in users, often with grave consequences. So, the effort to bring order to the chaos of images should also be understood in terms of its potential social impact.

IMAGE SEQUENCES

The students in my research seminar on light have vanished. Only four or five of them are showing up in class. The others, with or without valid excuses, are absent. What's going on?

As already noted, Harvard students are all in a big hurry: a hurry to understand and to create. Each is currently working on an individual project. They have already completed their experiments with plastics, transparencies, and the chromatics of light. They are acquainted with Young's work on mixing colored light.[60] They know everything about polarization. They have devised dozens of slides and studied image sequences. Now they want to put what they have learned into practice. The studios in the Carpenter Center where my class meets are underequipped; students are forced to take turns using tools. Whether individually or in groups, they've been forced to develop their own tools. They are anxious about one of their peers stealing their ideas before they mature.

A few weeks back some of the students confided in me that they had a special project in mind. They wanted to know how and where to bring it to fruition. I listened to their questions, helped them to sharpen their focus, tried to concentrate their attention on the core concept. I provided advice on how best to proceed: what needs to be done right away or done later; also, the techniques best suited to successful development of the core concept. Then my students disappeared. They did resurface every now and then outside of class time, checking in on a practical detail or two.

One of them is still showing up in class because, now that so many classmates are working offsite, he has access to multiple projectors. He's studying sequences of shapes and colors. He projects an initial slide, with an elementary red-on-black design. He then projects a second slide with the same shape over the first image but made up of fine green pinstripes overlaid on a black background. The first image is then swapped out with a successor image that is the negative of its predecessor. The operation is repeated with results that resemble what in film circles is known as a "cross-fade" carried out with images that can be freely sequenced. His next task is to study what sorts of stories can be told by such means. The effect of layering colored pinstripes is lovely and the projection (with a second projector) of images into the dark areas of the first slide is crystal clear.

Another student is experimenting with reflections of a single image and has succeeded in projecting six stills and one moving image through a sequence of semi-opaque walls. The effect is achieved by using sheets of Perspex which reflect the projected image while allowing the image to pass through to subsequent sheets. After traversing a given number of sheets, however, the image loses its luminosity.

A group of four students, one of whom is Italian, is developing a device that permits the controlled distortion of images. It uses colored lights (the three base colors—red, green, blue—employed by color televisions to generate other colors) with flexible, adjustable mirrors and movable opaque objects that can intercept the various lights and yield other colors in turn.

For over a month now, Cambridge's trees have sprouted little bundles of leaves ready to open under the spring-time sun. The bundles are small and tightly packed, composed of tiny green leaves. They barely stick out from the branches that have survived the winter. But spring still hasn't arrived. They say that it almost never arrives. Instead, summer explodes suddenly: leave home one day and you will find the trees all filled with leaves. In the meantime, the sun heats but the wind chills. Harvard students are in a hurry even during the spring. Barefoot or shod in sandals they traipse around Harvard Square eating gigantic ice-cream cones (a local specialty, it appears). Other students in my class are working in the dark-room printing prepared slides as if they were negatives. Some have success-fully shared their early results. In this manner one can generate up to fifty prints of varying color from a single polarized light glass slide without ever altering the composition, which is to say, the design of the slide.

Yet another student is experiment-ing with effects of transparency. Their work involves the layering of many strata of plastic together in an unstruc-tured sandwich and then combining the resulting image with other unstruc-tured images. Light travels through the multiple layers and makes their various components visible. The study of light as a means of communication has thus sparked the imagination of students who, perhaps somewhat ingenuously (given that they still believe that every-thing will be relatively easy), have set about building something they seek to master but don't yet fully understand. What matters is that each individual or group has developed its own distinct set of questions and is pursuing different solutions.

FOUR-DIMENSIONAL MODULATION[61]

A fly's eye, a sunflower, a quartz crystal, a corn cob, a pinecone, a beehive: all are four-dimensional modulated forms (with time understood as the fourth dimension). For example, I believe that the individual cells that make up a beehive don't originate as hexagons but rather as cylinders: cylinders that, when packed in the largest possible numbers into the smallest possible space, find themselves compressed into hexagons. Accordingly, the fourth dimension can consist in the transformation of a module with a round base into a module with a hexagonal base. The same occurs in the case of the almost cubical elastic modules that make up a corncob, whereas the seeds of a sunflower, arranged as a logarithmic spiral, have a rhomboid cross section. The curve of growth and the variations in the size of the module also need to be considered.

The seed of a sunflower is, thus, a module and the study of modules helps us to better and more deeply understand part of the world that surrounds us. Only "part of the world" because there exist other parts that aren't so rigorously or visibly modular. Maybe we haven't yet understood the "module" that shapes a river, an optical nerve, an amoeba, a cloud, a continent, or a vein. Maybe it's a matter of examining other dimensions, other structural principles that will be analyzed in future class sessions.

Meanwhile, after completing various exercises with modular surfaces and volumes (carried out hastily due to time constraints and the expectation that they will deepen their knowledge on their own), the students in my Visual Communication course are busy inhabiting the inside of modules. "Inhabiting" in the sense that they are operating on the inside of modules as they seek to characterize a given volume. Each student has built a tetrahedron out of wooden rods with sixty-centimeter cardboard sides. They have enlarged one of the small-scale modules that they developed during their initial compositional exercises. Working now within an empty, much enlarged version, they need to find a way to better define it by composing an array of surfaces and volumes which can, in turn, accommodate submodules.

Any shape made up of so many identical components is also determined—materially shaped as it were—by factors integral to the components themselves: determined either by their material composition or internal configurations that sometimes bear little relation to the shape of the base component. Our assignment consists in finding connective lines or planes strictly located within the model's constituent elements.

I explained to my students how one can make connections between various points marked equidistantly along the rods that establish the boundaries of one of these shapes composed of four equilateral triangles. I showed them how the resulting internal structure can be symmetrically bisected by a square plane and that the constructions that they complete need to be conceived and constructed by constantly changing the base of the structure. (Any facet of a tetrahedron can serve as its base, so internal compositions need to reflect this fact.)

A few students became suspicious at this juncture. One of them asked me: why don't we conjoin all these uniform components and compose one large modulated form?

As a matter of fact, this was exactly what I had in mind, so I was gratified that the idea arose spontaneously among the students. Continuation of the assignment necessarily pointed in the direction of teamwork. Up until that juncture, the work had been carried out individually; now it became collective. The shift was discussed as a group and required the selection of just one of the internal compositions and discarding of the others (now considered preparatory sketches). Only one student objected though agreeing to participate in the group effort. The compositions developed up to this point were examined one by one in order to evaluate the potential result of their further multiplication and integration into a single unified structure. A consensus emerged around a simple composition that could readily accommodate a variety of effects through the integration of multiple modules. All the students rework this same composition and, soon enough, I am surrounded by tetrahedra featuring a new internal structure. The work of assemblage begins: an exercise that teaches students how, by manipulating components, tetrahedra can be combined in space. A subgroup sets out to assemble these shapes as a function of possible continuities between their internal structures. They do so with tape so that it's easy to quickly "erase" a shape and devise a better alternative. Several three-dimensional structures emerge as a result. A vertical one is selected because it seems like the best illustration of the problem with which we have been grappling.

Some students complete the vertical structure while they dismantle the others. Some of them begin to say good-bye and depart: they have already understood that there's little point in hanging around to view the outcome. The most motivated students stick it out. They help to complete our work and bear witness to the end result: a three-meter-high structure. Noting an anomaly in the internal structure, a Chinese student points out that there may be a misaligned tetrahedron somewhere.

Everyone heads out. Good-byes are said. My teaching assistant reminds the students of what they need to bring for our next session. There's a wine (Italian) and cheese (Pecorino) reception in the Carpenter Center on the floor above. A majority of the group eventually reassembles upstairs, not with a tetrahedron in hand but instead

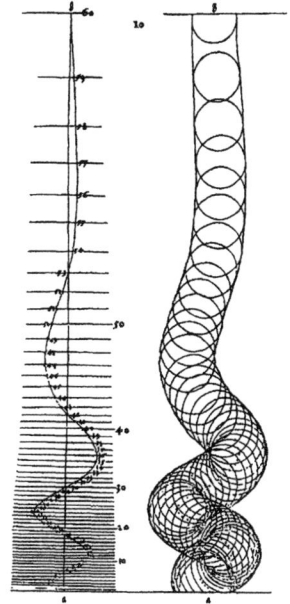

a bread square topped by a cube of cheese in one hand and the section of a cone filled with red wine in the other.

COMPUTER GRAPHICS[62]

Many visual artists, painters, and illustrators are terrified of machines. They don't even want to hear about them. They are convinced that, someday, machines will be capable of making works of art. They already feel as if they are unemployed. Even a celebrated critic writing about the programmed art movement in a major Italian daily posed the overblown question: will art be made by machines?[63] It's a phrase that attests to a deep misunderstanding of the problem. It's like asking whether we will have an art of the brush or art of the pencil. It's disappointing to see a solid, classically trained intellect demonstrate such complete ignorance when it comes to the here and now of contemporary culture.

Naturally, the machine that induces the greatest fear is the electric calculator or "computer" as it is known here in the USA. Computer art.[64] Computers have memory. They have a luminous eye and can see, even recognizing objects. They can manipulate these objects with an articulated metal arm. They can perform lighting quick calculations and, of greater concern to the above-noted artists, they can even produce images, draw with a light pen, erase, redesign, correct, turn a figure around, allow us to see it from above and below, display it

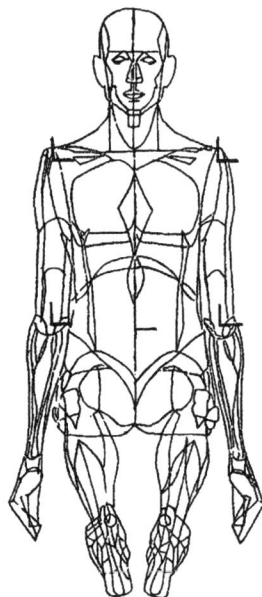

A drawing done by a computer

on its right or left side, rotate it, turn it at any speed, remove pieces, add others . . . In short, they can do a billion things. The electronic computers in question are referred to as computer graphics machines and can be used to visualize just about anything one wants to render in visual form, from a technical drawing to a diagram, from geographical to urban surveys, from features of city traffic systems to those of residential interiors.

How do they operate? Like embroiderers or mosaicists or anyone seeking to translate a design (or data set) from one medium to another, they have their own code which you must master. That's because the computer, despite the fear it induces in certain artists, is ultimately only a tool. If there is no one, no human being to give it orders and use it, it sits still and silent. A revolution or tornado can take place, snow may fall or flowers bloom, but the computer doesn't so much as budge. It's dumb and insensitive to that which can precipitate an artistic experience. And, to start with, it wasn't invented for this purpose. The computer's strength is that, when exhaustively programmed, when it has been told everything it needs to do and how, it executes everything quickly without ever becoming distracted.

What do embroiderers do when they need to transfer a drawing of a rose onto the fabric to be embroidered? They make use of two components: one vertical, the other horizontal. Together they form a grid. So, if there's a curve that needs to be drawn, it will be broken down into many small squares distributed across the grid in such a way as to approximate (as accurately as possible) the desired curve. In the case of embroidery which involves color but in only two dimensions the entire operation stops here. The computer, on the contrary, has other axes with which it can work beyond the vertical and horizontal: axes that allow it to perform varied tasks like rotating an image and anything else for which it has been programmed. In other words, computer graphics animate figures using the same system employed in cinematic cartooning. The figure to be animated is inserted (*input*) into the computer's memory with all the basics regarding its relative coordinates: up-down, right-left, front-back. Executing the commands it has received, the computer then generates (*output*) all the intermediary images between the figure's first and second locations, creating the illusion of movement. These images are displayed in various manners: usually via a cathode ray tube like that employed by television sets that trigger rays of light by means of ultrafast electric pulses. Along these same lines, Bell Labs has released several films in which three-dimensional geometrical images made from light can be seen rotating in a dark four-dimensional space.[65] Produced for research purposes, the films aim to promote a better understanding of the potential of these new tools.

Technologists are studying how to perfect such computers and enable them to work with color. In the not-so-distant future it's likely that artists will be able to employ computers in their research: particularly when prices fall (as is widely anticipated) and the universe of computer applications expands, giving rise to computing centers for large numbers of people who will also be able to engage in remote work.

But, most of all, when computer codes become as simple as those used in embroidery.

ORGANIC FORM

Like other rivers, the Po and the Tiber flow down from mountain summits. Two seconds later they reach their mouths. A river descends seeking out the lowest lying ground available. It flows through hollows, spreads out into spacious valleys, devises a serpentine path across uneven terrain, and runs straight over plains. A river has a natural organic form that can't be analyzed from the standpoint of the same structures we adopted in our study of other natural shapes. Modular structures are of little value. An alternative method is required. So, in my course on Visual Communication, we have set out instead to create a simulation. The students are trying to reconstruct a river's flow not by drawing from nature or copying topographical maps but building a model that allows for the study of how a liquid flows across an uneven surface. Each student grabs a piece of white paper, scrunches it up into a ball as if to toss it away, and then flattens it out. The sheet now possesses geographic characteristics like mountains, hills, and landslides.

The delta
of the Nile

65

It's like a section of the earth's surface that has been peeled off: what precise portion of the earth is represented or the artificial river's anticipated flow are of no importance. What matters is understanding how a given organic form takes shape.

Students are invited to carefully pour some India ink (diluted down to a medium gray) over the model landscape. The ink streams across the paper just like a river, choosing the lowest available path, branching as it moves, dispersing wherever possible and, eventually, coming to a rest. Soon enough the ink is dry. The sheet can now be flattened by wetting its verso and allowing it to dry. The marks left by the river are an organic sign that invites study. The gray isn't uniform. Where it lingered the marks are darkest. It varies in breadth. It's a self-generated sign.

Other forms of automatic drawing, drawing that involves a minimum of personal input and allows the ink a maximum of freedom, can be done on sheets of paper. One well known system involves placing a large drop of ink on a smooth sheet and then blowing across it through a drinking straw to shape branching patterns. The forms take shape on their own until the ink runs out.

These sorts of exercises excite the imagination of people who go through paper and ink as if they were being paid on a piecework basis. The entire floor of the main room in the Carpenter Center is soon completely blanketed in paper. To move around you have cross mountains and rivers, tree branches and root structures, electric discharges, blowups of nerve cells, tangles of twigs, islands and continents, and other unrecognizable shapes.

It's like looking out the window of an airplane from one thousand meters in the air: the landscapes of a black-and-white world. These drawings were produced so quickly that no one reflected on what they had done: they barely looked at their last one before moving on to the next.

This corpus of drawings—if we may designate them as such—was analyzed during our subsequent class meeting with the goal of defining the visual characteristics of these sorts of shapes: shapes that are, in fact, perfectly coherent, with every individual detail corresponding to the overall shape. I pointed out how forms branch outward in both rivers and blown-upon drop-lets. I called attention to the contours of the marks, the different grays that result from the ink sitting or running, the ends of the branch structures, the connections between parts. I noted that some marks didn't have a uniform gray color but instead a granular material-ity. I asked for an explanation and the author explained that he had mixed India ink with Coca-Cola.

I then invited my students to rip up their drawings into little shreds, especially where branching occurs (i.e. where marks branch off). They would subsequently be asked to recompose the overall drawing in another manner while retaining the same visual charac-teristics. The exercise was designed to

"Cloud" as written by a Japanese child

deepen their thinking about the nature of these organic shapes. Putting the pieces together and reconstructing the whole helps to better understand the overall process.

At the beginning of the semester, my students had a general sense of the kind of work they would be doing. In an ordinary art class, one would begin with points, transition to lines, and then continue on to study surfaces, colors, and three-dimensional volumes. In my course, instead, we moved from rigidly structured forms to modules to organic forms, from works developed on the basis of geometry to forms that self-generate. One can't understand the visible world only in terms of geometry: a large portion of the world is organic and we have to do our best to achieve an understanding of it as well.

EVOLVING TOOLS

Laziness drives progress. It's the stimulus that spurs us to achieve what we achieve while making the smallest possible physical effort. Maximum result for minimum effort has long been one of the founding laws of economics. It can be said that our being, our body, is composed of two distinct entities with two distinct characteristics. The first is our brain which moves at the speed of thought. The second is our muscula-ture which seeks to minimize fatigue. But given that it's usually necessary to activate our muscles to achieve ideas hatched in the brain and given that muscles tend towards indolence, the brain devises systems to achieve the same results while minimizing the muscular workload.

It's also the case that our brains give up on things because they require too much effort. To push a button and obtain whatever one desires while reclining on a comfortable sofa: that's the dream of every human being. Machines were invented to spare our muscles. We ride in cars instead of walking. We use lathes instead of working iron rods manually. The aim is to achieve our goals without exertion and with enhanced precision. Everyone knows that an iron object produced on a motorized lathe is more precise than the hand-turned equivalent or that a circle drawn by hand is less precise than one drawn with a compass. In fact, who still draws circles by hand after the invention of the compass? Hand-made objects that involve a lot of manual labor engender pity. The best acrobats never break a sweat.

Likewise, in the field of art, a work completed quickly can preserve all the vitality of the moment in which it was first conceived. The bamboo leaves in a Chinese or Japanese painting were executed in an instant but observed over an extended period. Long observation, deep understanding, instant execution.

When they are at their best, brains and muscles work together. The result is something that is alive.

Art is a mental fact, associated with the knowledge both of things and of visual communications media. Things are the reality we all inhabit. Media are the instruments employed to visualize what the brain receives from external stimuli. The law of minimum effort for the maximum result thus applies to art and, in this case as well, "minimum effort" means the proper tools. Among the tools that today's artists have at their disposal for purposes of self-expression, there are indeed tools that produce maximum results at minimal effort. It's a matter of getting to know them and understanding their affordances. Art is deeply intertwined with technique. To soldier on with old, laborious, and static techniques makes no sense, particularly when new modes of communication are involved.

Art is a mental fact whose physical execution can be carried out by any available means.

In art academies teaching is still tethered to old techniques yet, as students struggle with outdated techniques, their brains are already living in the near future. Even in more up-to-date "art schools" there's a need for change: to streamline teaching programs, to combat the belief that art implies only certain techniques, to embrace new techniques, to accept the fact that not all art is created for eternity, and to renounce the emphasis in teaching upon the creation of works reserved for social elites.

Most of all, it's time to stop talking about art. Instead, we need to talk about visual communication. If there is to be art, it will exist independently with respect to schooling. We can educate people to understand art (visual communication) but we can't train artists, not to mention geniuses.

Tools have evolved between the era of cave paintings executed with fingers and today, when artists neither make their own brushes nor grind their own colors. Some even employ the same jackhammers used on city streets. If such is the case, why shouldn't this progression continue? Why neglect the many tools available to visual practitioners today that minimize effort and maximize results? To do otherwise would be to be mentally lazy. So, let's draw up the plan for a technical school in visual communication dedicated to addressing the challenges of today (not yesteryear).[66] Such a school's mission would be to promote research on the future of visual communication as well as working methods. It would also teach—not for operational but cultural reasons— the history of art, alongside sociology and psychology. It goes without saying that "history of art" here means the history of *world art*, not the version that begins with prehistory only to leap forward to ancient Greece and then Italian art. Today, one needs to know about the entire world. In the not-too-distant future, one will probably need to know whether there is visual communication on the moon.[67]

Are values lost as a result? On the contrary: we are in the process of acquiring new values.

VISUAL CODES[68]

The drawings of architects, electrical diagrams, and the like are forms of visual communication. They are objective, perfectly intelligible to their recipients, often written in code (yet communicative all the same). If an architect were to orally communicate the plans for a home, describe them over the telephone, or weave all the measurements and instructions into a narrative, they'd be unlikely to be understood.

Accordingly, in many settings, visual communication proves a unique means for transmitting information between a sender and a receiver. The prerequisite for success is precise information, objective signals, unified codes, and the absence of misinterpretation. These are conditions that can be met only the two communicating parties share an instrumental understanding of their domain of expertise.[69]

Architectural plans are an obvious case in point. But there are many others, whether codified in part or not at all, in which visual communication occurs in a confusing manner. Confusion arises either because the exchange includes superfluous information, the visual solution that was adopted is "contaminated," or the codes employed weren't formulated or implemented with sufficient care. In a setting within which vast quantities of visual data swarm around us in disorderly and sustained fashion, visual communication seeks to determine the optimal relation between information and a given support on the basis of objective data.[70]

Even if it can be transmitted otherwise, every category of information has its own ideal support. It's a given that (most of the) data associated with a construction project need to be communicated visually, employing marks whose thickness and continuity are significant and correspond to precise measurements. Building materials are assigned distinctive textures in the visual codes of the construction industry. A road sign, on the other hand, requires a support whose optical-chromatic and figure-ground characteristics have been carefully considered with respect to the sign itself and its setting. A road sign can be improvised with a ballpoint pen and a piece of cardboard in an emergency, of course. It also goes without saying that the ideal support is the one most familiar to us.

So, visual communication involves two components: information and supports. The two can be detached from one another and studied separately. A proper support needs to be determined based on visual codes and materiality. These codes, in turn, may be artificial, a priori creations or ones that emerge on their own within a given setting. Examples of artificial visual codes are maritime signal flags, roadway signage, military rank markings, industry seals. Examples of spontaneously emergent codes are those that help individuals to recognize one another visually: the gray suits worn by office workers, the beards sported by members of the Alpine brigades [of the Italian army], long hair, etcetera.

Like a box that contains maritime signal flags, supports for visual communication can exist on their own without information but will still convey information when put to use. Such supports include marks, colors, light, movement . . . all employed as a function of the recipient of a given message. This is why it's so important to study the support best-suited to conveying the information being transmitted effectively on every occasion. A recipient's character and their physical and sensory surroundings (which may filter or impede the transmission of information) need to be considered as well. Case in point: the cultural sophistication of mass audiences. This is a question that needs to be approached with care and not in the manner of the many advertisers today who, dismissing such audiences as stupid, consider them best suited for stupid messaging. The opposite is true: such messaging requires greater clarity which implies, in turn, research of a sort that is uncommon. Children require simplicity and extreme clarity, not stupidity. Otherwise, children and unsophisticated individuals won't understand. This is a matter about which anyone who authors good children's books is acutely conscious: clarity and simplicity are top priorities. A lot of work goes into removal rather than addition. Removing the superfluous to convey only essential information rather than adding and complicating the information at hand.[71]

MANY IMAGES IN ONE[72]

Getting to know visual communication is akin to learning a new language: a language made up exclusively of images, images that mean the same irrespective of nationality or the languages that people speak. Visual language is a language. Perhaps it's a bit more limited than spoken language, but it's surely more direct. The cinema is perfect example. When a film is good, no words are needed: the images tell the story.

We are all continuously receiving visual messages upon which we reflect and learn in the absence of words. Visual communication isn't reducible to the visual arts; it also encompasses people's behavior, the ways they dress, the orderly or disorderly nature of a dwelling, the way in which someone handles a tool, combinations of colors and materials that suggest poverty or luxury. These modes of visual communication prevail when it comes to designing settings that need to convey a sense of privilege or seclusion, of productivity or comfort. Even illiterates readily perceive the meaning of consecrated materials and colors such as the color red, marble, and precious metals, or, at the other end of the spectrum, burlap bags and plastics. Generally speaking, Italian schooling remains literary in character and the communicative power of images has always been undervalued by literati. This might explain why, when it comes to their latest books, so many contemporary authors fail to object to grossly incongruous covers and page layouts: books that remind me of someone dressed in a red mantle and ermine cloak like a king who is holding forth on the subject of misunderstandings between fourteenth-century Turks and the ceramists of Albisola in a public phone booth.

Acts of visual communication built upon images that haven't been objectively defined are just as confusing as sentences that lend themselves to multiple meanings. This is why the careful study of such images is required; one needs to gauge their expressive power, the relationship between multiple images, and the setting within which they occur. Psychologists have studied our modes of visual perception exhaustively. The perceptual limits of an elementary image, moiré effects, optical illusions, the persistence of images on the retina, illusory motion, images that take shape inside the eye . . . all these phenomena (and many others) are covered in my courses at the Carpenter Center: both in my Foundations of Visual Studies course and my Advanced Course on Visual Communication.

Artists from prior eras were the visual communication experts of their times. They were intuitively familiar with many of the same questions and confirmed their intuitions by means of testing. Their technical rules were sound principles of visual communication: the juxtaposition of colors to intensify brilliance or some other desired effect; the adoption of compositional rules that encompass the harmonic ratios of the golden section; and everything else the Dadaists (quite rightly) discarded because it conflicted with the new sensibility: rules wearily applied within the setting of static schools that, still living in the past, had become purely academic. (As a matter of fact, the art from this period so narrowed its scope that it became an art for elites, meaningful only to highly educated, specialized individuals. This is still true today: we need interpreters, otherwise known as art critics, to explain the intentions of artists to unschooled audiences.)

Artists have followed the same path, locking themselves up in ivory towers and ever more hermetic languages. The result is that we now find ourselves in the midst of a chaos from which we can only emerge by establishing new rules for visual communication: flexible and dynamic rules that aren't fixed for eternity but that are instead forever mutable, responsive to all available technical and scientific tools. These rules need to be objective, which is to say, valid for everyone. Only such rules will foster models of visual communication that don't rely upon expert interpreters to be understood.

Once upon a time, we knew the Adige River because, as kids, we had explored it in boats. Our visual memories, accordingly, were framed within a given horizon, limited to certain landscapes along its shores. Today, soaring above the river, we can perceive something different even if it remains a single river that presents in two different manners. A photographer using infrared-sensitive film could surely provide us with yet another set of images in addition to portraying the river under the sun or wrapped in a storm. The more aspects of something we experience, the better we understand its reality beyond any single representation.

Today's technologies allow us to see and, thus, to experience multiple facets of a single object. This makes exercises like studying the multitude of shapes, lines, and elements that can be found by moving the point of a pencil around within a single overall shape interesting. Likewise, we can photograph a three-dimensional object from every conceivable angle so as to discover whether a hidden structure emerges that reveals its nature.

A deep understanding a single object's every facet enables practitioners to select the best possible images for purposes of visual communication. Sometimes they can even achieve aesthetic effects by embracing deliberate visual ambiguities, not unlike certain poems in which words have been chosen to convey not just information but also to stir up memories from infancy that had been long forgotten in the minds of readers.

part two VISUAL COMMUNICATION[73]

Is it possible to define what we mean by "visual communication"? Almost everything that our eyes experience is visual communication: a cloud, a flower, a technical drawing, a shoe, a poster, a dragonfly, a telegram qua object (leaving aside its content), a flag. Images that, like other images, take on value and convey information as a function of the setting within which they are embedded. All the same, the multitude of messages that reach us through our eyesight can be divided up into two categories: random or intentional communication.

Random visual communication is exemplified by a cloud that moves across the sky without the intention of warning me that a storm is approaching. Intentional visual communication is exemplified instead by the smoke clouds used by Indian tribes to relay precisely coded information.

A random act of visual communication can be freely interpreted by the recipient, who can decode it in a scientific, aesthetic, or other key. An intentional act of visual communication, on the contrary, needs to convey the full significance intended by the sender.

Intentional visual communication can be further broken down into two sub-categories: aesthetic and practical information. Practical information, unlike aesthetic information, is exemplified by technical drawings, press photographs, television news programs, roadway signage, and the like. Aesthetic information is exemplified by messaging that, for example, informs us about the harmonic lines that make up a shape, volumetric proportions within a three-dimensional construction, the timeline of how one shape is transformed into another (as when a cloud disperses or changes form).

Random visual communication

Photo by Ugo Mulas.[74]

Intentional visual communication

Drawing by Rino Albertarelli.[75]

It goes without saying that aesthetic norms aren't uniform. There are as many aesthetic solutions as there are peoples and even, perhaps, individuals in the world. So, one can indeed pinpoint aesthetic choices in a technical drawing or press photograph. But, in such cases, the visual practitioner must convey aesthetic choices alongside readily comprehensible objective facts.

Let's establish the following rules for purposes of convenience but remain open to alter or break them as we pursue our exploration of these questions.

Visual Messages

Visual communication takes place by means of messages that belong to the great family of messages that strike our senses: acoustical, thermal, dynamic, etcetera.

The standard assumption is that a sender emits messages and a recipient receives them. Yet the recipient is immersed in an environment filled with forms of interference that can alter or even cancel out certain messages. Some examples: a red light installed in a space where red light prevails will be barely visible; a dull poster pasted up alongside a legion of other equally dull posters along a city street will get lost in a sea of uniformity. A storm will disrupt an Indian who is trying to send smoke signals.

Let's assume that the visual message has been properly crafted to ensure that it can't be distorted during transmission. It is certain to reach the recipient. But here there are new obstacles to overcome. Every recipient has his or her own idiosyncratic attributes—let's call them "filters"—through which every message must pass if it is to be received. One of these filters is sensory. Case in point: a colorblind person doesn't perceive certain colors and, as a result, messages that rely entirely upon chromatic differences will find themselves altered or canceled out. Another filter could be described as "operational."

It reflects the psycho-physiological characteristics of the receiver. An example: it's obvious that a three-year old will analyze a given message very differently than a mature individual. A third filter could be defined as "cultural."

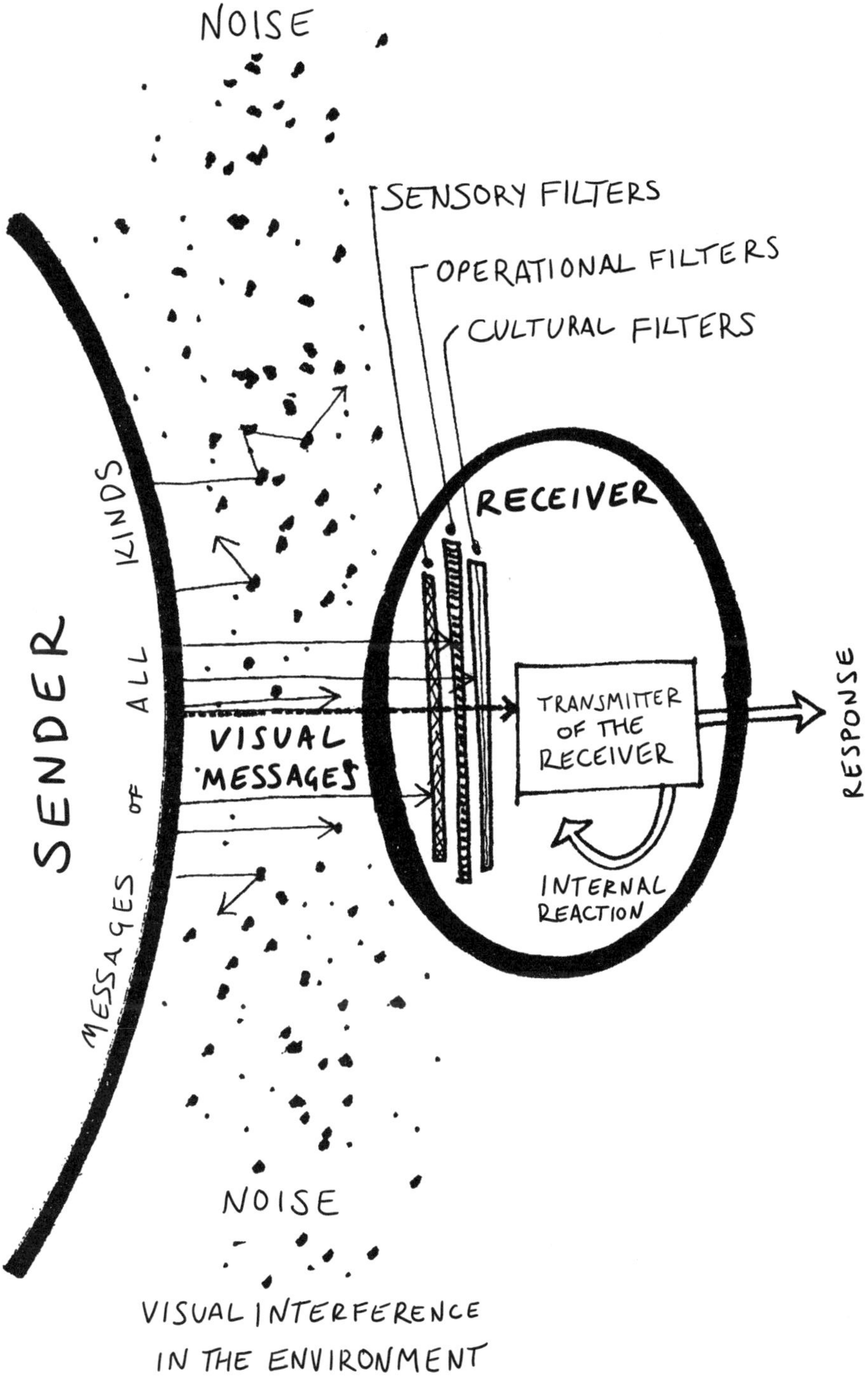

NOISE

SENSORY FILTERS

OPERATIONAL FILTERS

CULTURAL FILTERS

RECEIVER

SENDER

MESSAGES OF ALL KINDS

VISUAL MESSAGES

TRANSMITTER OF THE RECEIVER

RESPONSE

INTERNAL REACTION

NOISE

VISUAL INTERFERENCE IN THE ENVIRONMENT

85

It allows only recognizable messages, messages that belong to a recipient's own cultural universe, to make it through. An example: many Westerners won't recognize Asian music as music because it doesn't conform to their cultural norms; for them "music" is necessarily and exclusively the music they were exposed to since childhood.

There aren't always clear distinctions between these three filters. Their order is reversible and sometimes they comingle. So, let's assume that our message has made it through all the ambient noise and individual filters, reaching an interior zone within the recipient that I am calling the "transmitter of the receiver." Here there are two possible responses to the message: one internal, the other external. An example: if the visual message declared "there's a bar here," the external response might instruct the receiver to drink; the internal response, however, might be to say, "I'm not thirsty."

Decomposing Messages

If we truly wish to understand visual communication, we need to study these sorts of messages and analyze their components. To start with, messages can be divided up into two parts: the first is the information being conveyed; the second is the visual support. The latter consists in the combination of elements that render a given message visible: the elements that need to be assembled and refined to ensure maximum communicative efficacy and coherence. They include Textures, Shapes, Structures, Modules, and Movements. It's hard, if not impossible, to neatly separate these out given that they are often interconnected. When we scrutinize a tree, we perceive the texture of its bark, the shape of the leaves and tree itself, the leaves' veins, channels and branches, the structural module that characterizes trees, the temporality of a tree's cyclical evolution from seed to plant to flower to fruit again to seed. We are also aware that were we to examine a texture with a magnifying glass, we would perceive its structure whereas, from a distance, the module disappears: all we see is a texture. For this reason, given that we are talking about visual communication, I propose that we consider the human eye as a categorical point of reference.

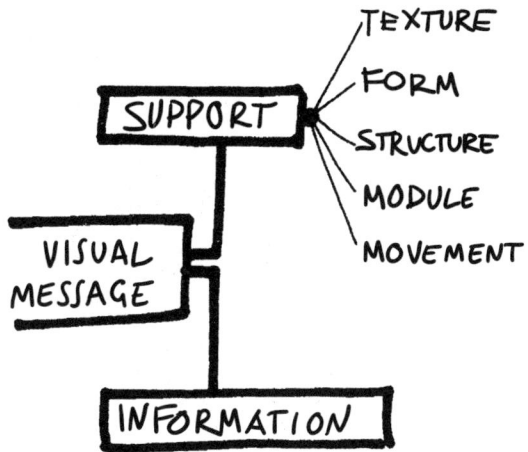

As such, we can state that when the eye perceives a surface that has been characterized materially or graphically as uniform, that surface can be considered a *texture*. When, on the contrary, the modules that make up said texture become visible and are recognized as being composed, in turn, of submodules, then we are dealing with a *structure*. Reflection on how shapes evolve over the course of time should then allow us to envisage how a texture could become a structure or how modules with distinct internal components could be devised that, assembled into structures, eventually emerge as textures with distinctive characteristics.

The textures, module, shape, structure, and temporal dimensions observable in a tree.

When we draw a bounded shape on a white sheet of paper, be it a square or a rectangle, we usually fill the space with a uniform scattering of dots in order to render the zone of visual interest, even before sketching out any images. By this means we have established a clear disjunction between the area within the sign and the rest of the sheet. This is one of the most basic and instinctive ways to render a surface communicative. There are many ways to render a surface communicative and what Americans refer to as "textures," we [Italians] would refer to as the "grain" (in the sense of granularity) of plasterwork and walls, the "knurling" of sheet metal, or the "weave" of textiles.[76] I don't believe that the [Italian] word "weave" [*tessitura*] or, for that matter, our word for "texture" [*testura*] would be allowable if one were referring to plasterwork.[77] So let's embrace the [English] word "texture" for the time being just like we have embraced the word "design," which isn't translatable into Italian.[78] (By the way, I'm a big fan of borrowing as many words as possible from the world's languages so that, in a not too distant future, only a few of our own words will be needed for us to forge a hypothetical international language.)

It's time to experiment with making textures using every available method, from traditional to mechanical, from spray cans to pastels or whatever else you're inclined to try. The experiment will allow us to determine how many kinds of textures exist, always with the understanding that our aim is to create absolutely regular and uniform but highly varied surfaces.

Once we have developed a better sense of what, visually speaking, textures are, the second phase of our efforts will consist in collecting a wide variety of sample textures, both natural and artificial, in the world that surrounds us: tree bark, textile samples (particularly ones from male garments that don't involve printed patterns), wallpapers, cross-sections of expanded plastics, paper, and cardboard. The bas relief textures of ancient and modern buildings can be photographed. A wide variety of samples of knurled metal plates can be gathered. So can sheets of patterned glass and so on and so forth.

Rubbings can be done over some bas relief textures, like those of metal coins, in order to record them.

Thus far we have assembled and produced an array of textures using a variety of materials and tools. The exercise could go on forever, but the goal is deepening our understanding. In the wake of these hands-on experiences, everyone perceives the surfaces of objects with greater intensity. Many objects that were once only perceived as shapes are now perceived as having distinctive textures. We now also perceive the differences between organic and geometric textures. Every texture is composed of many identical or similar elements distributed evenly across a flat or very slightly raised surface. Textures are characterized by uniformity. The human eye always perceives them as a surface. But what happens when this condition of uniformity is altered?

Visual phenomena of rarefaction and densification can be analyzed in textures. How far can we rarefy the marks that make up a texture and still have it read as a surface? What's the limit of density? What happens if we densify and rarefy the same surface in two different areas?

Experiments with camouflage also become possible. To varying degrees, a given texture may be visible within another texture, with whole or partial overlaps giving rise to mixed textures. These are frequent in architectural settings in which the natural grain of a material is overlaid with an artificial texture. Many buildings make use of double textures, chiseling uniform, artificial bas relief patterns that become visible in the sun into the natural grain and color variations found in stones like granite. The result is that, from a distance, we may perceive a texture in bas relief while, from close up, we experience it instead as a "material" texture.

The same processes involving the densification and rarefaction of textured surfaces can be observed in halftone prints and almost every form of printing that involves the use of relatively visible screens, particularly when printing on irregular paper surfaces. When you examine such prints under a magnifying glass, you immediately discover that the same image that, viewed from a distance, assumes a recognizable shape is actually made up of dots of varying sizes packed into more or less dense clusters.

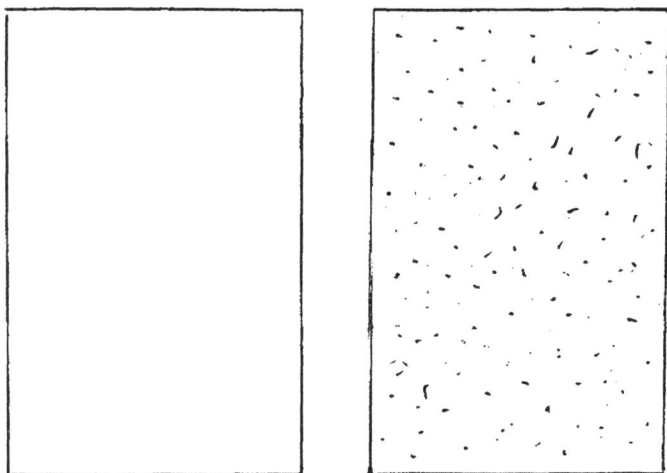

Rendering a surface expressive.

A texture obtained by spraying black paint at a distance of eighty centimeters from the paper.

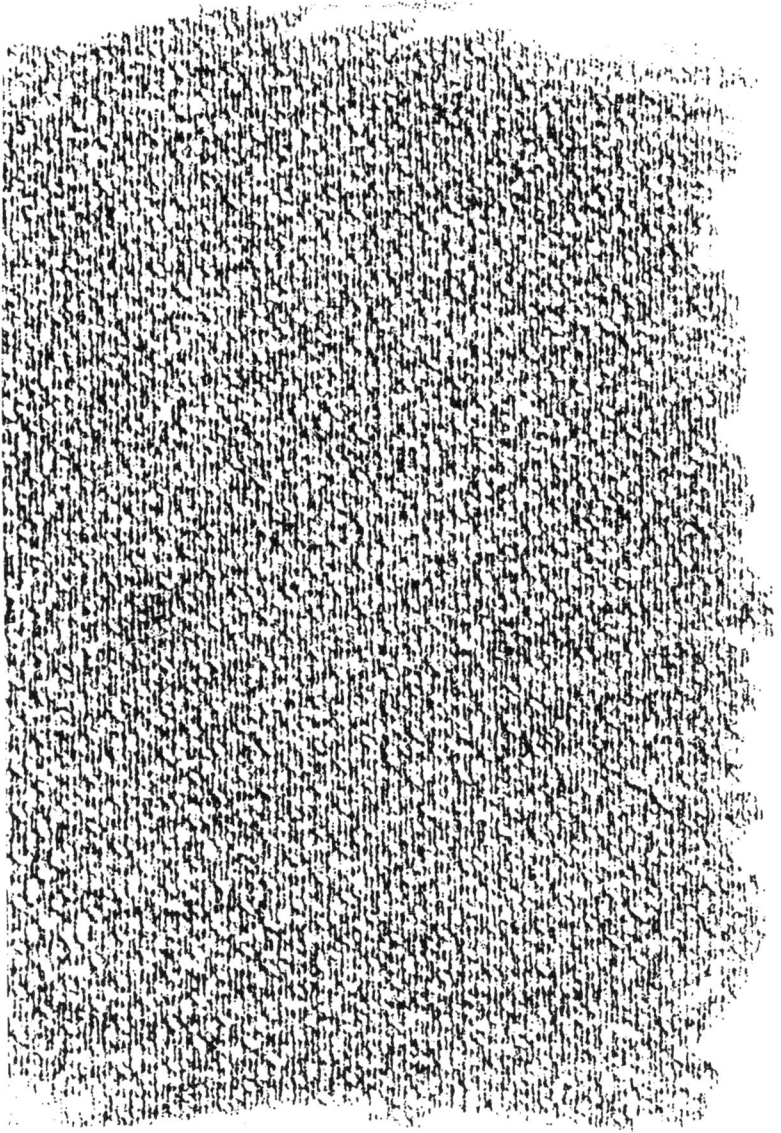

A texture obtained by running a flat wax crayon over granular paper (as used by Seurat in his drawings).

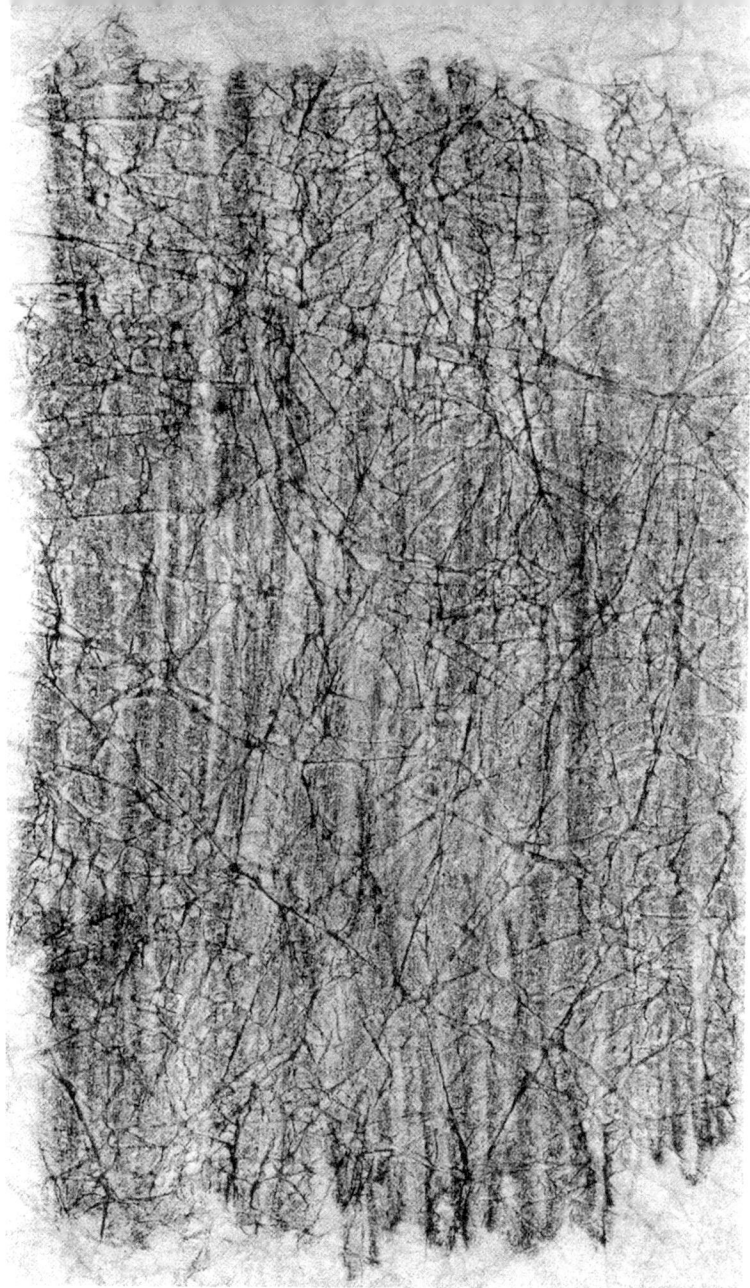

A texture obtained by crumpling a sheet of paper and then running a flat pastel across the surface.

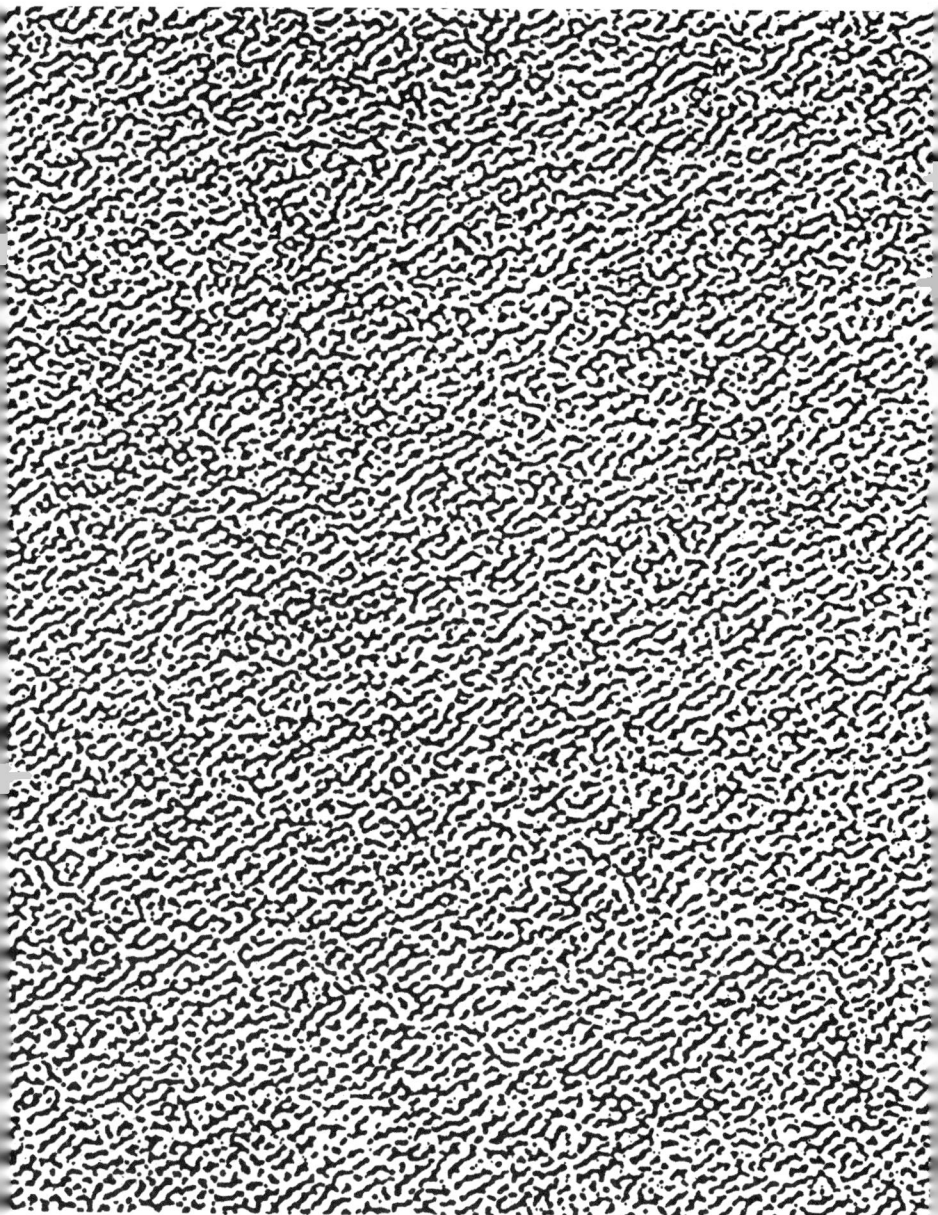

Some commercially available textures from Letraset.

Other kinds of commercial textures found on adhesive films.

A complex texture created by overlaying two similar textures.

An example from the visual arts: François Morellet, *Double Frames*, 1958.

Every surface in the interior of traditional Japanese homes (which are still in use) is rendered expressive by means of the judicious use of textures that reflect the structural logic of the very materials that constitute the whole.

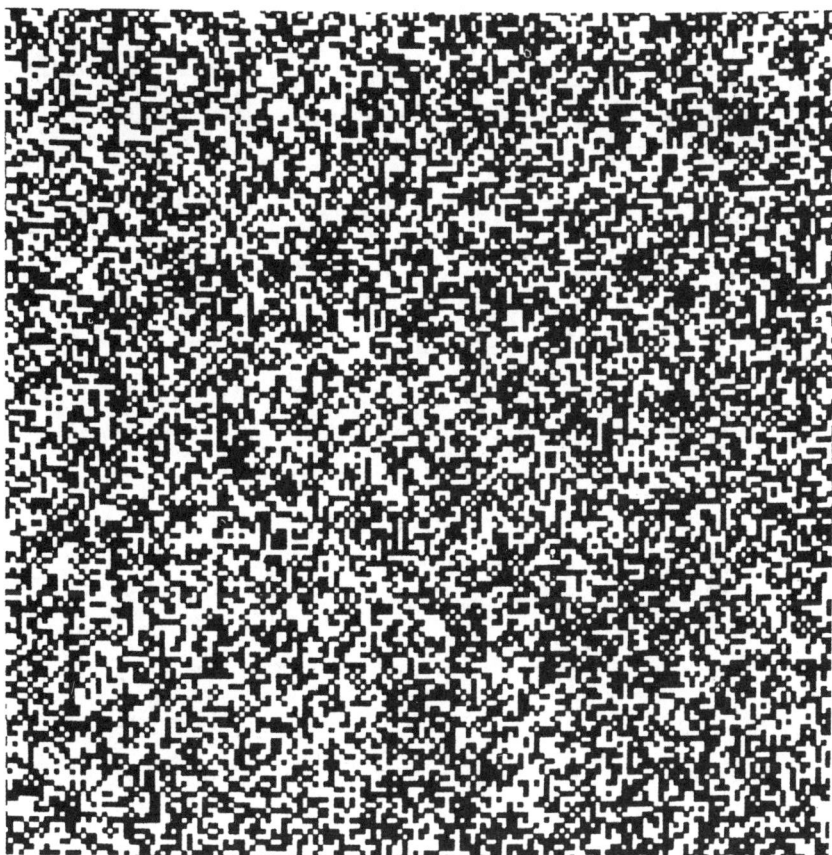

Two more works by François Morellet. The image on this page displays
the random combination of forty thousand squares organized according to
the even and odd numbers printed in a telephone directory.

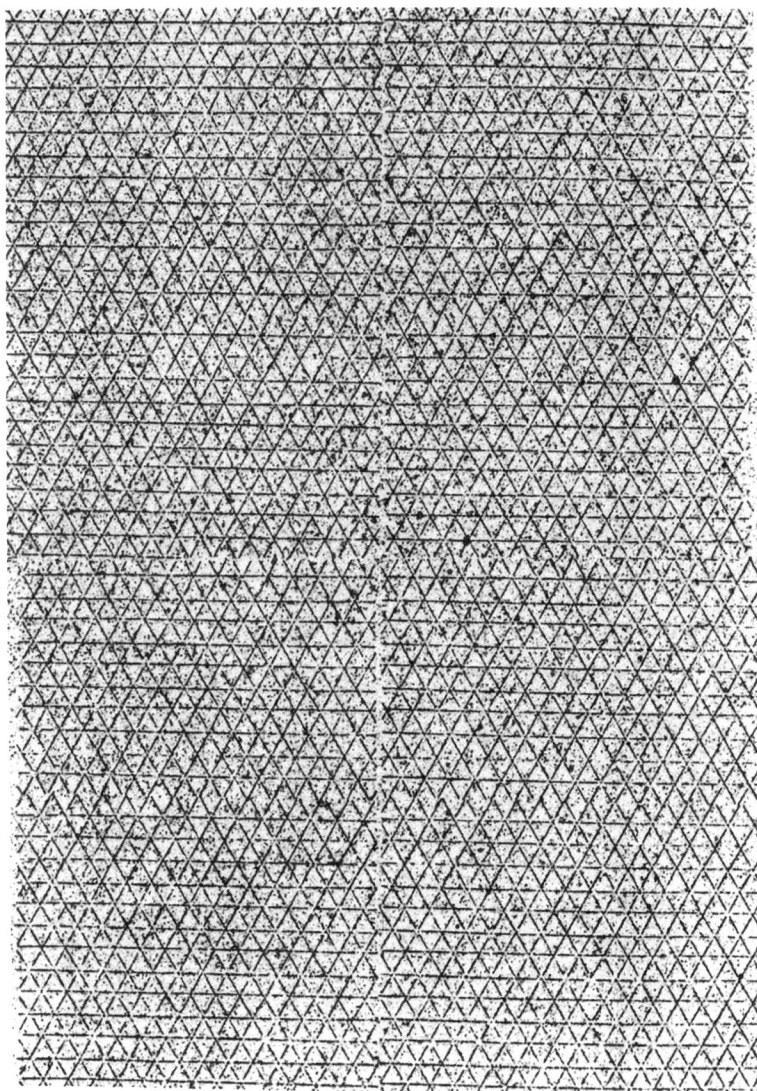

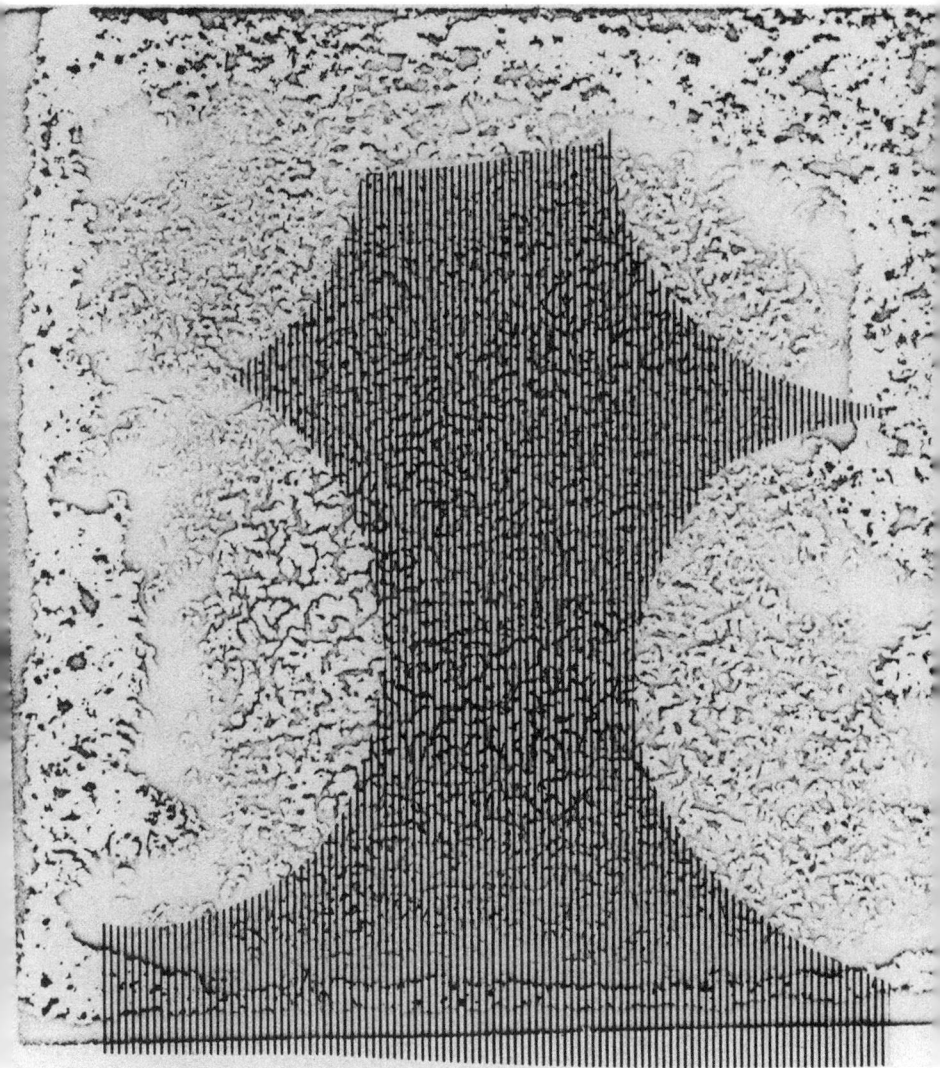

Examples of overlaid organic and geometric textures.

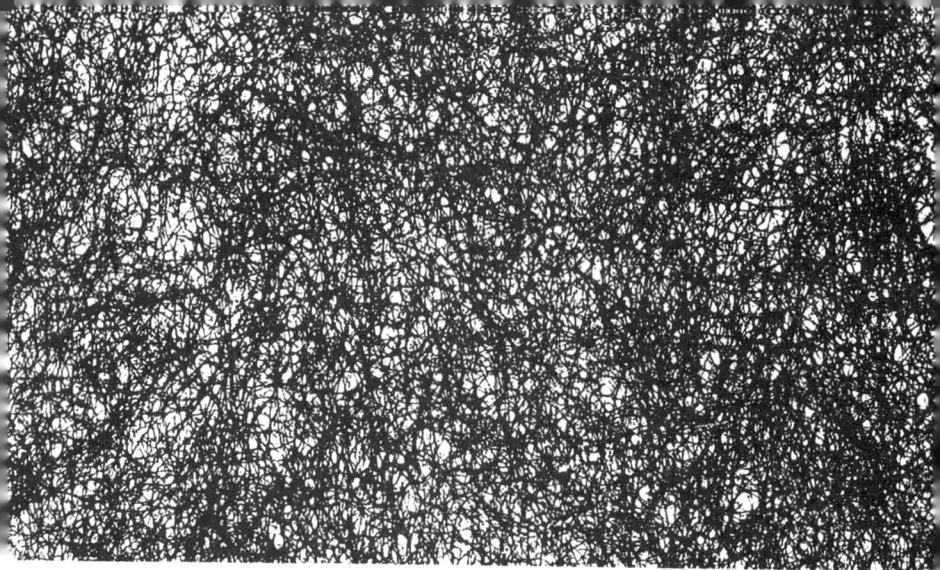

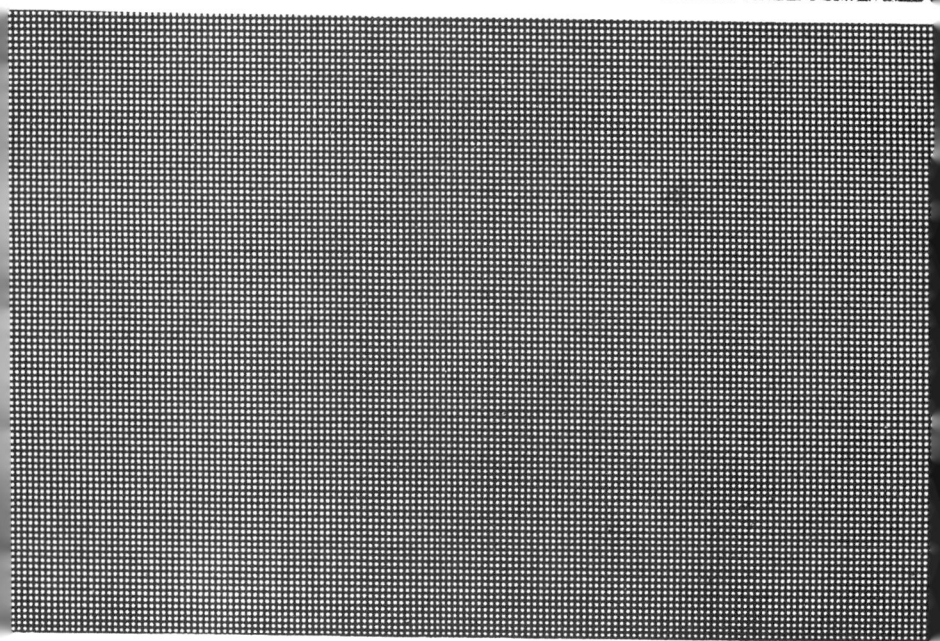

We can divide textures up into two large families: the organic and the geometrical.

106

A texture created by superimposing typographic texts.

Images arise within textures as a function of the rarefaction or densification of the elements that make them up, whether they are geometrical (as in the case of typographical screens) or organic in origin.

The creation of textured images on a Rank Xerox photocopier. The original was a conventional photograph. As seen in these two pages, thanks to multiple intermediate steps, the photographic chiaroscuro has become textured.

110

These illustrations show the various stages of development of a sound print created by means of piezoelectric crystal oscillators. A layer of purified quartz sand was uniformly applied over a horizontal five millimeter thick, 31 × 31-centimeter steel plate. The vibrations generate the patterns. From Hans Jenny, *Cymatics*; photography by Hans Peter Widmer.

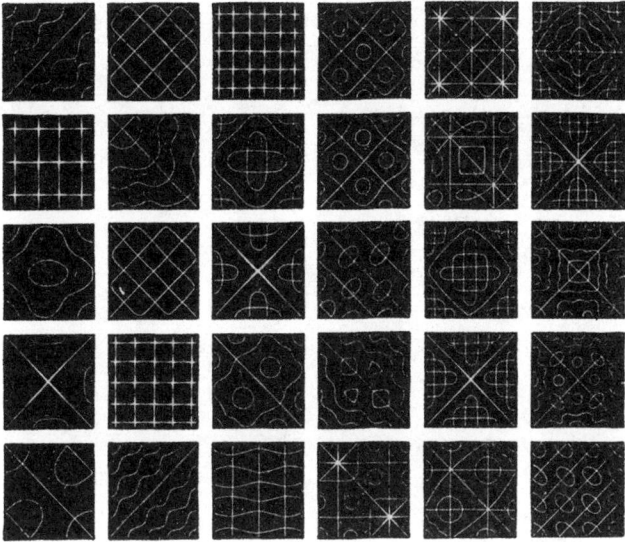

Other figures produced by means of vibrations.

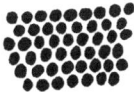

The density and rarity of gas molecules and atoms in liquids and solids.

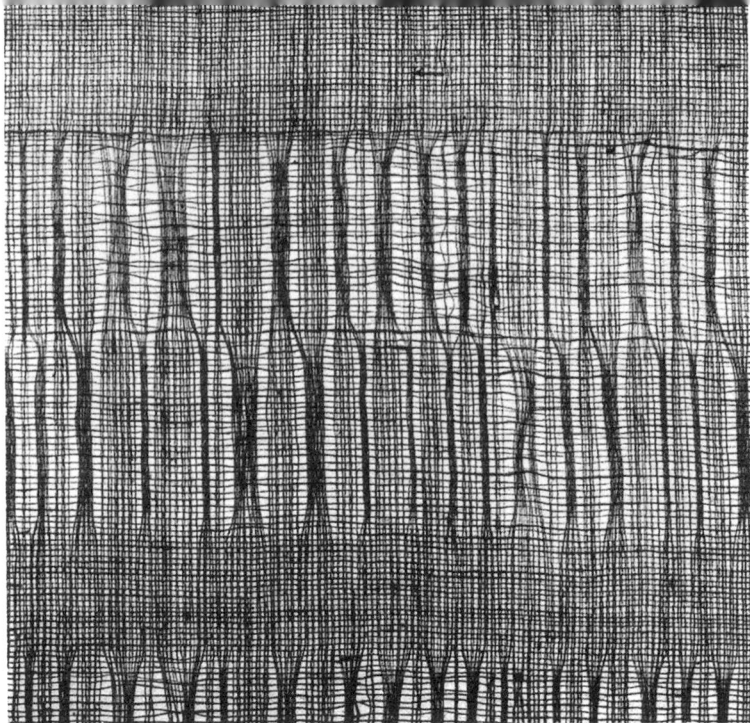

Density and rarefaction in the weave of a curtain and concentration of light points at the center of a rug by Renata Bonfanti.[79]

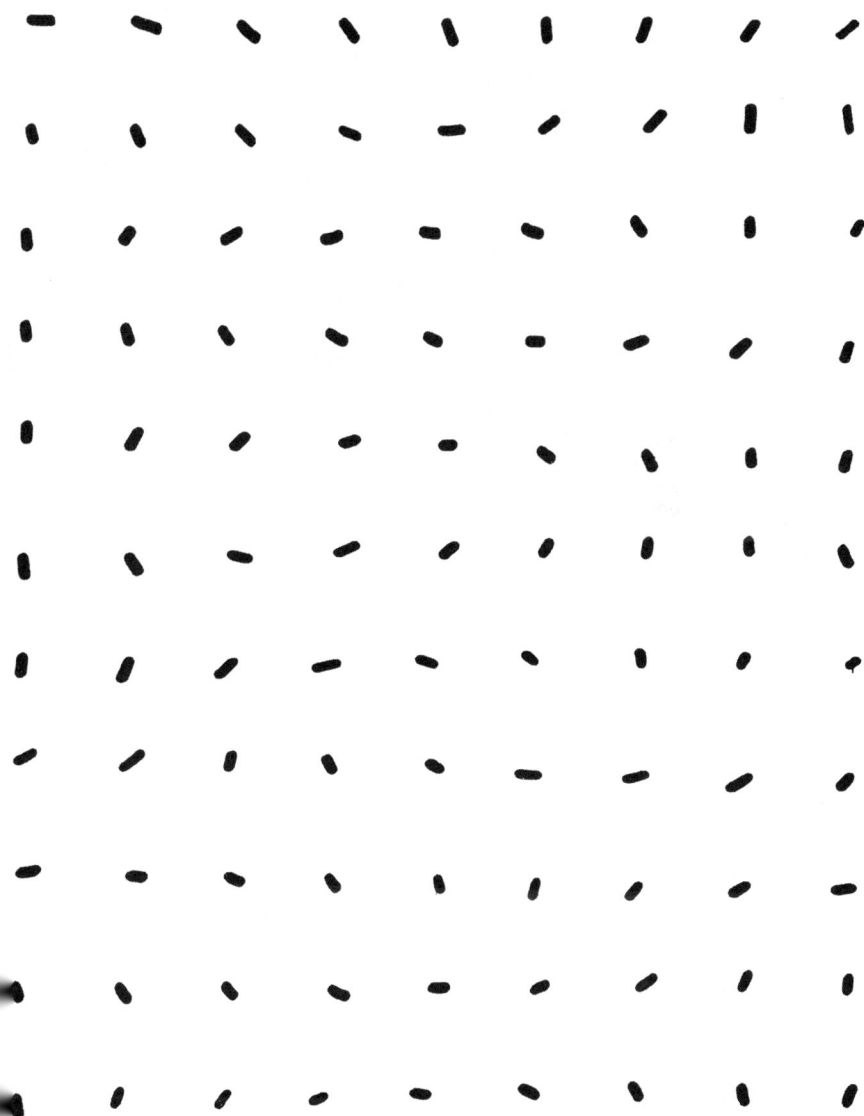

The illusion of motion in a texture obtained by sequentially altering the orientation of components. Bruno Munari, 1960.

Study of textile textures. Plain fabrics with macramé weave, 550 thread, weave ratio 8 threads per 8 wefts, 4 heddles.

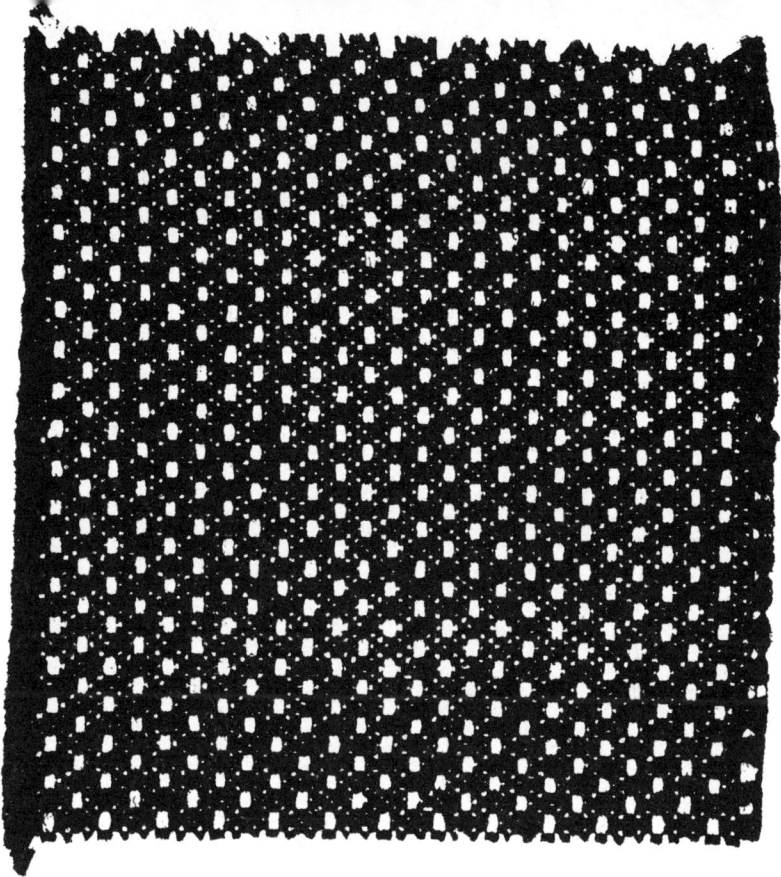

weave

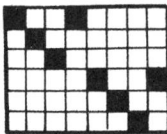

heddles

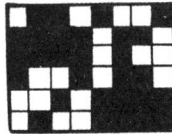

cards

Plain fabric with patterned herringbone; same weave ratio, threads and wefts as in preceding example; 6 heddles. From the Art Institute of Isernia, directed by Prof. Mario Vittorio Garofoli; instructor Prof. Tonino Petrocelli.

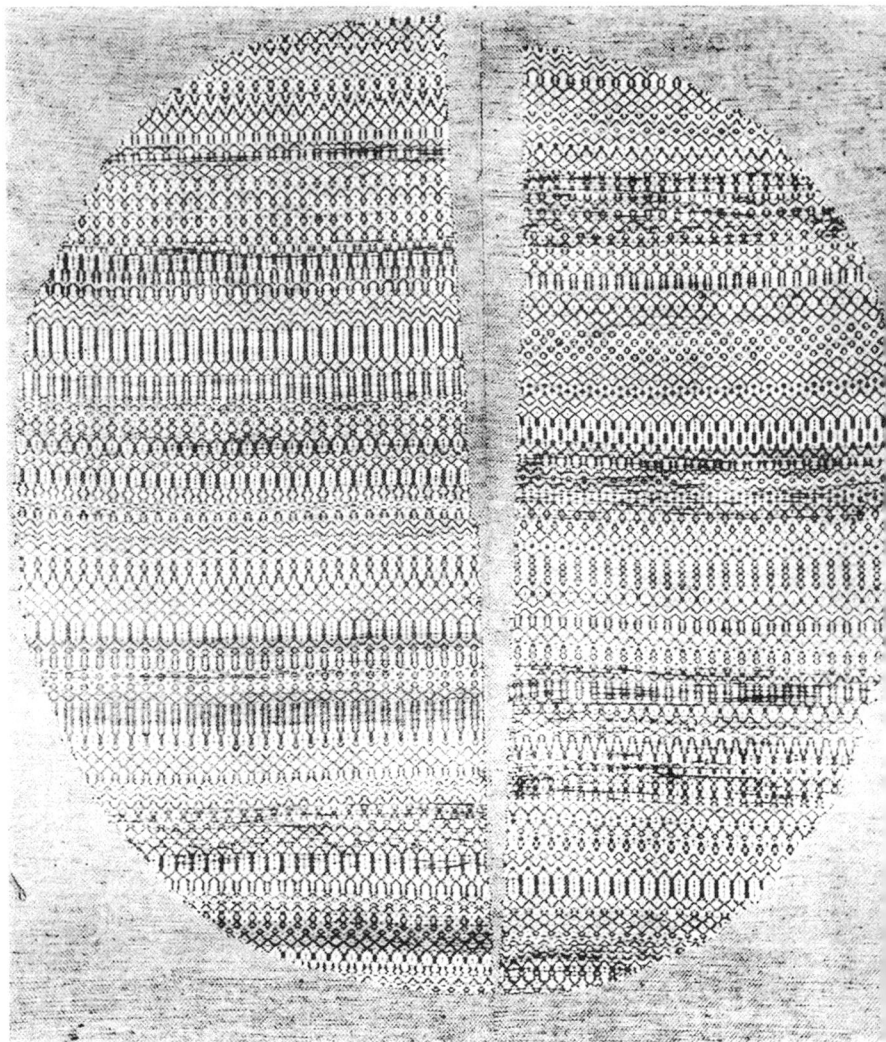

Variations in a series. An example of rigorous programming combined with random variations. As shown by the horizontal lines of the illustration, the warp of these textiles is programmed while, as a function of the textile worker's interests, random variations are introduced through the repetition of stable programmed motifs. The outcome is a set of varied patterns generated by means of the variable repetition of the base design.

The resulting design is, therefore, a collaboration between its creator, Renata Bonfanti, and the various workers who participate actively in the shaping of the final work.

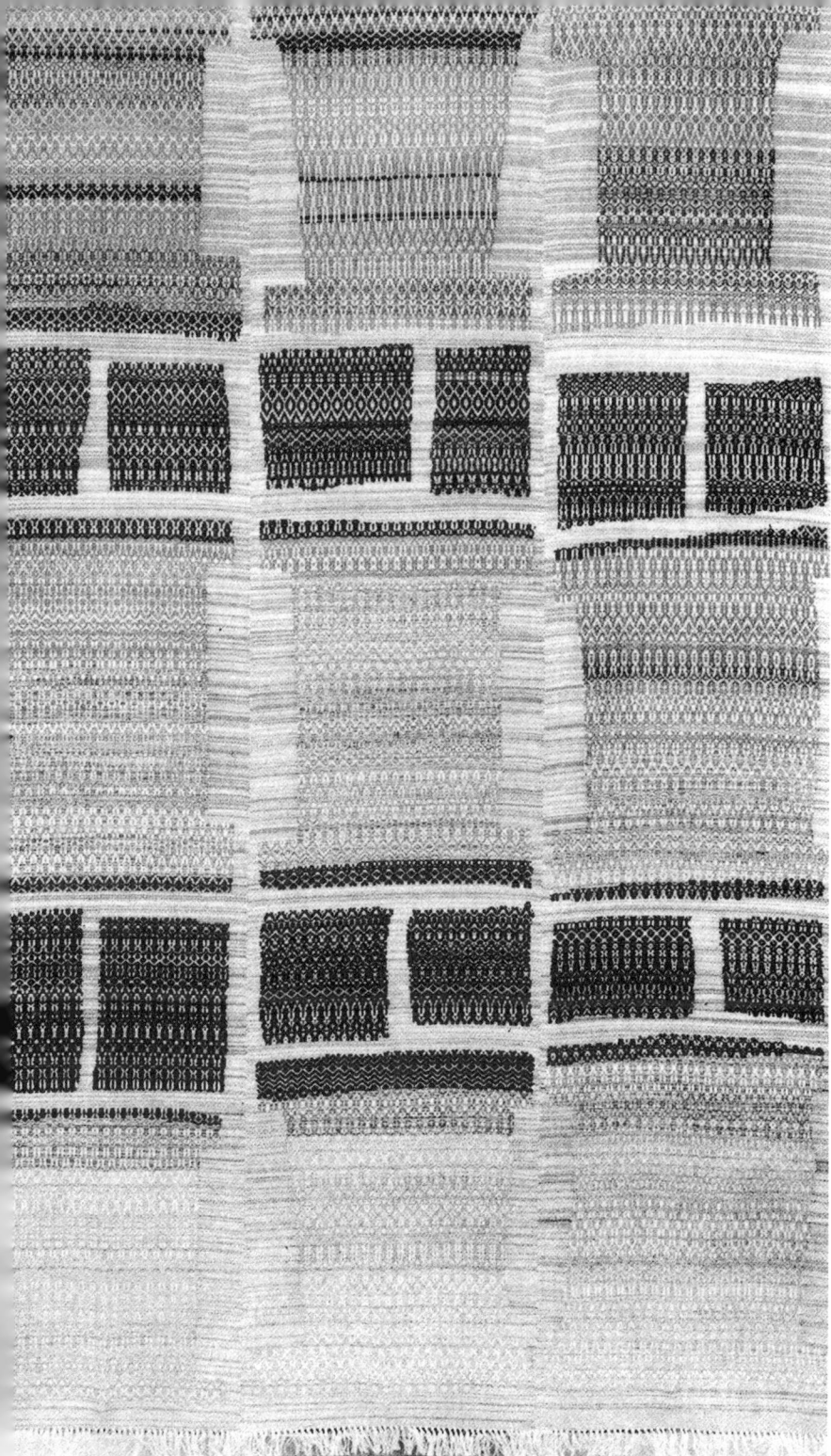

Photographic textures created by Franco Grignani by distorting uniform textures through patterned glass.[80] Despite the appearance in some areas of the texture of divergent elements, the visual field retains its overall unity.

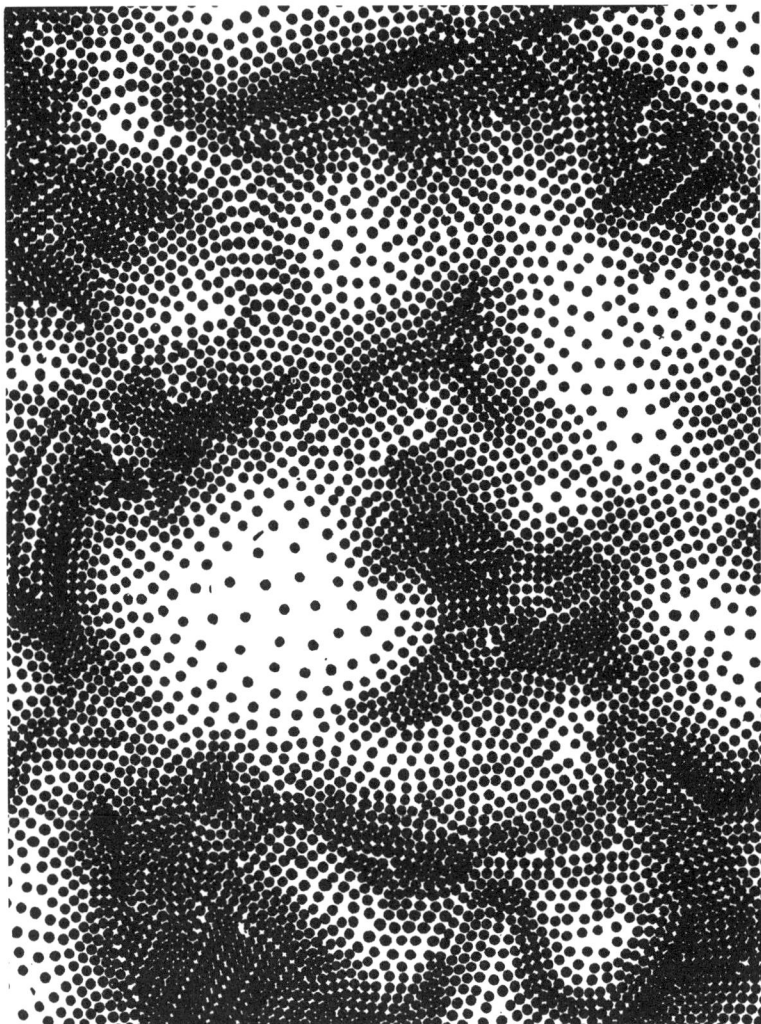

Densification and rarefaction of the same surface. From exercises carried out at the Carpenter Center for the Visual Arts, Cambridge, USA.

A densification and rarefaction achieve by means of the superimposition of two chessboard-patterned transparent screens.

Three examples from the Ulm School involving variations on an isometric grid: by regularly varying the space between the square points they tend to cluster into groups.[81] Another variation can be obtained by altering the dimensions of the dots themselves. When the illustration below is viewed from a suitable distance, one can observe some of the geometrical shapes obtained with these procedures.

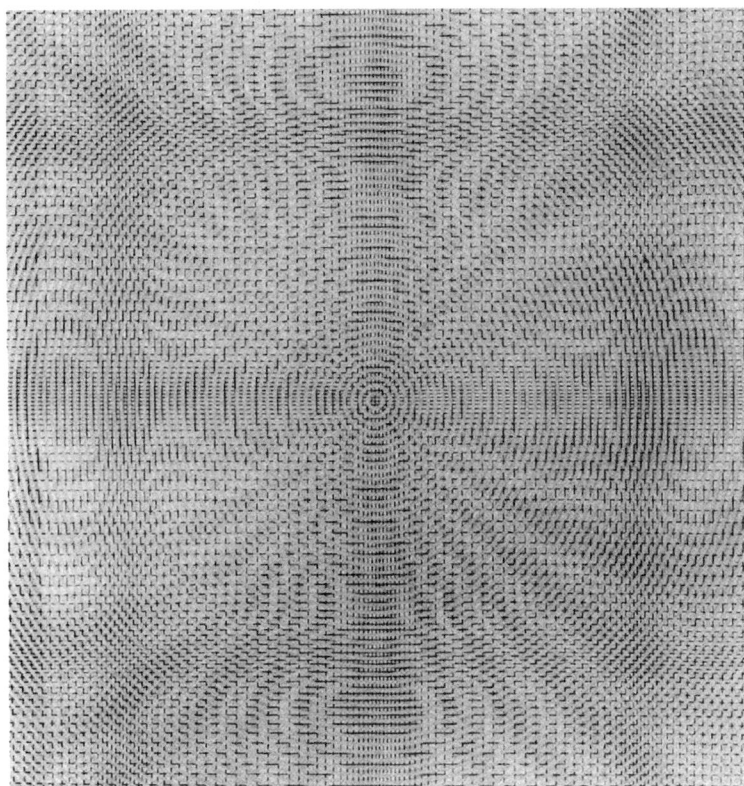

An image created by placing a square grid over a series of concentric circles. From the teaching assignments of Prof. Robert Preusser's course on Visual Design at the Massachusetts Institute of Technology.[82]

A common rough texture from the building industry (Algadian IMP).

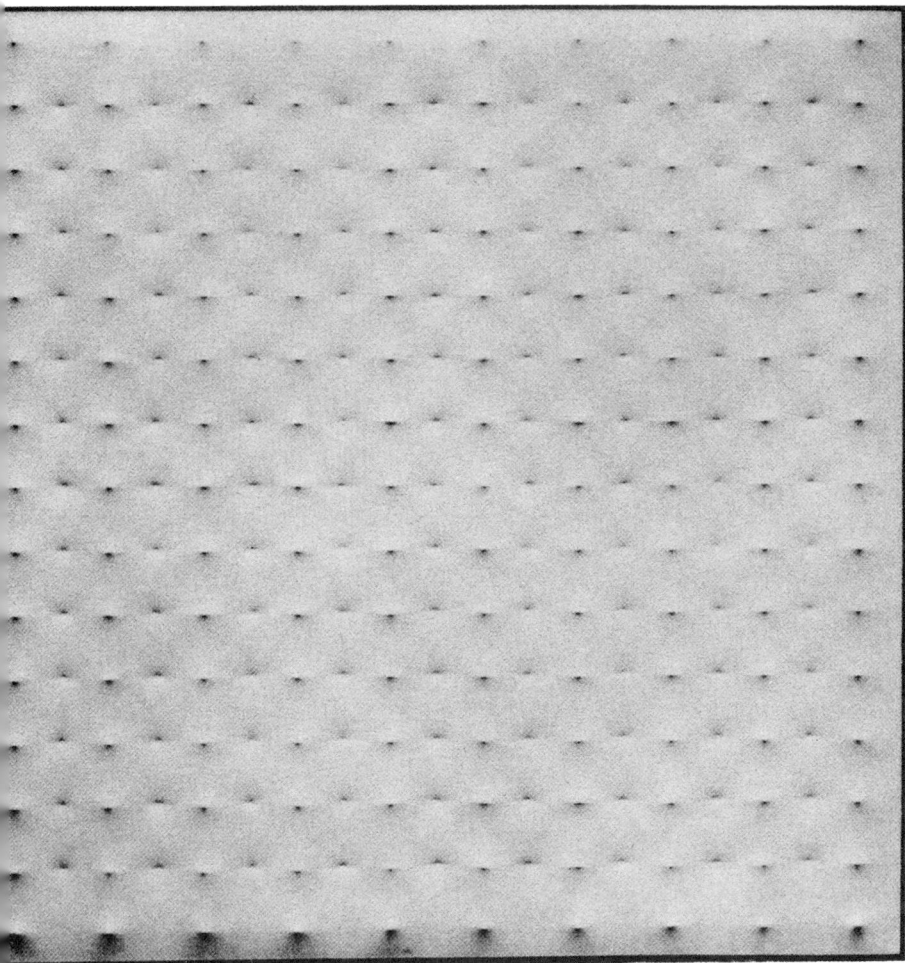

Enrico Castellani, *White Surface* (1965).

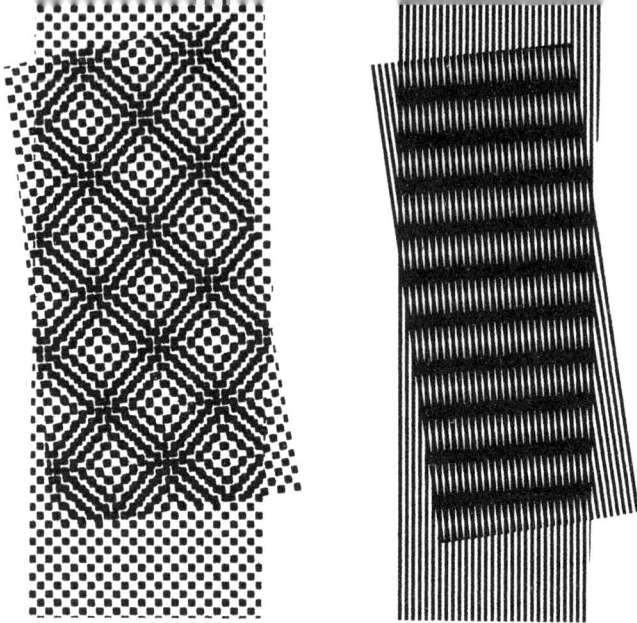

Variations on textures obtained by superimposing transparent screens or pinstripe patterns of the same size over one another and rotating them a few degrees.

The images are generated through variations in the isometric field of the textures, in the density or rarefaction of the components, and also in scale.

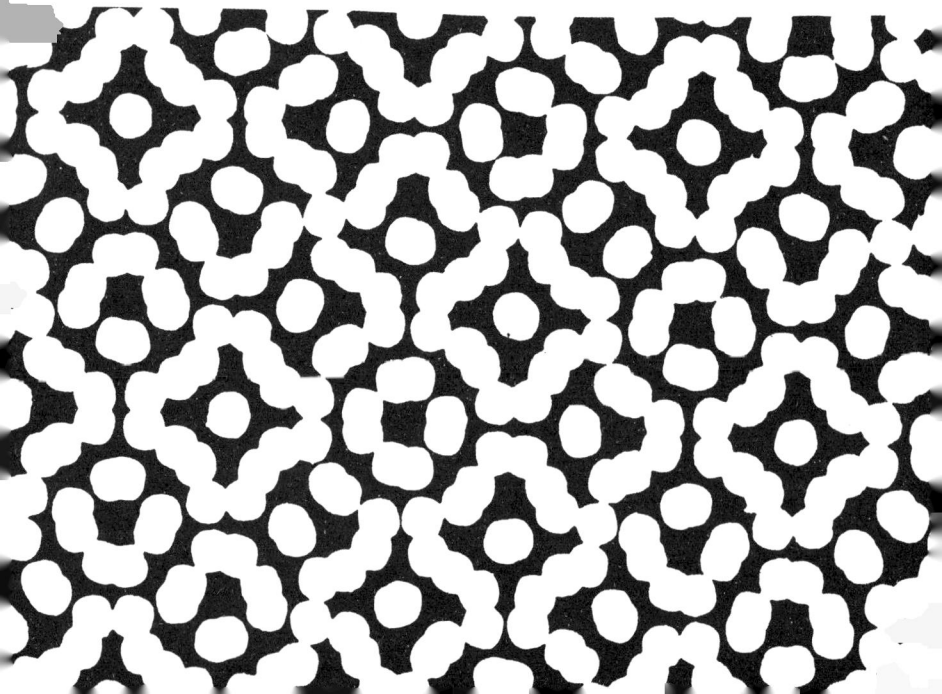

FORMS[83]

If usage of the word "texture" poses some difficulties, the word "form" [*forma*] presents even greater semantic challenges. Of course, diplomatic formalities, the shape of Parmesan cheese wheels, the morphology of shoe trees, or the shapes and counter-shapes that printed matter can assume are of no interest to us here. Our concern is with geometrical and organic forms. Geometrical forms are familiar to everyone thanks to textbooks. Organic forms we encounter in such objects or natural occurrences as the roots of plants, nerves, electrical discharges, rivers, etcetera.

As already stated, the transition from textures to structures is sometimes a matter of scale. If we momentarily abandon the human eye as our perceptual guide and make use of an alternative instrument, textures can be enlarged to the point at which their constituent elements become visible. Among this array of shapes, let's single out the essential ones to streamline our work: the basic shapes from which all other shapes can be generated by varying their component parts.

These basic shapes are three familiar ones: circle, square, and equilateral triangle. In addition, I'd like to add an organic shape whose identity is uncertain but could serve as the basis for experimentation.

Because they are so simple, these basic shapes are underestimated by most people. They appear to have many characteristics relating to the very nature of form—corners, edges, curvatures—so it's worth exploring them using a method that they themselves suggest. Each of these shapes has a different origin, its own internal proportions, and behaves differently when examined. Assemblages made from a number of identical shapes (interconnected to one another by their edges along a flat plane) can generate a variety of shapes as well as clusters of shapes with distinctive characteristics of their own. We encounter instances of negative/positive contrasts, double images, ambiguous images, incredible topological shapes or impossible figures . . . all accurately and rigorously drawn but never buildable. We also encounter growth patterns, branching structures, patterns of decomposition and recomposition, visual recession, visual rhythms, pneumatic forms, liquid shapes, both shapes that are immobile and shapes that bear within them signs of movement.

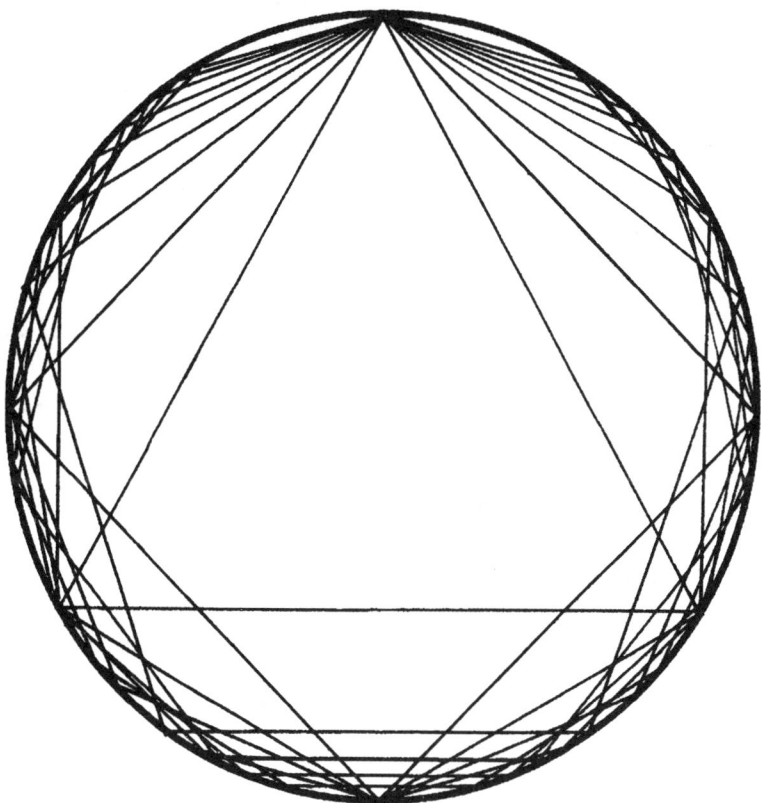

Ten polygons inscribed into a circle, starting with an equilateral triangle in ascending order. The circle is a polygon with an infinite number of sides.

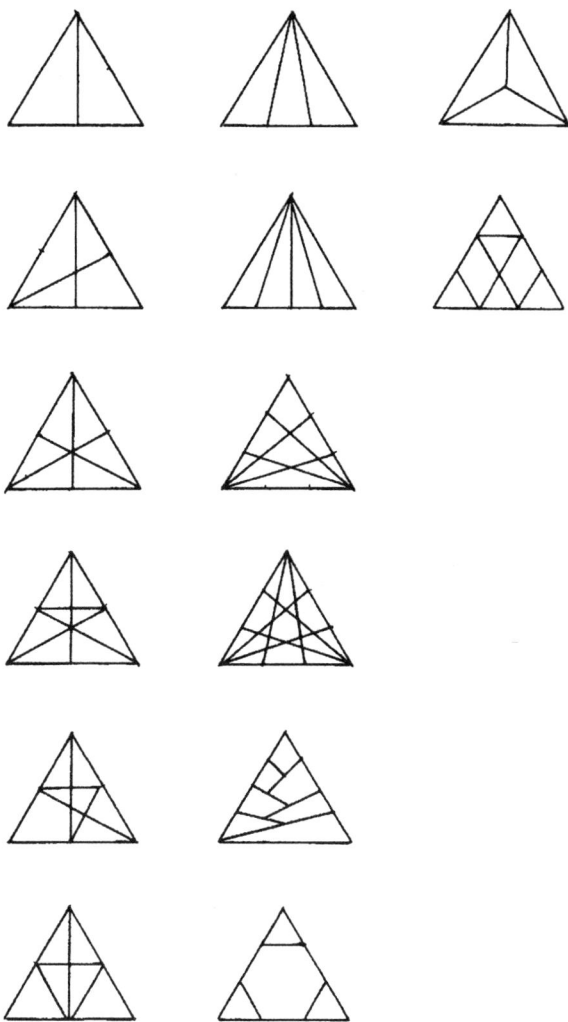

Some internal divisions of circles and triangles carried out by working with the proportions of the overall figure or on parts that have been evenly divided.

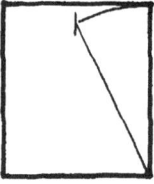

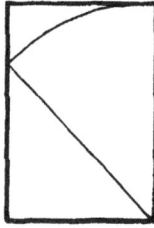

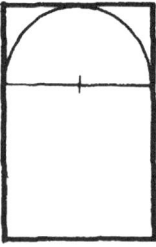

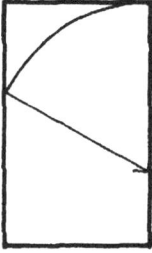

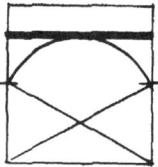

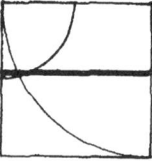

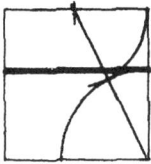

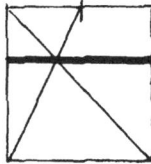

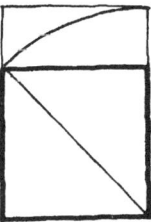

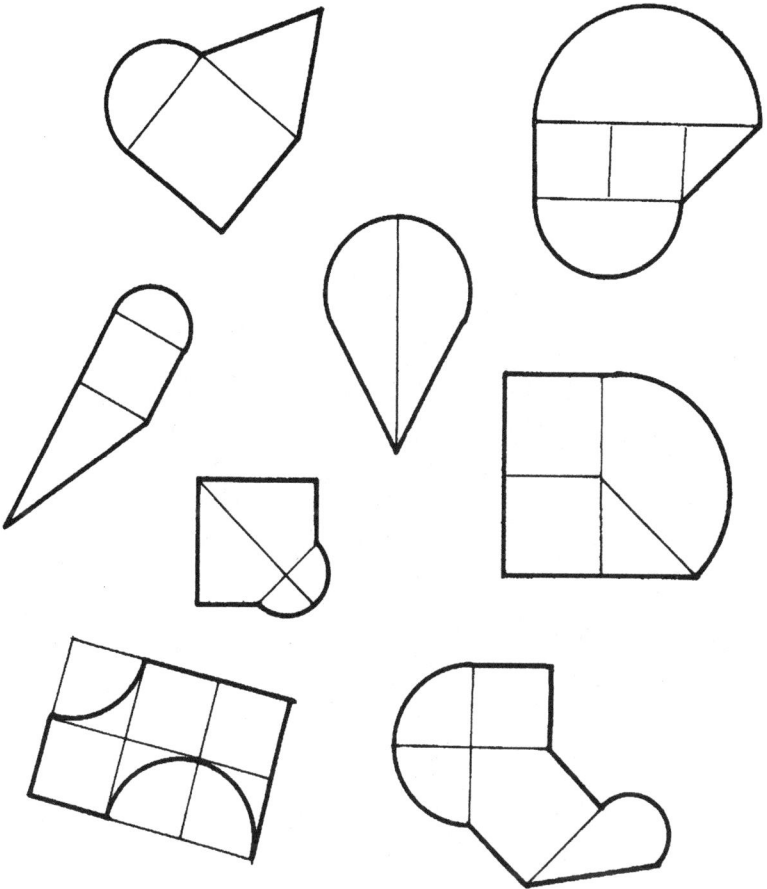

Internal divisions of squares and rectangles based upon their measurements.

Figures created by means of the conjunction of circles, squares, and triangles.

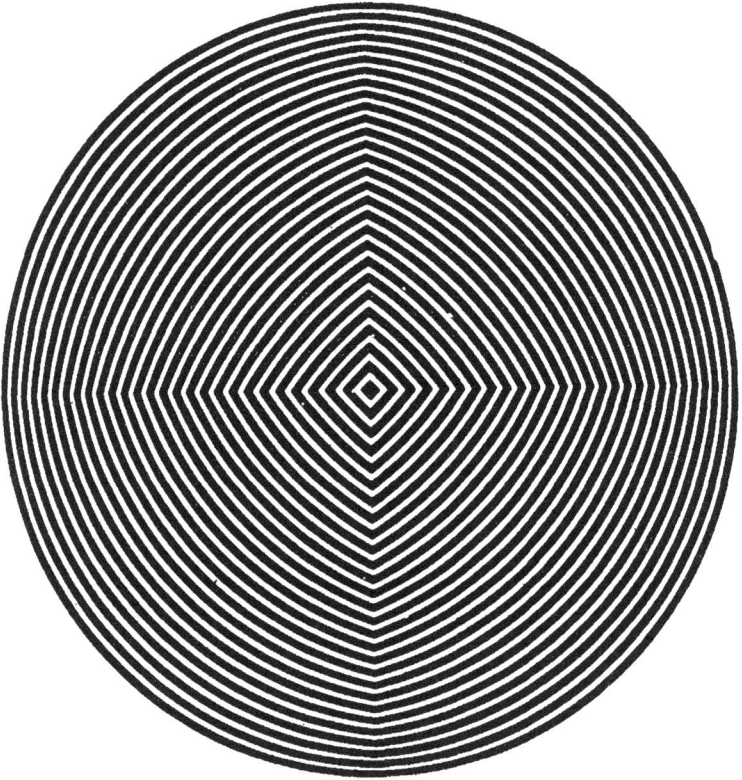

A square expanded into a disk. Marina Apollonio (1960).[84]

136

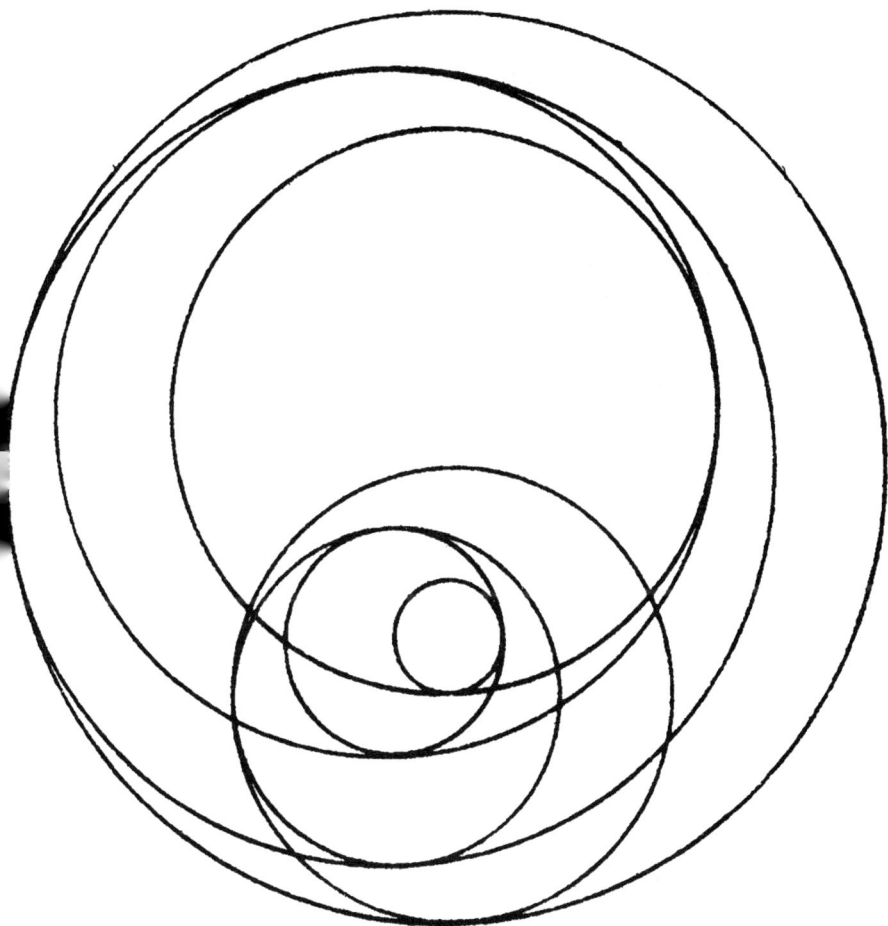

Eight circles with diameters varying from one to eight have been assembled so that four are tangent to two other circles and four are tangent to three other circles. Lanfranco Bombelli (1950).[85]

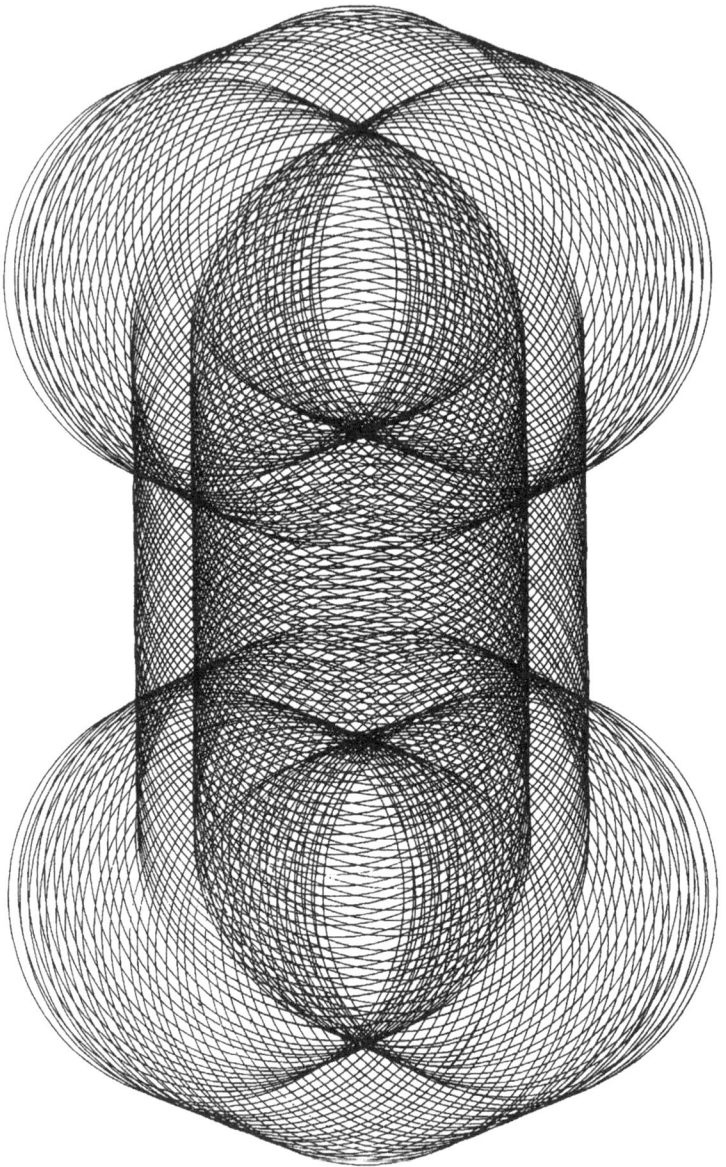

Designs obtained by superimposing a series of equal circles, arranged at modular distances on the basis of an internal structural path. Art Institute of Isernia, directed by Prof. Mario V. Garafoli, instructor Prof. Edilio Petrocelli.

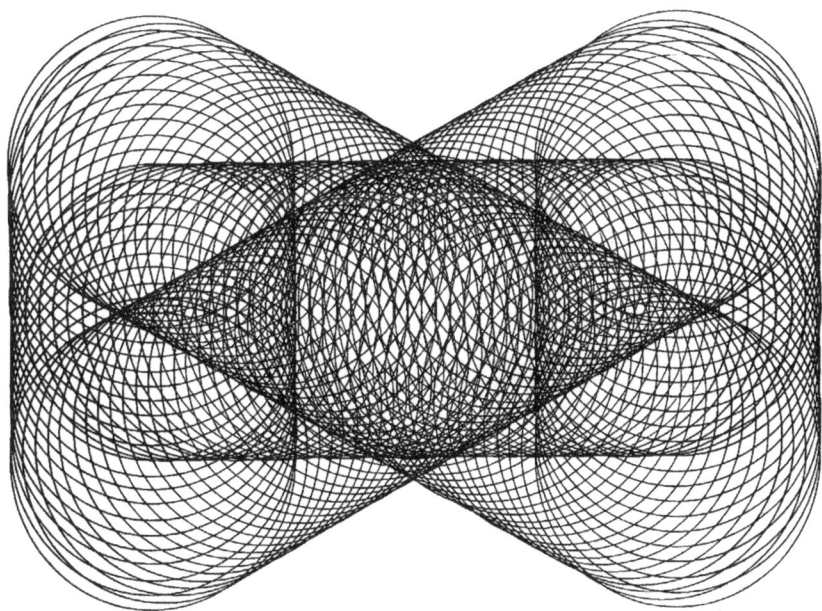

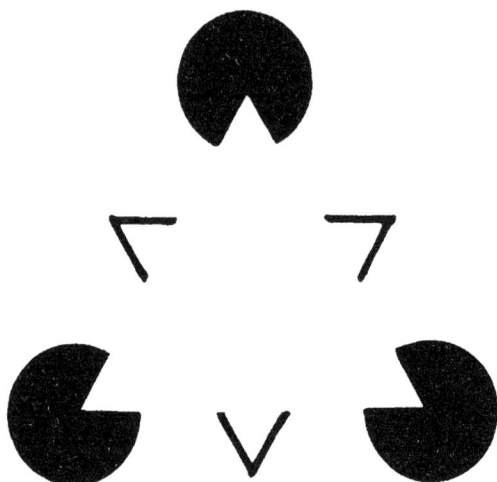

In an article published in *Rivista di psicologia* 1 (Jan.–March 1955), Gaetano Kanizsa from the Psychology Institute of the University of Trieste, describes phenomena of "quasi-perceptual edges in fields with homogeneous stimulation":

"Consider the figure above as a case in point. Objectively speaking, it is made up of three black circular sectors and three black angles laid out in a certain order on a completely uniform white backdrop. Despite this, not only did my test subjects clearly perceive a white triangle superimposed over and partially covering another triangle, but many claimed that the white triangle was cut out of a sheet of paper whiter than the white backdrop and pasted on top. They couldn't differentiate between the borders of the geometrical figure and the physical borders of a surface different from the background."[86]

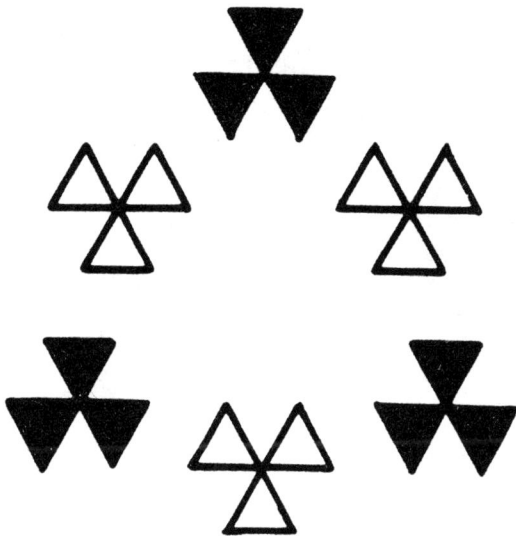

The illusion ceases when each element in the whole is formally auton-
omous and complete such that it is perceived not as a shape that is
missing something, but rather as a bounded form. In such an event, the
uniformity of the visual field is restored.

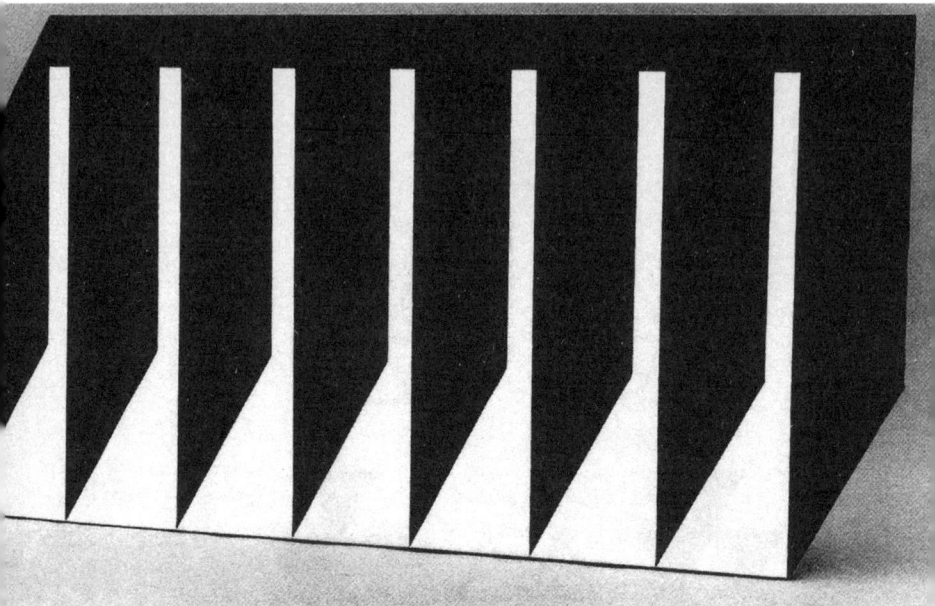

Marco Cordioli, Cadence, 1968. Though a 2D painted image, the 3D effect is the same as that of impossible objects.

A composition with double images.

The logo of Studio Nizzoli Associati. The two squares separated by a triangle in this manner form the letter N in white. The designer was AG Fronzoni.[87]

Perceptual phenomena involving double images are encountered not only in scientific experiments on visual perception but also by chance in a wide array of human and natural objects. A well-known [Italian] weekly magazine featured such double images as found in nature. The ghost image that appears in our example above, depicting a set of wheels devised for travel along a custom rail bed, is obvious: a pair of monkey faces appears within the drivetrain, creating a strong semantic disturbance.

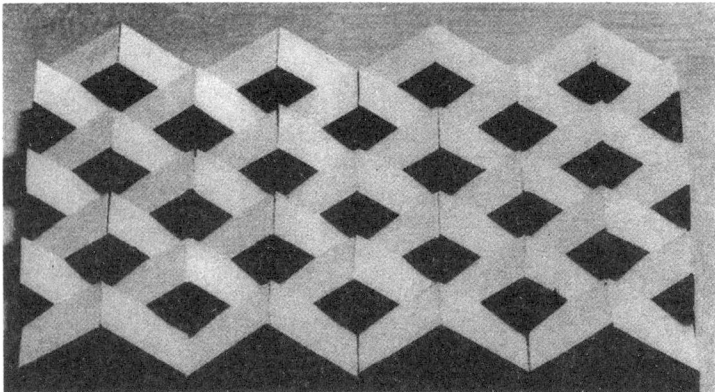

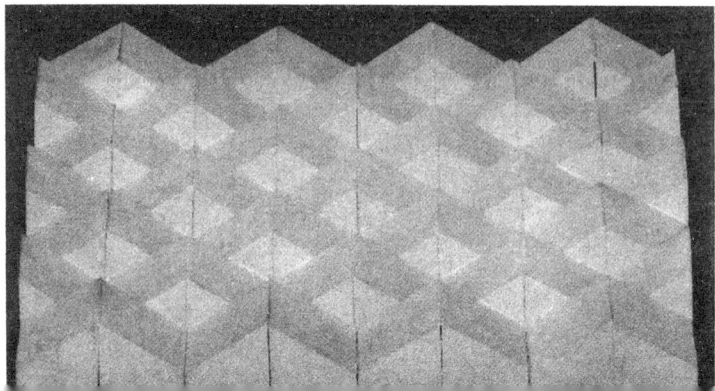

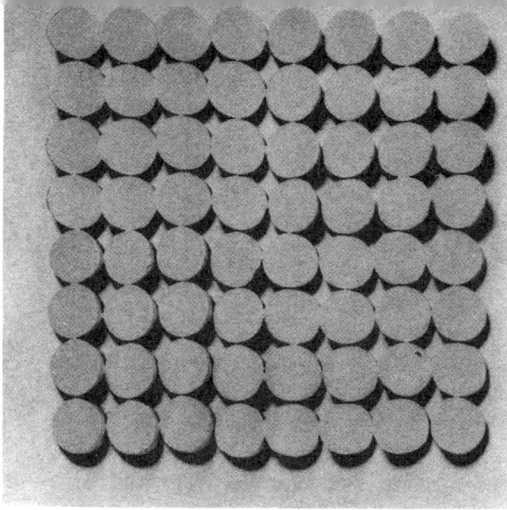

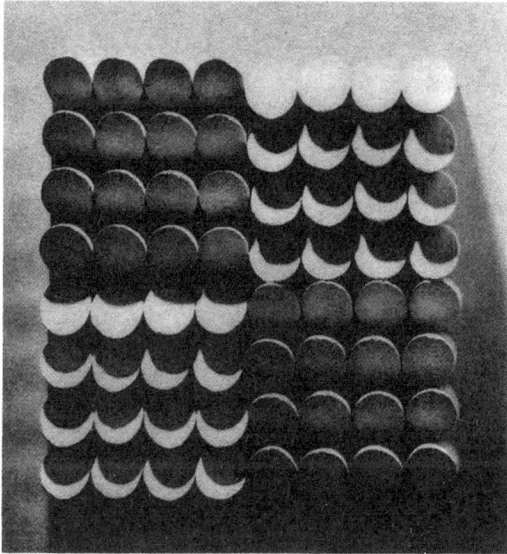

Panels designed for purposes of visual education, developed by students at the Romano Lombardo Middle School (teacher Elio Cenci). Depending on the light, the panels appear in relief with their shadows giving rise to a variety of apparently two-dimensional images of the same object. Because they were made out of colored wood, the color also becomes part of the visual information. (Photo by Carlo Leidi.)

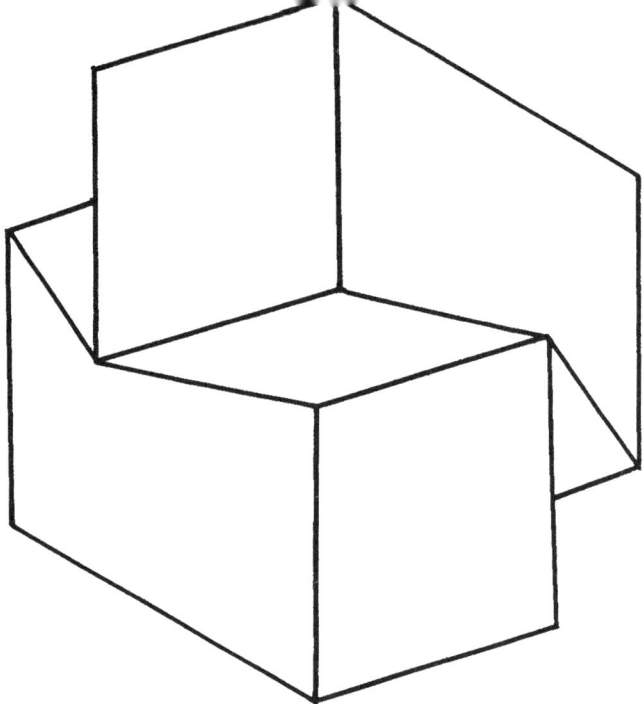

Ambiguous objects are characterized by double perceptions: the relief effect can be reversed by inverting the volumes of the shape itself. Drawing by Joseph Albers, *Structured Constellations*, 1953–58.

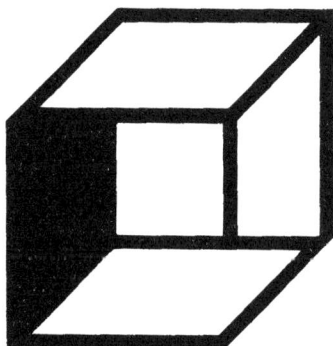

Lanfranco Bombelli, drawing.

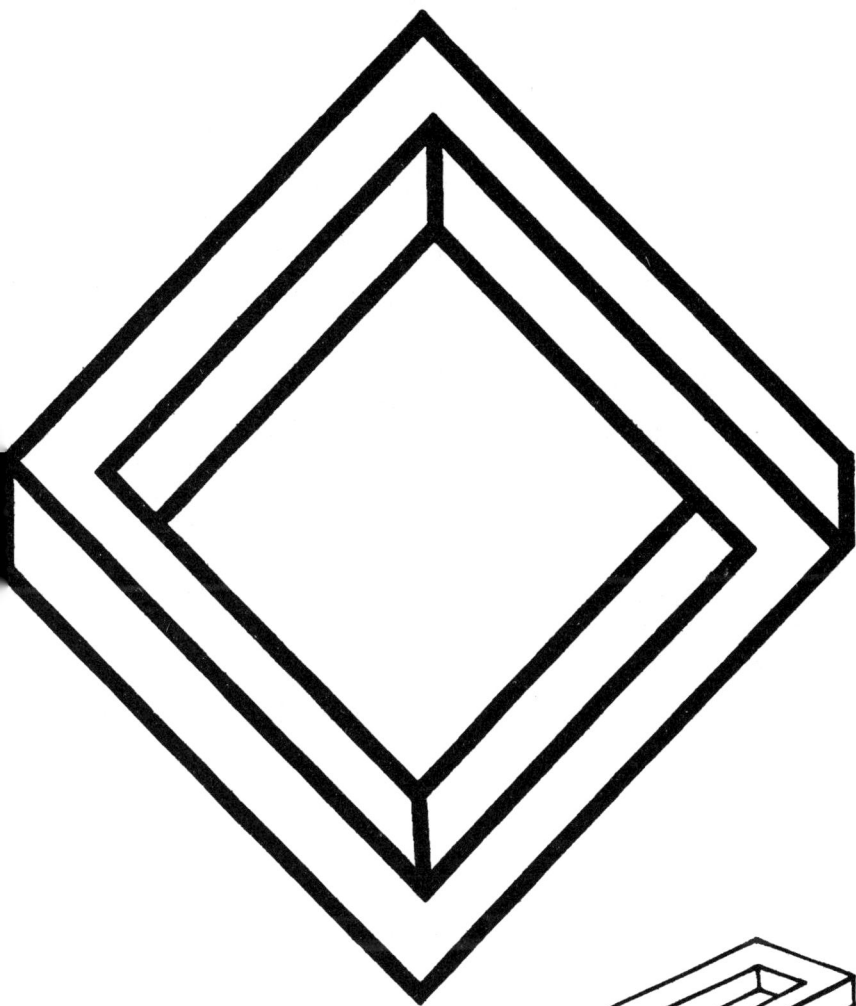

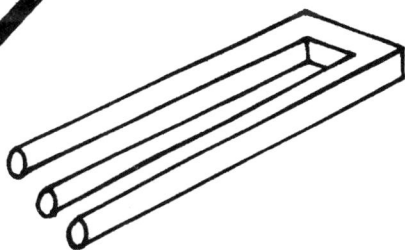

Impossible objects can be perfectly and rigorously drawn on a piece of paper but can never be built in three dimensions. The smaller illustration shows one of the most famous impossible objects. The larger one was drawn by Martin Krampen.[88]

Impossible objects in the paintings of the Spanish artist [José María] Yturralde.

Marcello Morandini, "Formal Progression," 1965. A sequence of quarter sphere volumes. The image is to be read left to right, starting in the upper left-hand corner, all the way down through the squares.[89]

A sequence of formal transformations involving four semicircles in continuous motion. Each semicircle moves towards the center and then crosses over into the opposite position, where it appears inverted. During the passage, the four identical shapes are superimposed such that they give rise to a series of additional shapes made up either of the curved portions of the semicircles or the straight lines of each disk's diameter transformed into the side of a square. The sequence is by Helmut Zimmermann (1970).

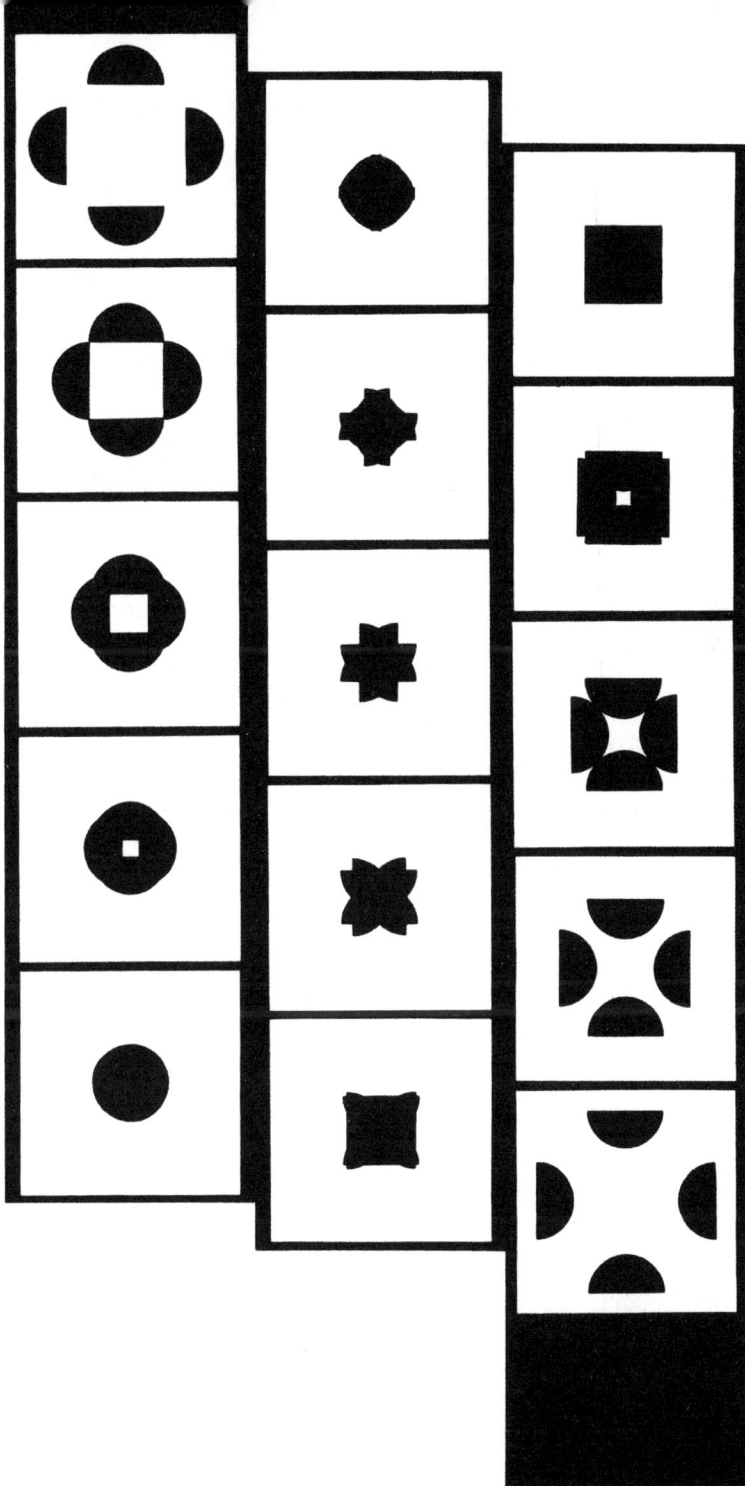

Variations on the theme of the circle. Student project by Mirella Quaretta, Novara School of Design.

A group of four images of textures that move through a square space at a different pace in each image. To be read from left to right and vice versa.

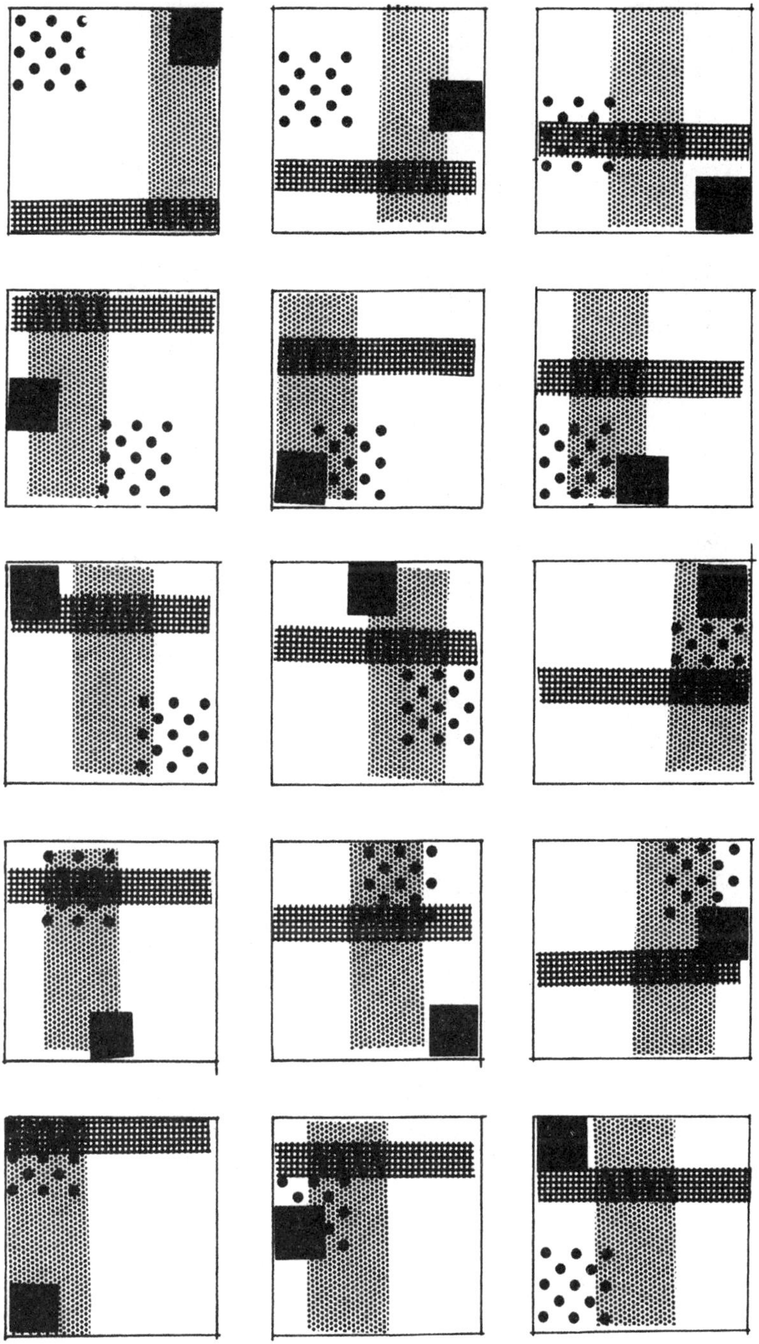

An image sequence based on a disk shape. One can obviously perform many exercises of this kind.

154

Effects of visual recession achieved by diminishing the size of the base and sides or the intensity of the texture. These forms of visual recession can also be devised by altering the gap between components (which can be either fixed or involve some sort of progression).

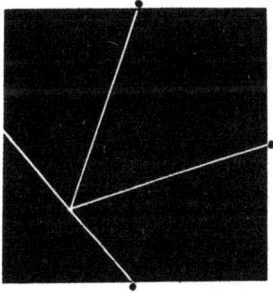

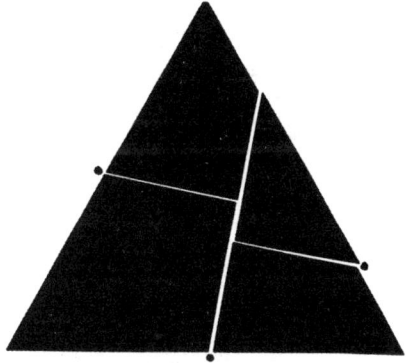

A square sectioned according to the white lines and hinged at the indicated points can be transformed into an equilateral triangle.

155

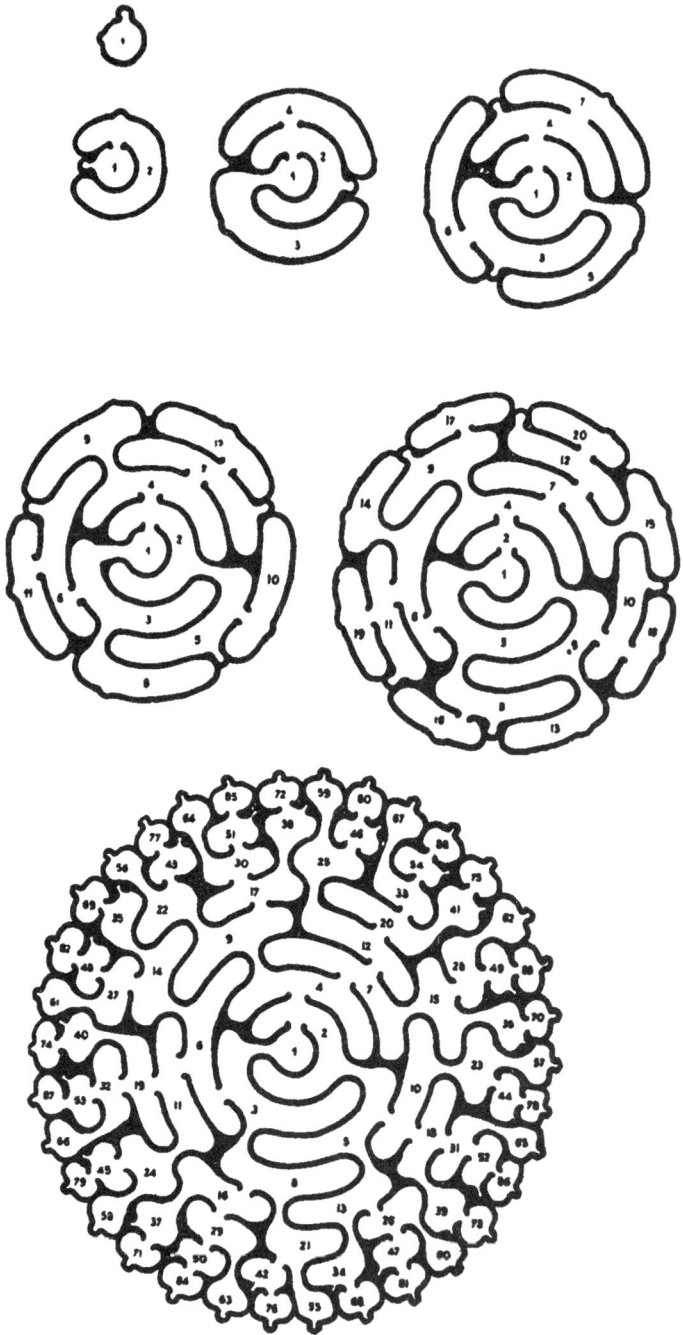

Diagram of the generative core of a vegetable at various stages of growth.

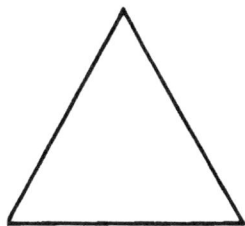

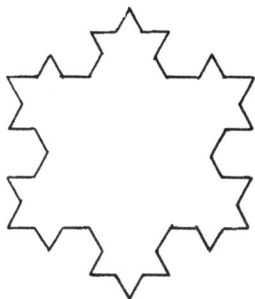

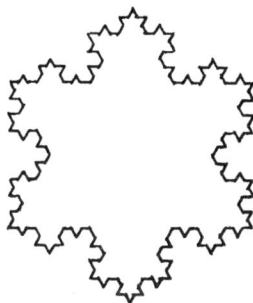

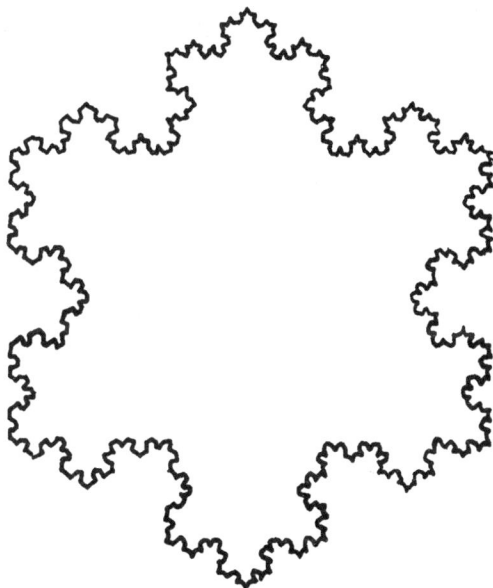

The second figure is obtained by dividing each side of an equilateral triangle into three parts and drawing a triangle on the outside of each side. If one continues the same procedure on each of the resulting new sides the eventual result is the so-called snowflake curve. The same operation can be performed by drawing triangles on the inside, but the resulting shape will be different.

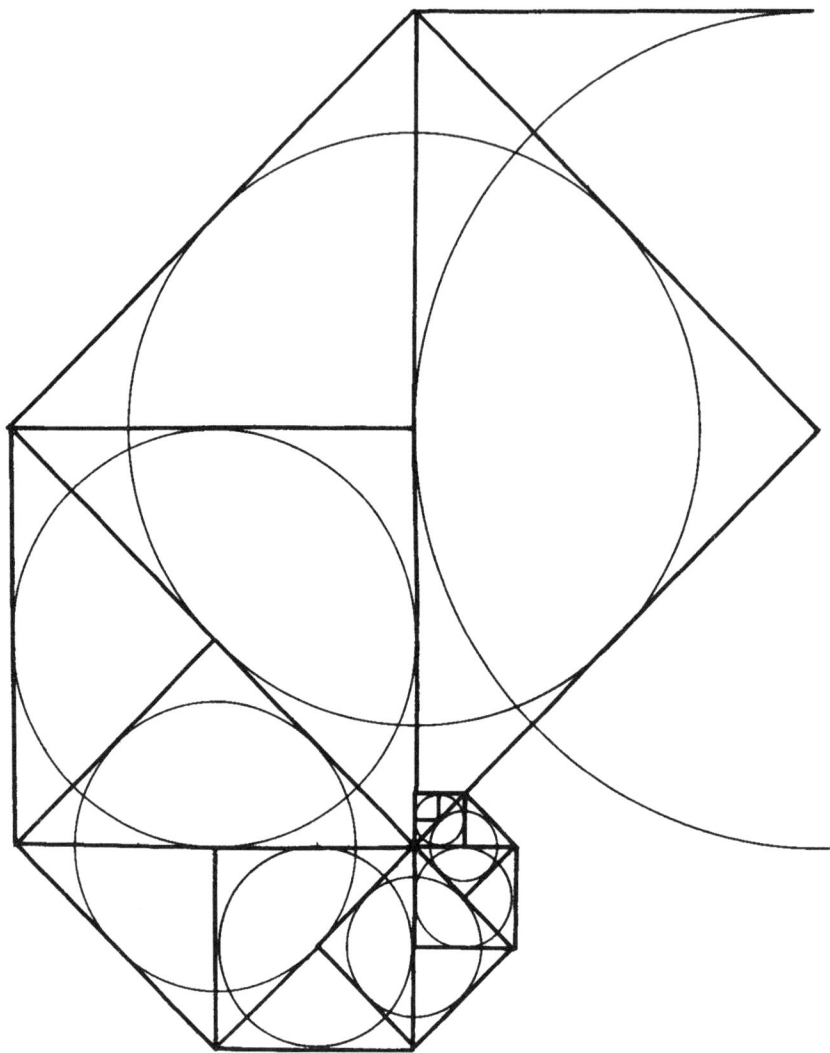

Simultaneous growth of a square and a circle according to a spiral pattern. This type of spiral is constructed by tracing a circle on the vertex of a small square whose radius is half the diagonal of the square itself. The square is then built upon this circle (which has the diagonal of the previous square as its side). Etc., etc., until your paper runs out.

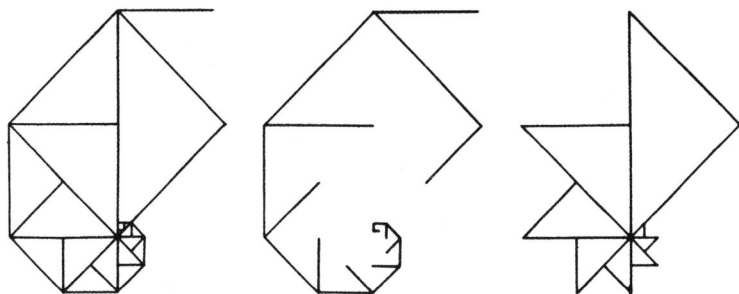

Exploring shapes contained in an overall shape. The drawing below of a leaf is the mirror image of a portion of the penultimate drawing above. Other images can also be created by coloring or covering bounded areas within the drawing as a whole.

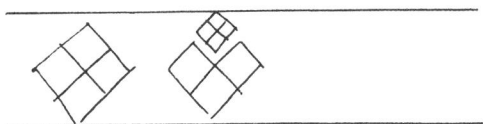

The unidirectional growth of a square. The same exercise can be performed with any basic shape, working with most elementary internal subdivisions of the figure itself. In this case, the texture of the square is uniform but could be made to reflect the growth pattern through densification or rarefaction.

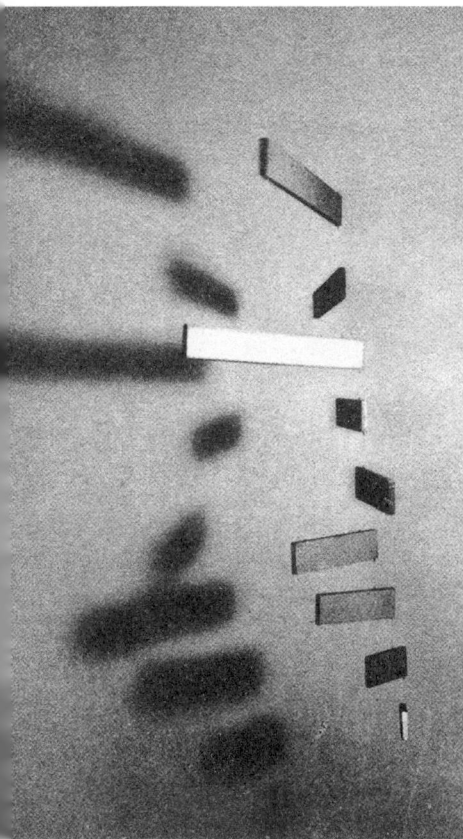

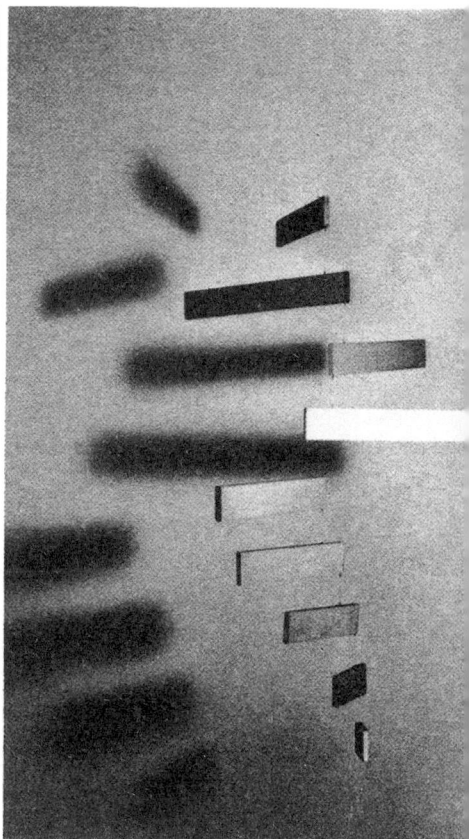

Suspended shapes: a square and a series of rectangles that are multiples of the square are hung beneath and attached to one another, with the uppermost one suspended from the ceiling. The spontaneous rotation of the components alters the composition. Any basic geometrical shape can be built out as a function of its internal proportions, recomposed, and hung in an open space. Bruno Munari (1948).[90]

A symmetrical hexagonal ceiling light made out of anodized aluminum slats of decreasing length. When the light is stored, the slats, hinged to a series of hexagonal metal rods, lie flat and the lamp takes up little space. When the light is hung, due to gravity, the slats deploy vertically. Design by Bruno Munari, produced by Danese.[91]

The distortion of an image can generate new images that sometimes don't recall the source image. This white line captures the reflection of the white mast of a boat in the water as photographed by Mario di Biasi.[92] Distortions can be used to study deformations of regular images under controlled conditions or to produce new images.

Distortion of a 2D texture over a 3D volume. Photo by Mimmo Castellano.[93] The projection of textures onto objects (even small textures pressed into glass slides) is a useful experiment.

Fold a sheet of cardboard just like Castellano did and then project uniform lines onto it. You will see how the thickness of the lines (or the components of a texture) are altered. Such exercises have numerous applications, especially in the fields of graphics and advertising.

Franco Grignani: distortion of a texture seen through a lens and sheet of patterned glass.

Any image can be distorted. The optical apparatus documented on the facing page is called a Fotomaster and can freely and quickly transform any source image: in this case the word FOTO. It thus accelerates work that used to have to be carried out manually: work that was onerous and whose outcomes were unpredictable. In the column to the right the same distortions as reinterpreted by a Xerox machine.[94]

166

FOTO FOTO

FOTO FOTO

FOTO FOTO

FOTO FOTO

FOTO FOTO

FOTO FOTO

FOTO FOTO

FOTO FOTO

FOTO FOTO

FOTO FOTO

FOTO FOTO

MASTER

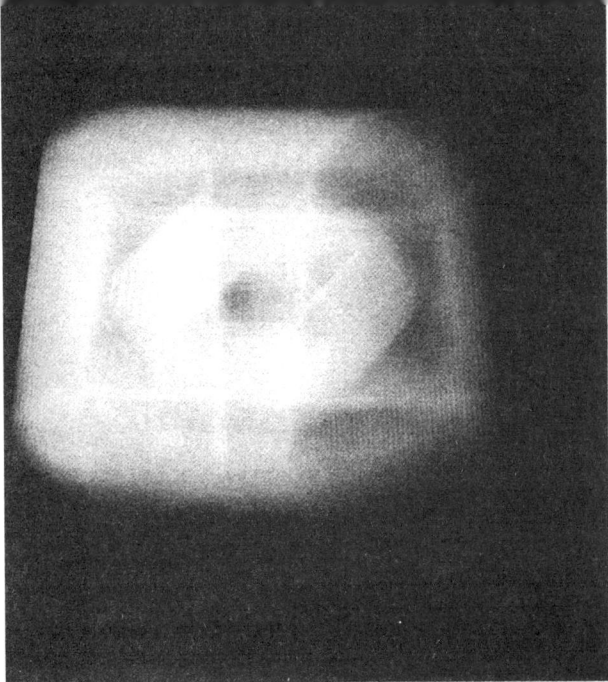

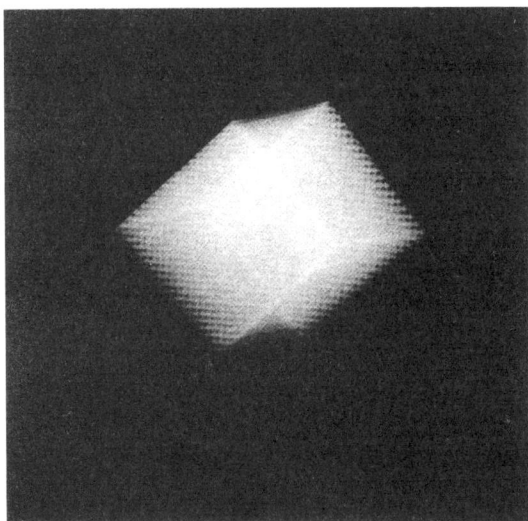

Rafael Martinez, *Immaterial Volume* (1969).[95] These images were created by subjecting an elementary shape—in this case a cube—to vibration. Painted in white and seen against a dark background, the core shape generates various "immaterial volumes" as a result of the directionality of the vibrations. As the vibrational thrust decreases, these volumes diminish in size from the expanded contours they assume under maximum vibration down to their actual static form.

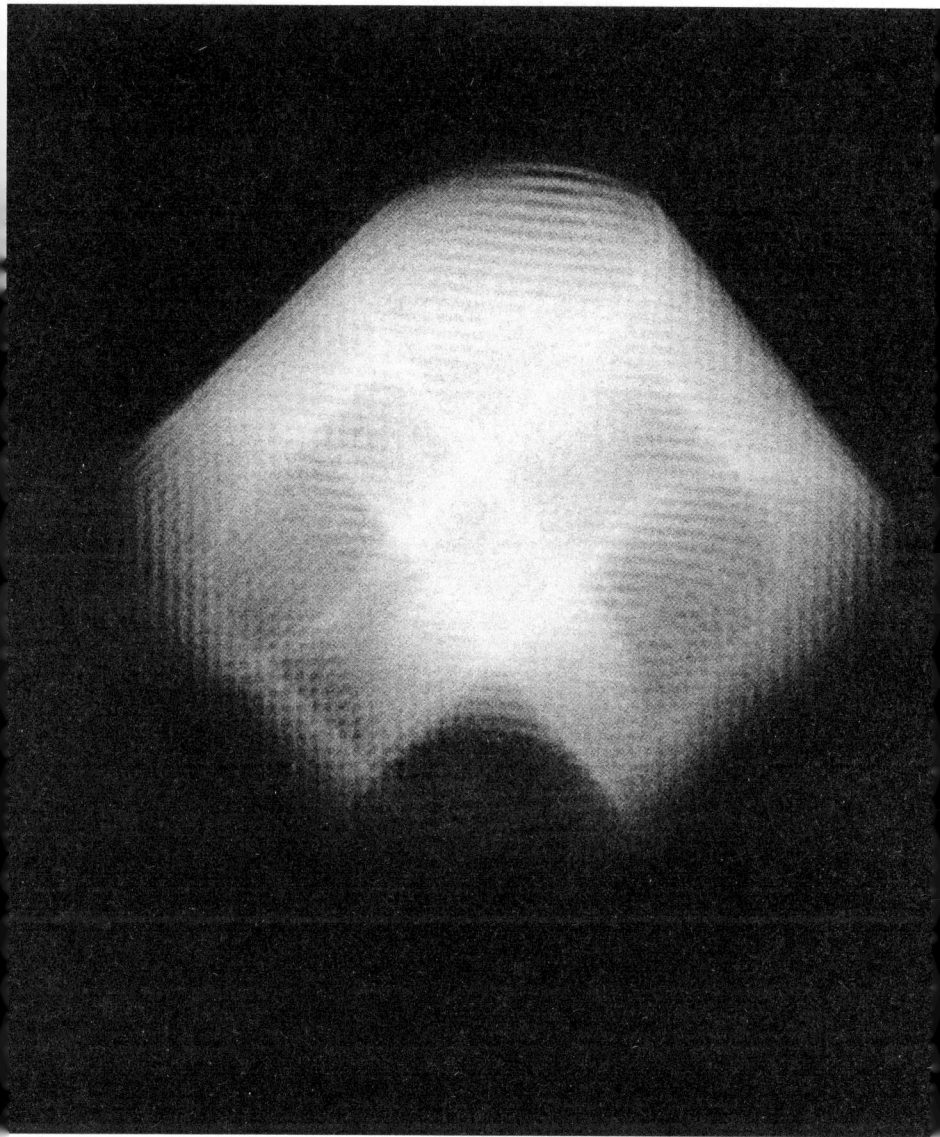

Three-dimensional distortion of a two-dimensional grid. Object by Ugo La Pietra (1967).[96]

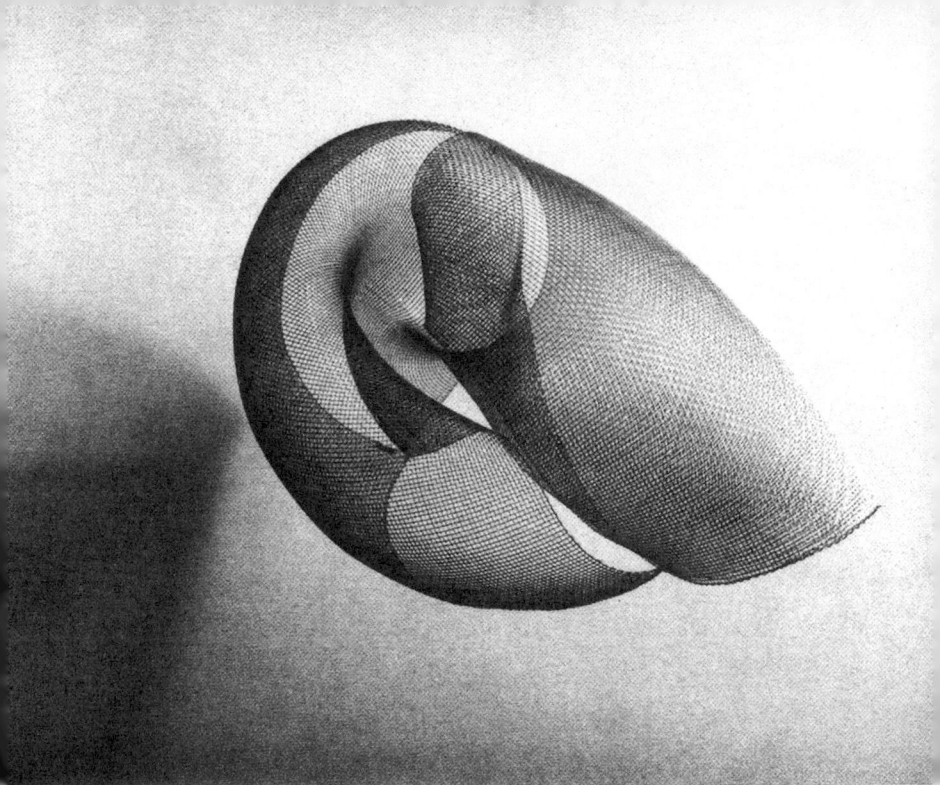

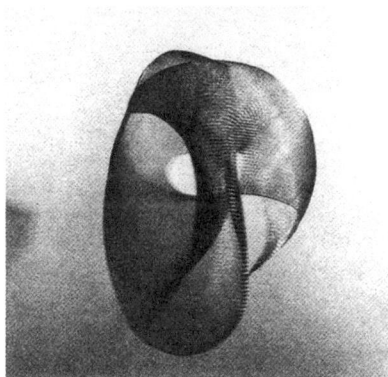

Three views of a three-dimensional object fabricated from a square, flexible metal mesh that has been bent and then fastened at predetermined points. Bruno Munari, *Concave-Convex* (1948).

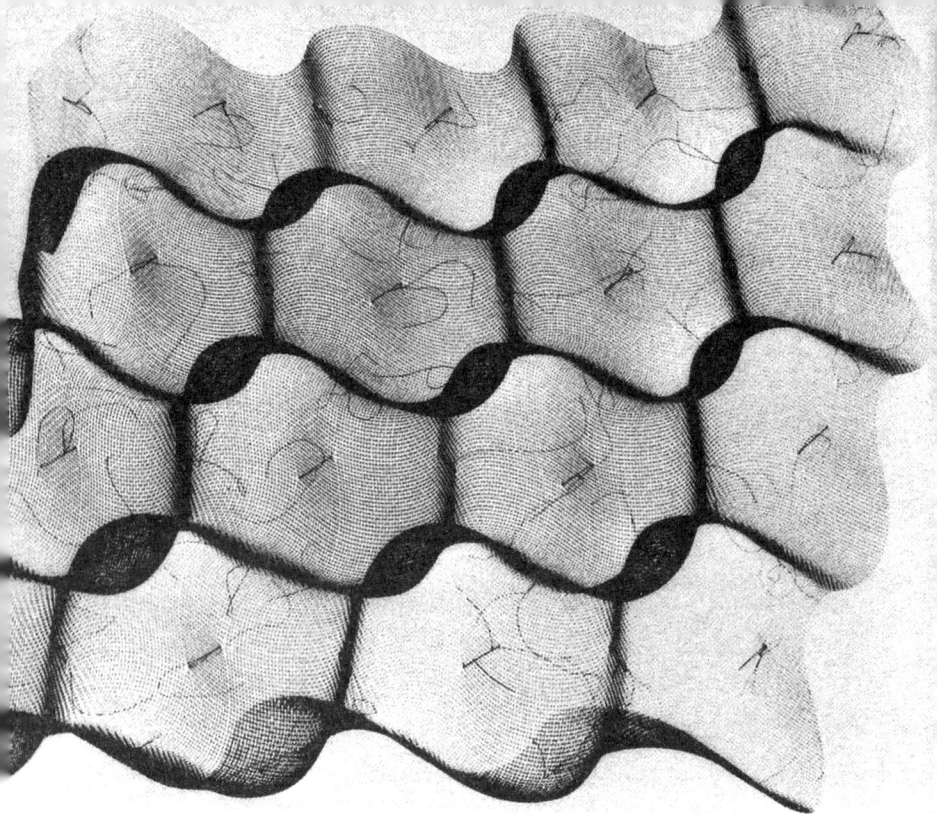

The work of a student at the Carpenter Center for Visual Arts (1967).

A bowl created from a square metal sheet that has undergone four cuts (as indicated in the diagram).[97] The edge of each of the sections marked A has been cut and superimposed over points B and spot-welded. The object's shape is the result. Below are other three-dimensional shapes that can be created by folding a square surface.

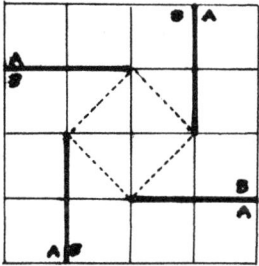

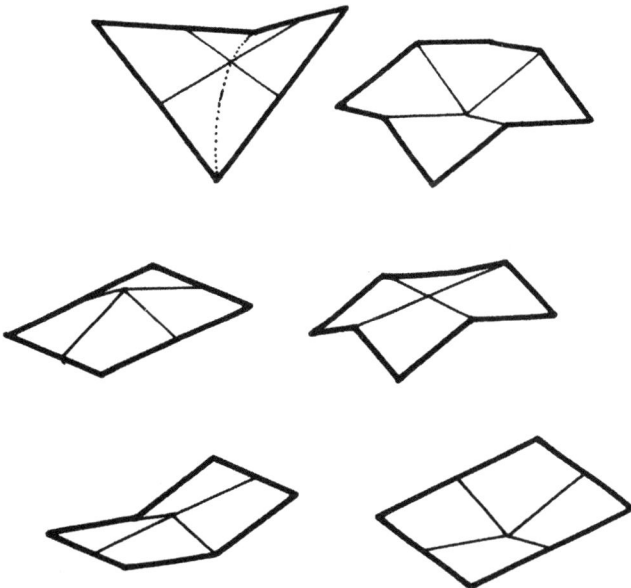

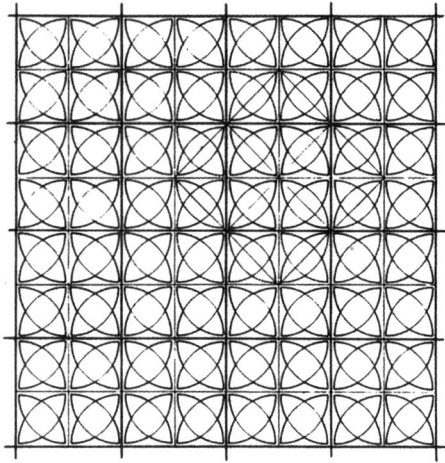

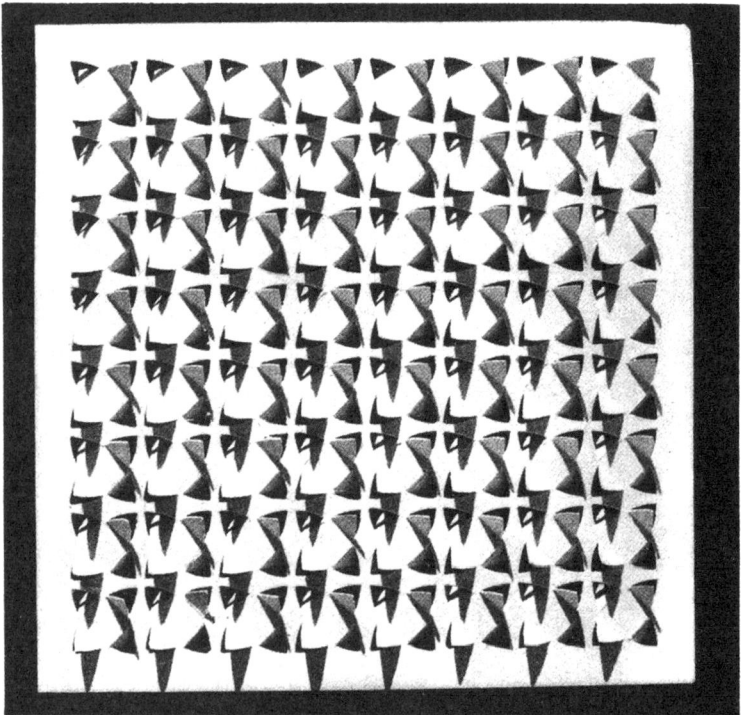

174

A modular panel created by superimposing circles over a square grid. The three-dimensional effect is achieved by highlighting some of the symmetrical elements from the resulting design by means of 45-degree folds. From the Art Institute of Isernia.

A textured bas relief shape. The large black triangle reveals the actual size of the paper sheet that was cut and folded to produce the effects of a textured bas relief. Claudio Majoli (1967).[98]

Bruno Munari, *Travel Sculpture* (1958). A foldable work made out of a single sheet.

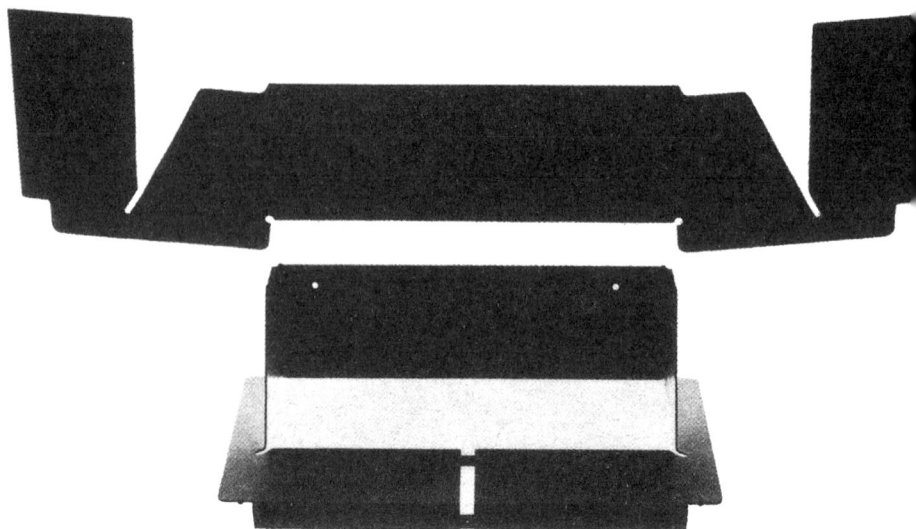

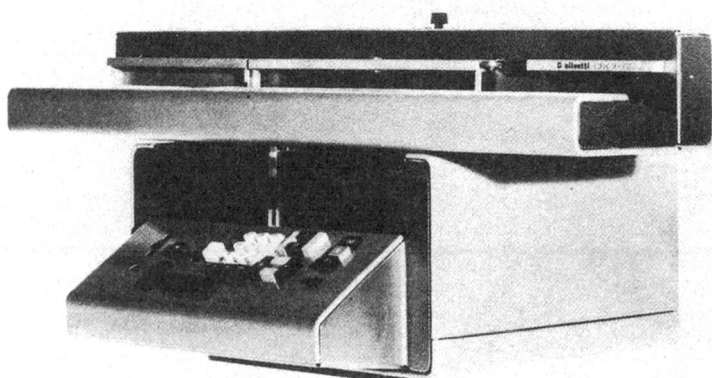

All the parts that make up the body of the Olivetti CMC7-7004 program-mable magnetic printer result from the cutting and bending of plasticized sheet metal on a single side. With three successive bends, the pieces are stiffened, finished, and ready to be assembled to form the bodywork of the machine. Designer Mario Bellini.[99]

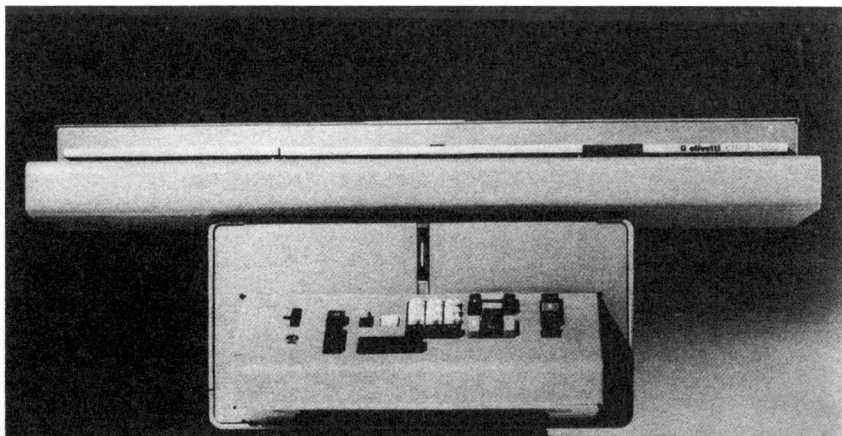

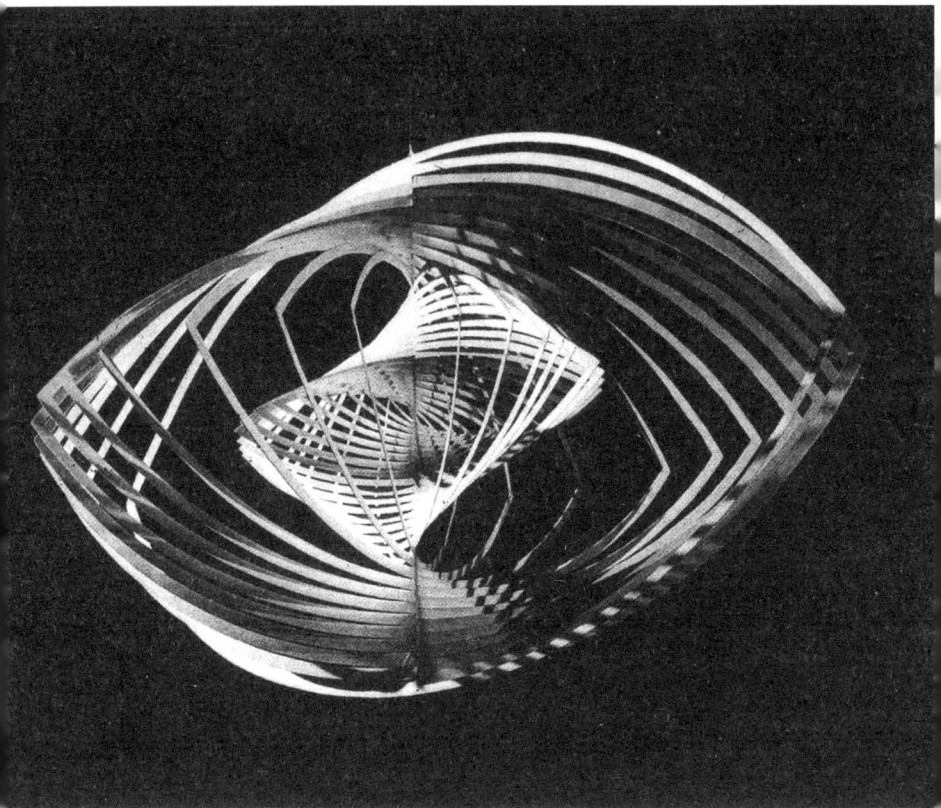

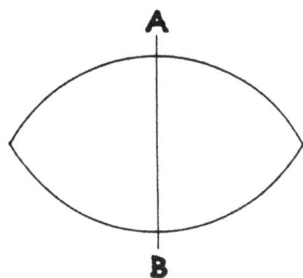

A two-dimensional shape cut into thin strips, held together along the central A-B axis, can generate a three-dimensional shape by fanning out the individual parts. Altering the initial two-dimensional shape using the same procedure, other spatial shapes can be created. The example is from Prof. Joseph Zalewski (1952).[100]

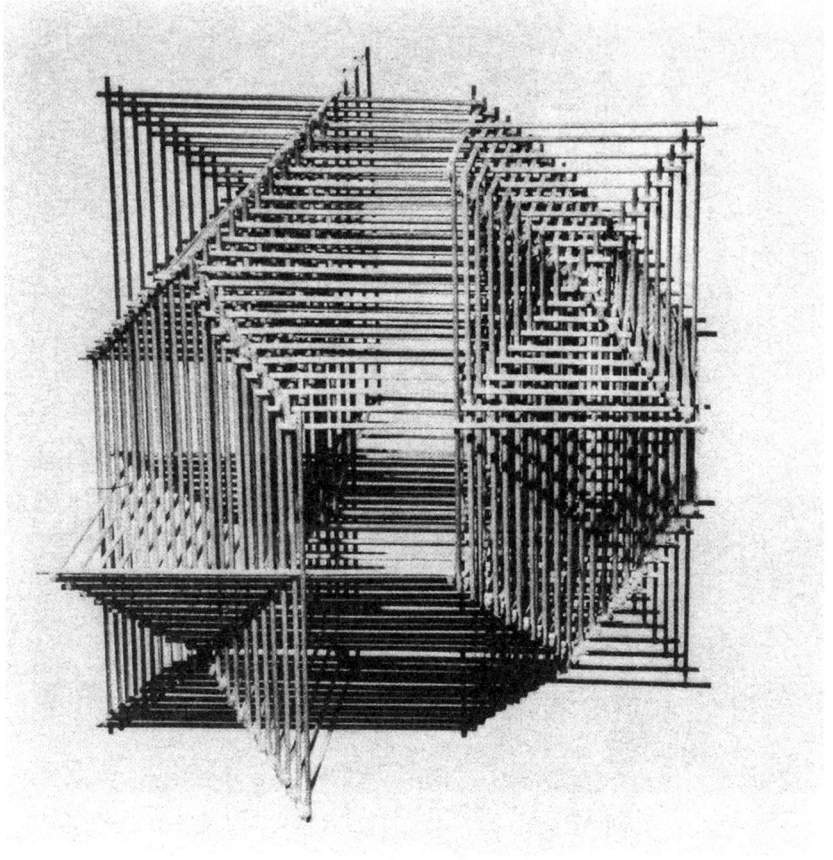

A complex three-dimensional form obtained through the repetition of two right-angled signs—in this case, two sticks—and the uniform and constant displacement of the third dimension. Carpenter Center for Visual Arts, Cambridge, USA.

A set design for Italian television by Gianni Villa. The spatial effect is achieved by means of the equidistant repetition of a simple form. The character of the sheeting and its weight determines the curvature. Thanks to the skillful use of lighting, the set projects light and dark stripes onto the floor and actors.

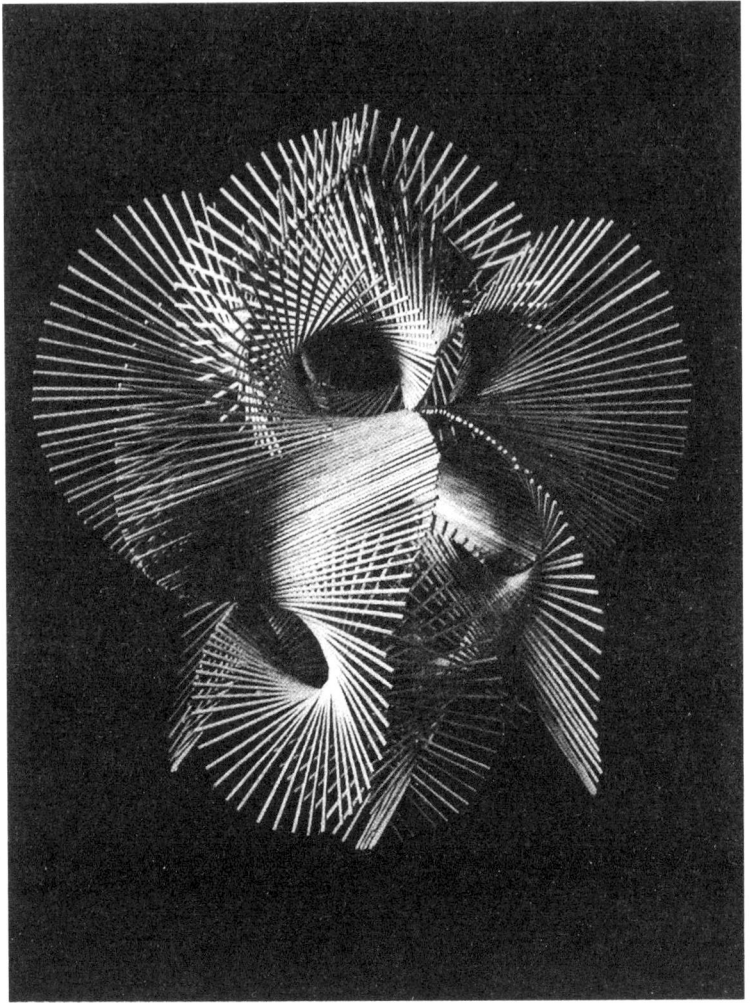

A complex shape achieved by means of the rotation of a uniform segment.
Carpenter Center for Visual Arts, Cambridge, USA.

A complex shape achieved by joining together simple three-dimensional shapes generated by rotating a single segment. Carpenter Center for Visual Arts, Cambridge, USA.

The study of form leads to the creation of increasingly complex shapes or objects by means of the accumulation of two or more identical shapes. Symmetry is the study of the ways shapes can be added together and, therefore, of the relationship between a source shape and an end shape generated by means of repetition. Our goal here, once again, is to determine whether there are elementary modes of aggregation from which a maximum number of complex forms can be derived.

According to the laws of symmetry, there exist five basic modes:

1 – identity
2 – translation[101]
3 – rotation
4 – reflection
5 – dilation.

"Identity" refers to the superimposition of a shape upon itself or its 360° rotation around its own axis.

"Translation" refers the repetition of a form along an axis that can be rectilinear, curvilinear, or other.

"Rotation" refers to the turning of the shape around an axis that can be either internal or external to the shape itself.

"Reflection" describes the two-way symmetry that arises when one places an object in front of a mirror and looks at both object and reflection as a single visual unit.

"Dilation" denotes an increase in scale that doesn't modify the shape itself, but only expands it.

Combining two or more of these modes makes it possible to develop or explain highly complex shapes. A case in point: the Procuratie Palace in Venice's Saint Mark's Square is an instance of the translation of a shape at equal intervals. The spokes of a wagon wheel are examples of the rotation of a shape while spiral staircases embody both rotation and translation (rotation of the steps but also repositioning of each step as it rotates around a central axis). We encounter reflection in insects, leaves, and the like. Dilation, accompanied by translation, is found in many seashells.

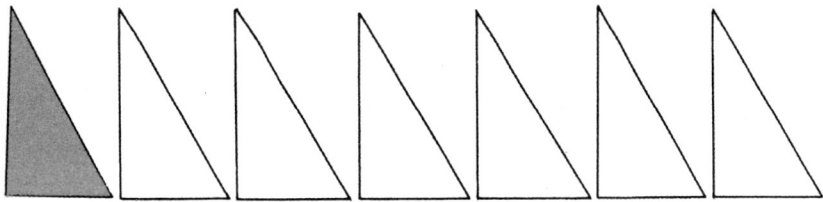

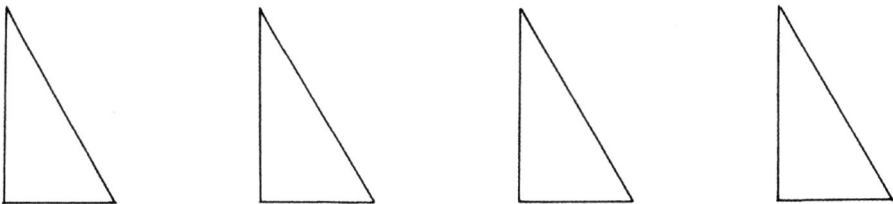

The translation of a right-angled triangle along a straight line. Variants are possible while still respecting the principle of translation. A variety of combinations are possible by modifying the gap between the components. Proportions can increase or decrease, whether at calculated intervals or alternating rhythms . . .

As concerns our own formal research and experiments, unusual elementary shapes can be devised that yield interesting results in the wake of multiple combinatory operations.

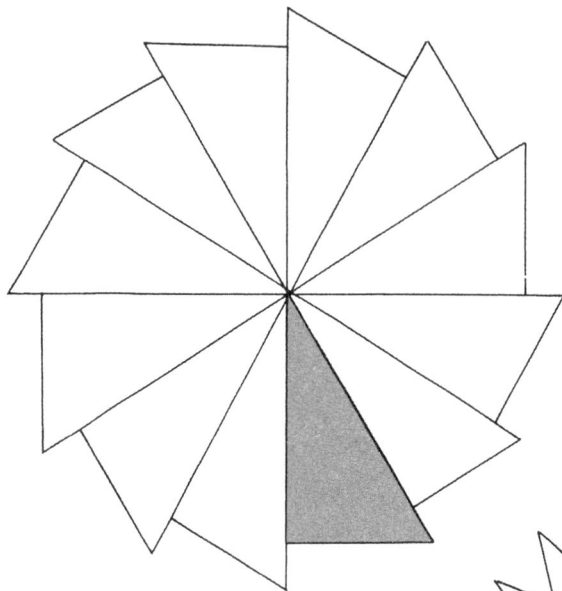

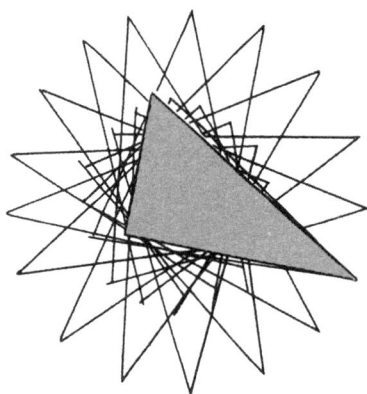

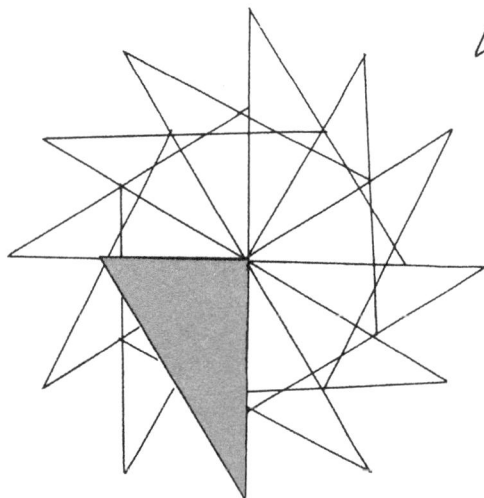

The rotation of a right-angled triangle around its 90° angle, which is to say its center. A spiral staircase comes about thanks to the rotation of stairs and their translation up and down a central axis.

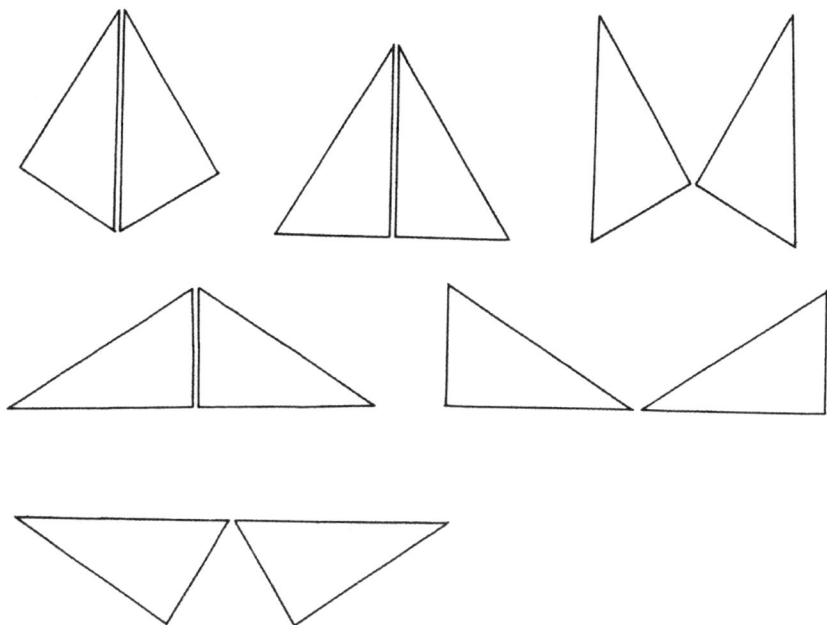

The mirrored image of a right-angled triangle in varying positions. The above illustration is binary but symmetry encompasses 3-, 4-, 5-, 6-, 7- . . . fold symmetries as well. A 3-fold symmetry is exhibited by clover leaves, cucumbers, iris flowers, etc. A 5-fold symmetry is found in starfish and numerous flowers.

A mirrored organic shape.

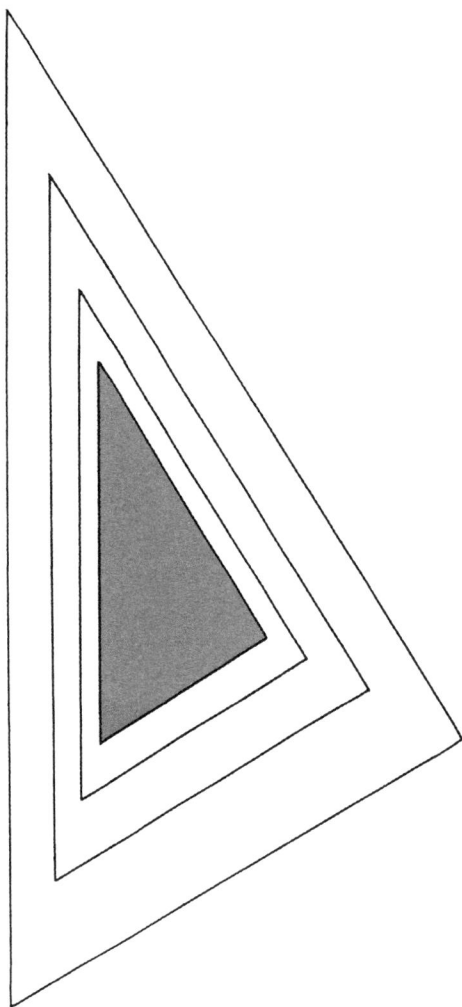

Dilation of the same right-angled triangle. It's clear that this shape should be considered elementary and, accordingly, that other shapes can be generated if it were rotated, translated, and reflected.

An assemblage of similar expanding shapes. Thea Vallè, *Macroextension* (1968).[102]

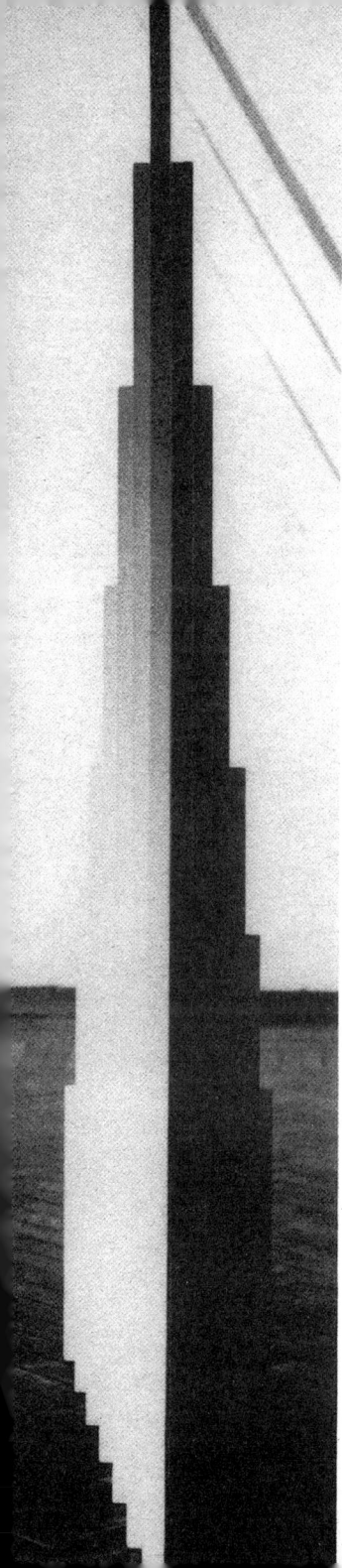

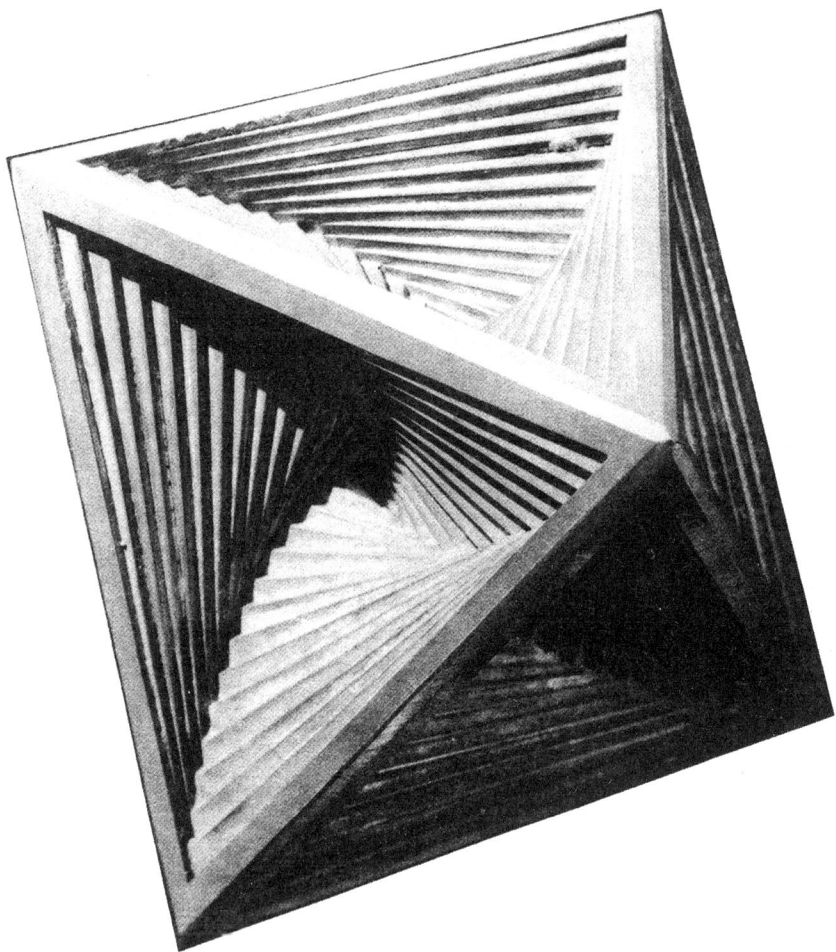

Shapes created by means of the accumulation and rotation of an elementary shape. Charles O. Perry, *Plastic* (1964).[103]

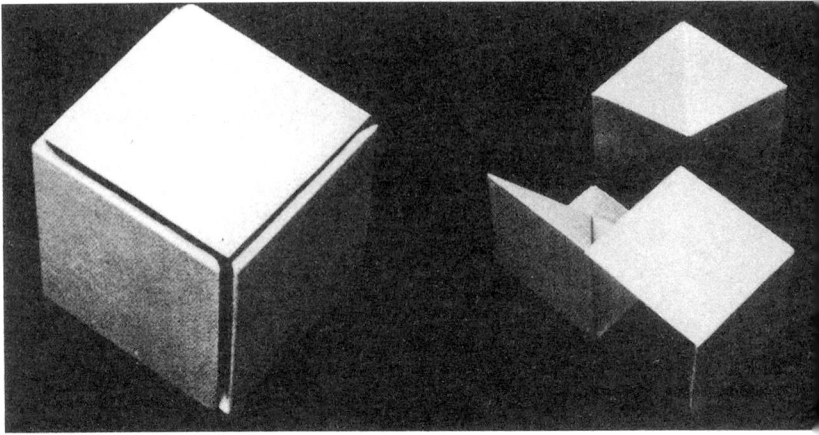

Spatial construction exercises with regular solids carried out in the Spatial Form studio run by Mary Vieira at the Kunstgewerbeschule in Basel (1966–67).[104]
The illustrations show the subdivision of a cube into three equal parts. To imagine a cube divided into three equal parts might appear difficult given that its sides are square and, therefore, imply separation into four parts. But a cube is six-sided and can be divided by three yielding a result of two. So, the entire surface of the cube is divisible

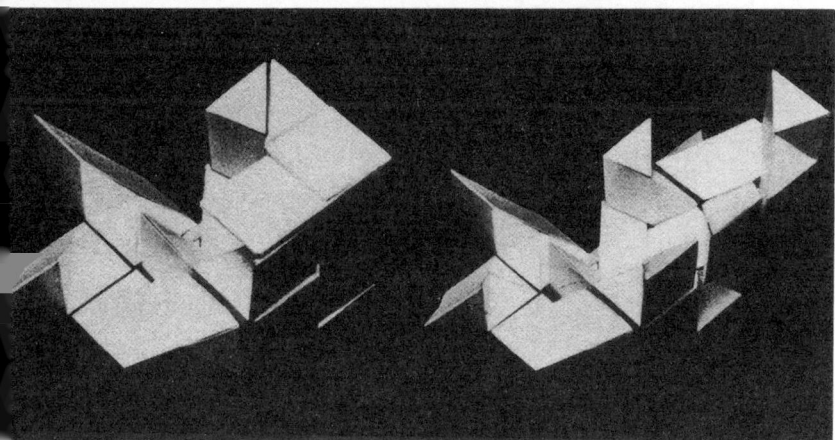

into three units each made up of two squares joined together along a single edge.

But what is especially intriguing about the exercises carried out in Mary Vieira's studio is the fact that the work involves not just the cube's surface but instead its entire volume. By exploring the rhythm of spatial vectors within the cubic form—lines that join opposing vertices or other designated points—other shapes emerge that are rigorously related to the initial overall shape.

The exercise makes use of claylike materials, both for reasons of economy (reuse once the exercise has ended) and because clay makes these explorations readily visible. Such exercises develop a student's spatial-structural awareness thanks to the determining role performed by the spatial vectors within the cubic form. This promotes the gradual development of associative and analogical skills for three-dimensional spatial

design, a precondition for authentic forms of inventiveness. Introspection is thus encouraged on the part of students, so that they come to understand themselves as the producers of questions rather than the reproducers of givens.

The cardboard models in the photographs were reconstructed based on exercises carried out with claylike materials.

197

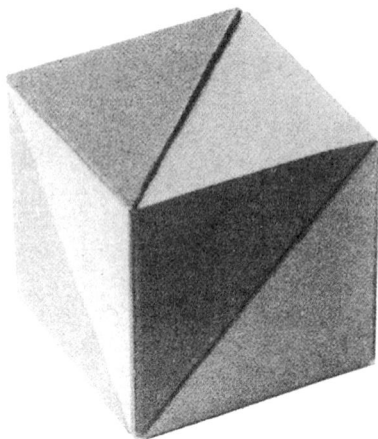

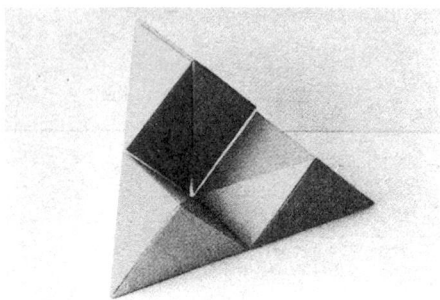

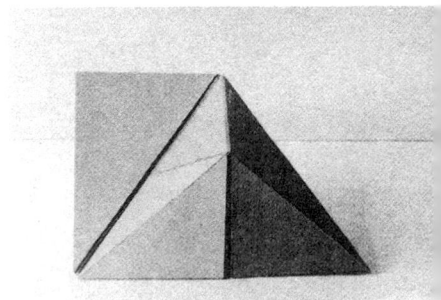

A cube divided into equal hinging parts can generate a series of other geometrical figures when the parts are moved and recombined, as illustrated above. (From Giorgio Scarpa's topological research.)[105]

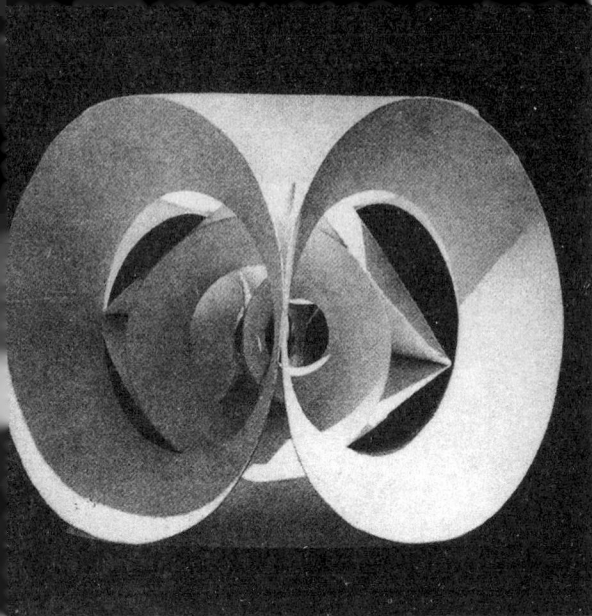

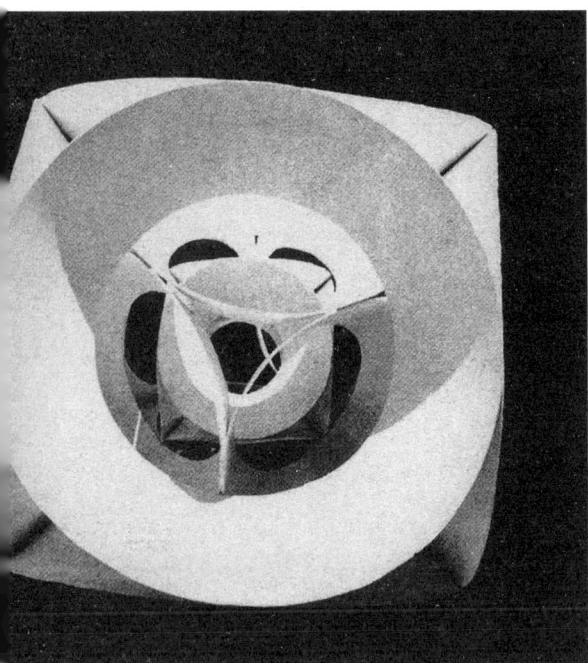

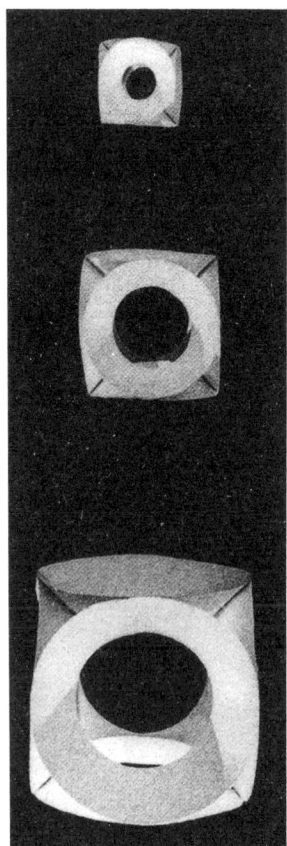

200

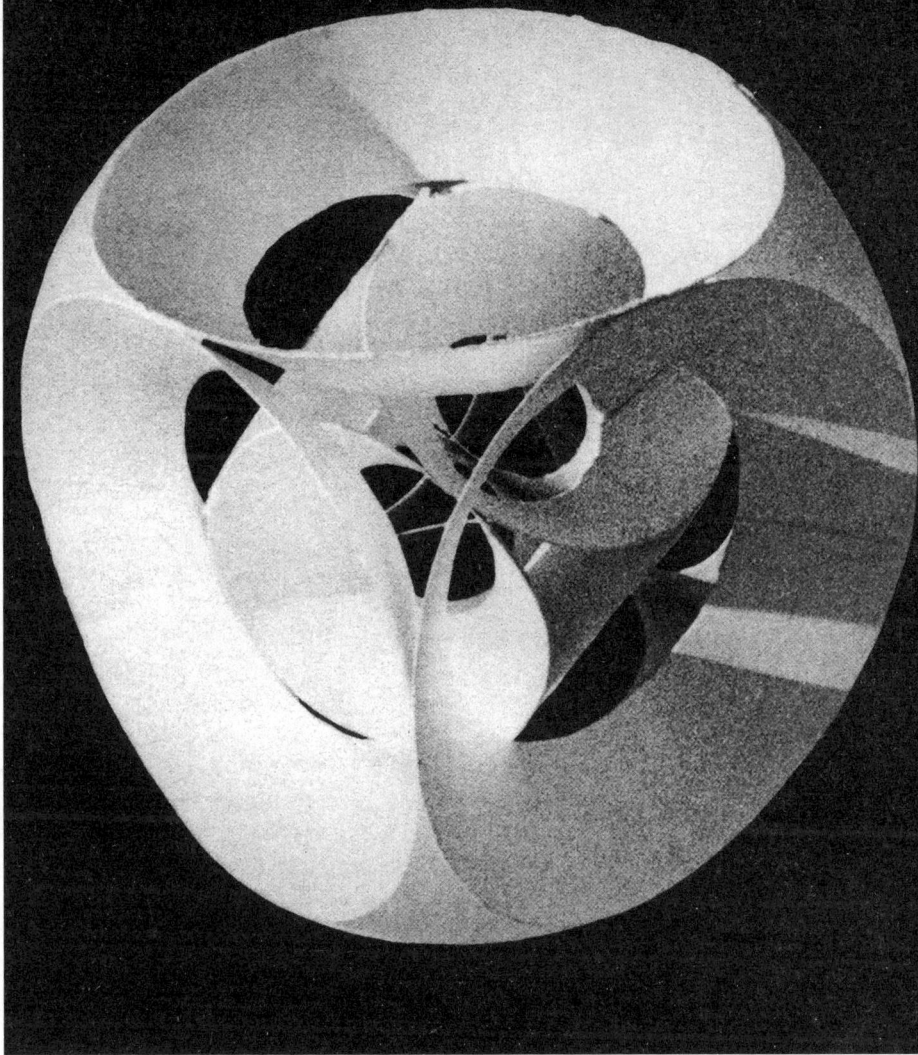

A complex cubic form made from three modules of diminishing size. Each module is composed of six conical crowns affixed to one another in such a way as to form a cubical space. Each shape is contained within the other. Edilio Petrocelli, Isernia.[106]

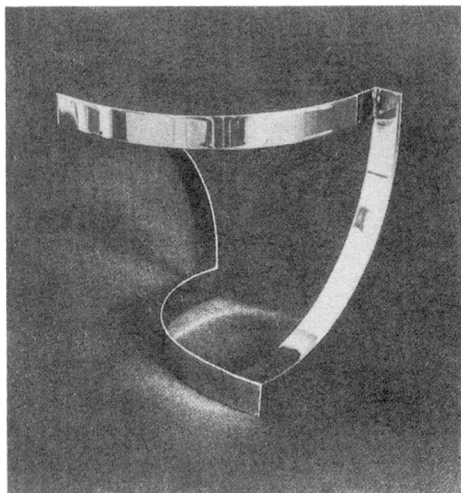
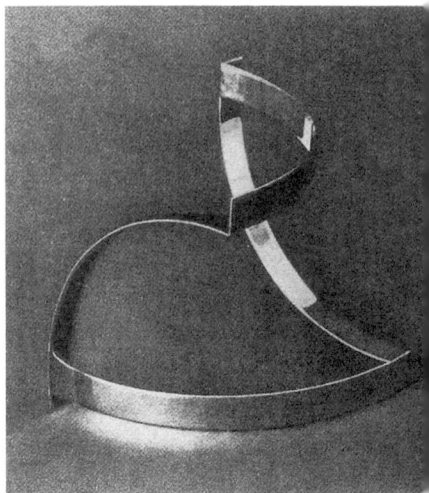

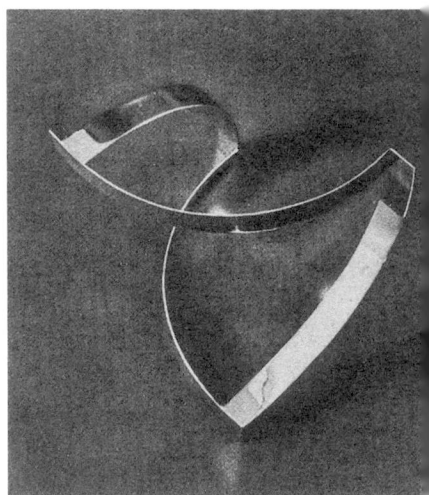

A logical geometrical shape carved out of a cube. On the opposing page, instead of being sculpted from a metal plate, the same shape is made from a tubular frame wrapped in nylon. (Made by Giorgio Crippa [1970].)[107]

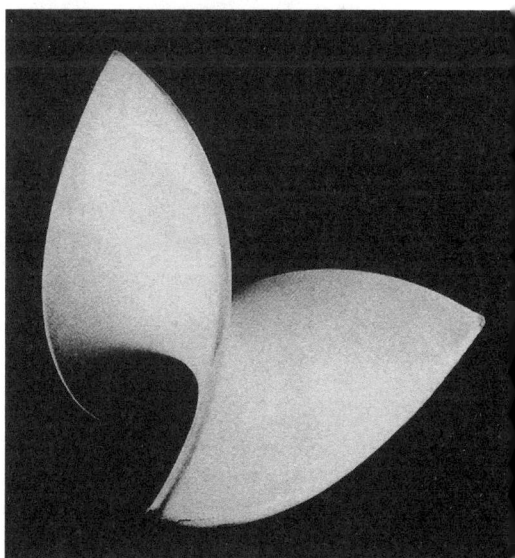

Marks on the sides of a cube that reflect its dimensions show the results of accumulation within a three-dimensional space. (A first-year exercise from the Istituto d'Arte in Trieste; Marcello Siard and Emilio Banko, instructors.)

Exercises involving the development of a cubic module, carried out by first year students at the Istituto d'Arte in Trieste, directed by Professor Romano Barocchi. The cubic module is sectioned in various ways to study compositional variants.

Models of objects created by reworking industrial extrusions. This sort of metalwork with a focus on design has been embraced by various art schools, displacing the "artistic" approach that informs the embossed hammered copper artworks upon which our once exuberant national craft traditions have relied for far too long. The challenge here is to explore the various ways in which industrial extrusions can be sectioned and assembled for purposes of production. (These examples are from the Art Institute of Sulmona, directed by Professor Italo Picini [1969].)

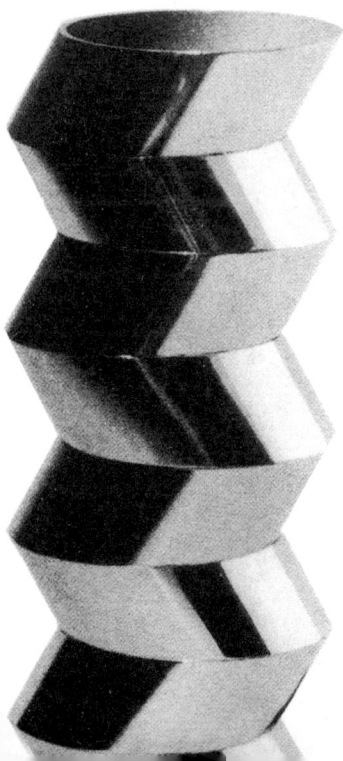

One of the pathways readily available to designers is the crafting of shapes out of industrially produced extrusions. Among these, the simplest and the one best suited for such explorations, is tubing, whether in metal or plastic. Cuts and openings can be mechanically executed on sections of tubing in order to yield purpose-built finished products (much as the Japanese have always done with bamboo). These flower vases by Enzo Mari are cases in point.[108] Also by Mari is this umbrella stand and coat rack combination: a 1.5 meter tube with a 25 centimeter diameter that has been sectioned so as to create an umbrella stand below (the tube has a base), an intermediate shelf for the placement of objects when one returns home, and projections on top upon which garments can be hung.[109]

Lino Sabattini has long produced practical objects based on industrial extrusions. This vase and ashtray were created by cutting a tube and bending it inwards.[110]

Franz Sartori fabricated this 6-meter-tall, 6-ton shape for the Dalmine corporation's stand at the 1968 Fiera di Milano; it was crafted from an industrial pipe with 30 mm walls by means of two very long cuts.

Topological shapes made with two-dimensional materials. Such shapes diverge from ordinary forms because they don't possess a well-defined front or back, inside or outside. Their inner surfaces remain indissociable from their external surfaces, giving rise to a continuum.

A topological shape. From the Ulm School.

A study of junctions between two shapes. From the Ulm School.

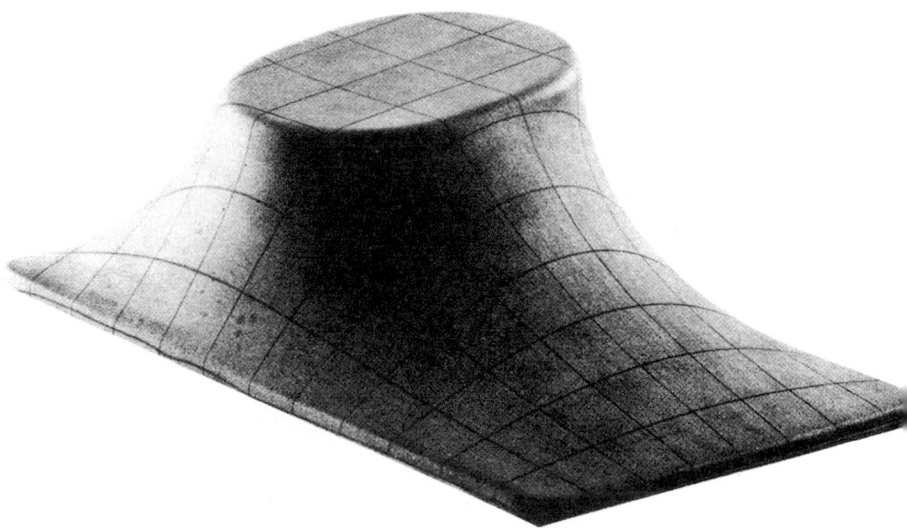

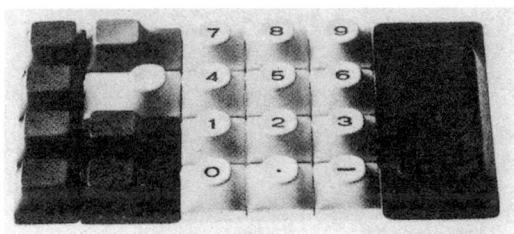

A study of junctions between two different shapes involving elastic membranes. The study was carried out with the goal of finding the smoothest transition between an oval (the surface on which a fingertip of a typist rests) and a rectangle (the base of a key). The photograph below shows the full keyboard with the size of keys determined by their function. Designer: Mario Bellini.[111]

A workstation for a mainframe computer permitting the exchange of messages on a television screen. Olivetti TCV250 model. Designer: Mario Bellini.

The roof of the German pavilion at the 1967 Montreal World's Fair.
Architects: Otto Frei and Rolf Gutbrod.

A portable pavilion in the form of an air-supported dome, developed for the Radio Televisione Italiana in 1967. Achille and Pier Giacomo Castiglioni, designers.[112]

Pneumatic shapes become visible in foams. Small air bubbles enclosed within ultrathin membranes cluster together in complex shapes that are always spherical in nature with the junctions established as a function of the equilibrium of forces. Such shapes are particularly noticeable in milk and beer foam (as seen within bottles). Thanks to plastics, it's now possible to produce large air-supported structures based on the same principles that structure soap bubbles.

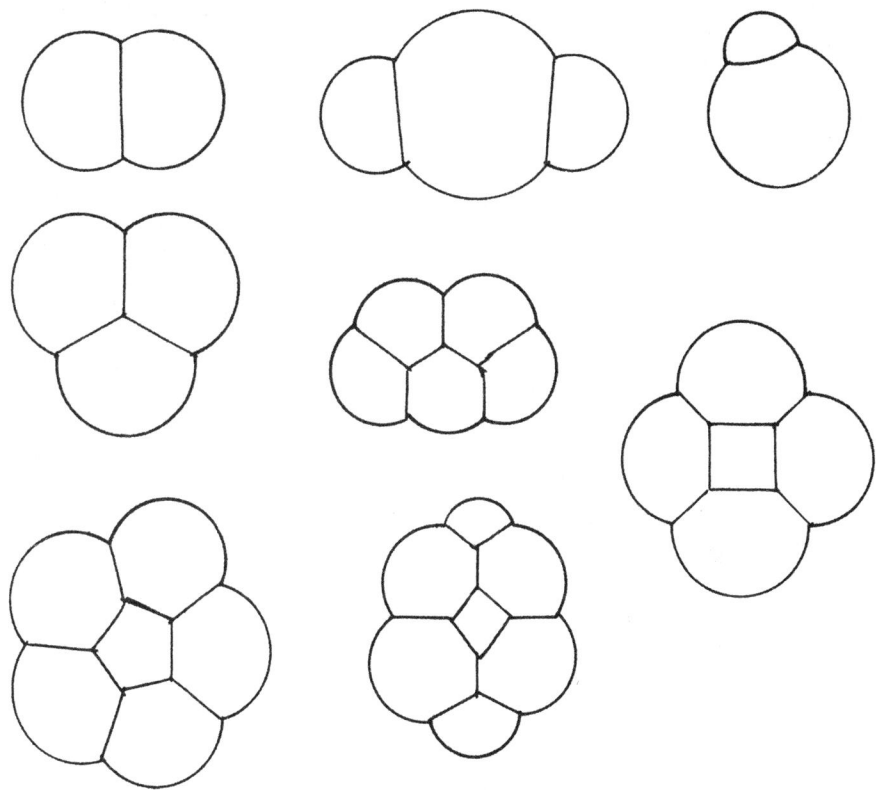

Studies of pneumatic surfaces. A dedicated device protruding from a circular opening inflates an elastic membrane; a grid is projected on the resulting shape that renders its various sectors visible. The blurred marks are the result of the structure's rapid deflation, during which the camera shutter remained open. From the Advanced Course in Industrial Design and Visual Communications, Institute of Art, Rome, directed by Prof. Osvaldo Calò; faculty: Andries Van Onck (designer) and Ernesto Rampelli (architect).

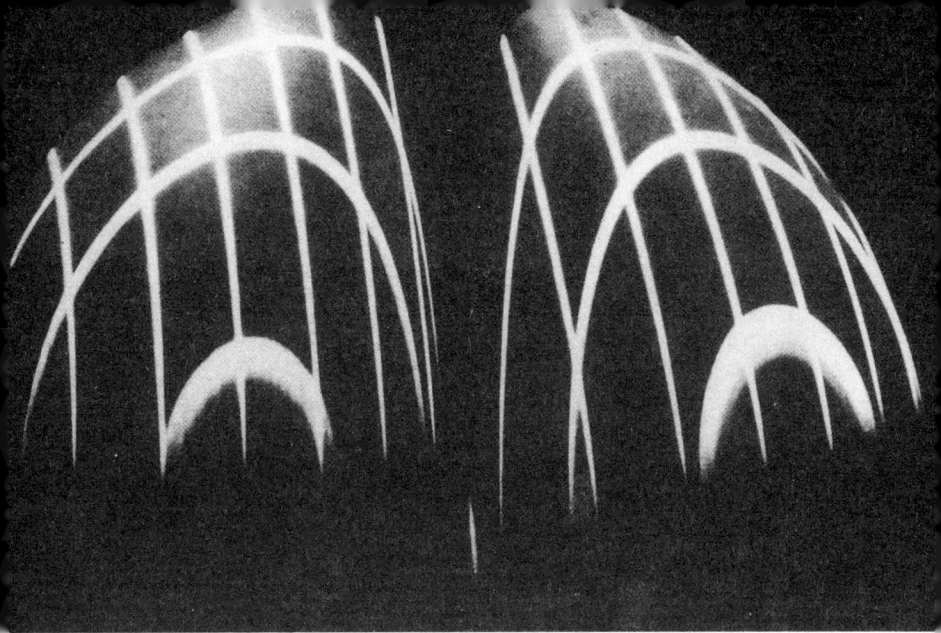

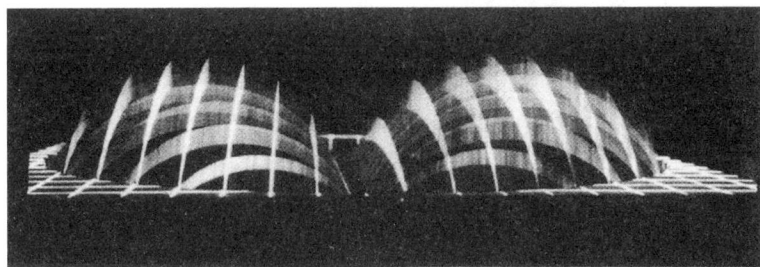

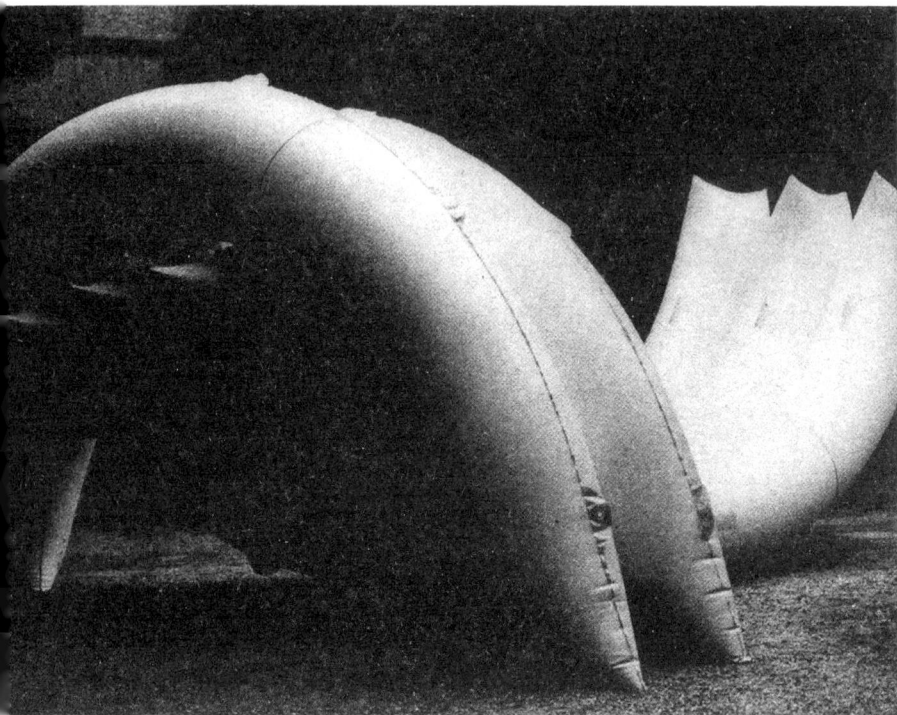

A floating 2 × 2 meter pneumatic structure, built by Franco Mazzucchelli in 1964. Other 3 × 7 meter shapes made in 1969.

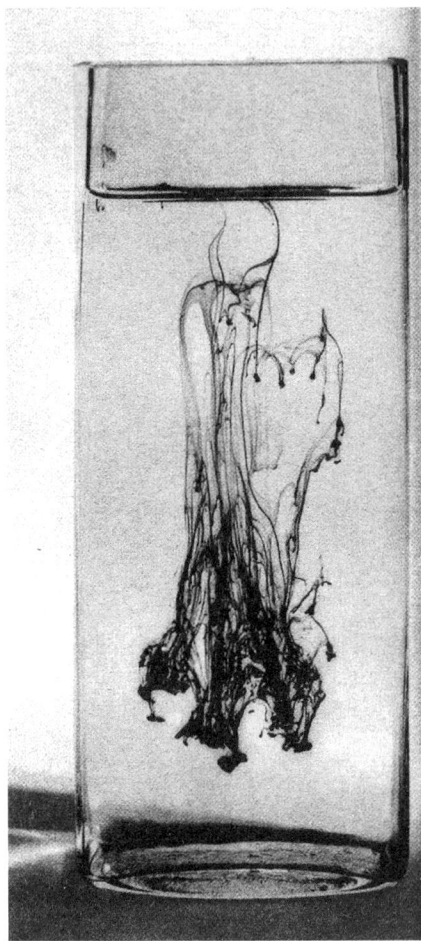

Shapes within liquids, which is to say the behavior of liquids within liquid mediums, can be studied by means of a simple device. Distinctive shapes result from differences in density, viscosity, weight, and other factors. Here we can observe the growth and transformations undergone by a shape until the instant of its disappearance. These images document three moments in a drop of India ink's passage through water. Photos by Michele Picardo.

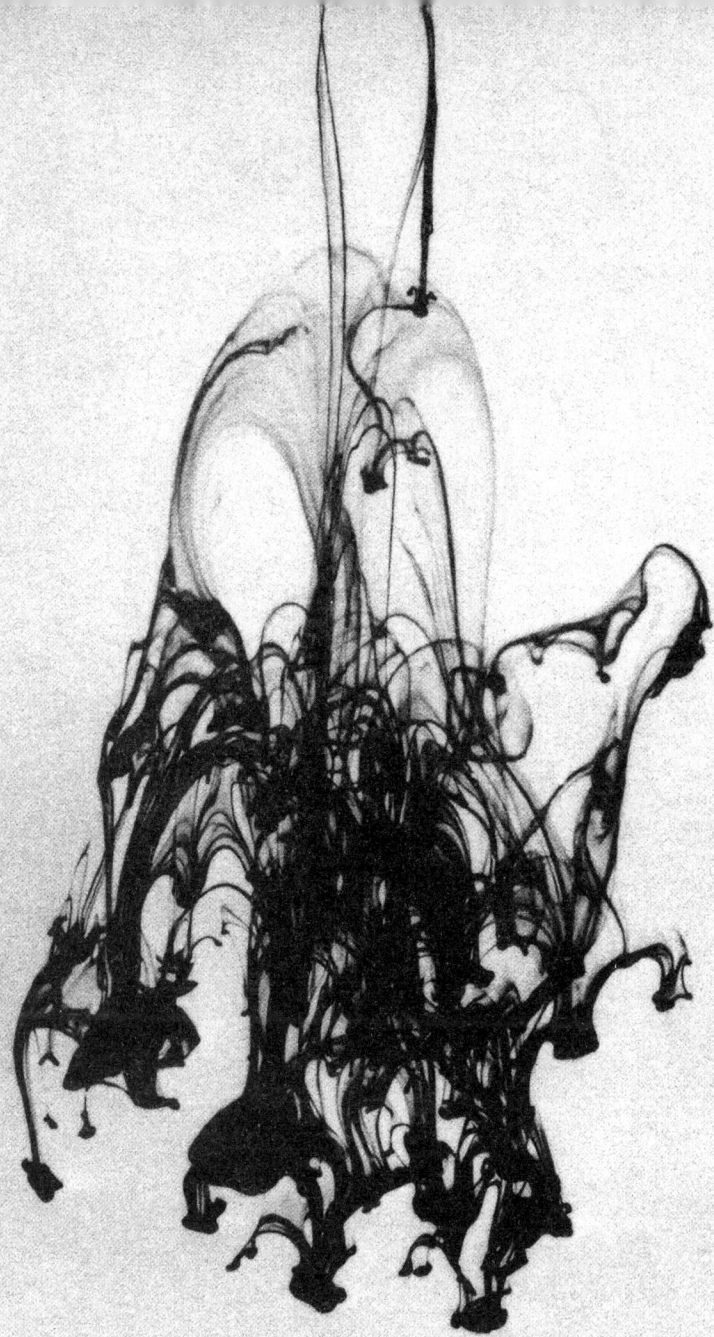

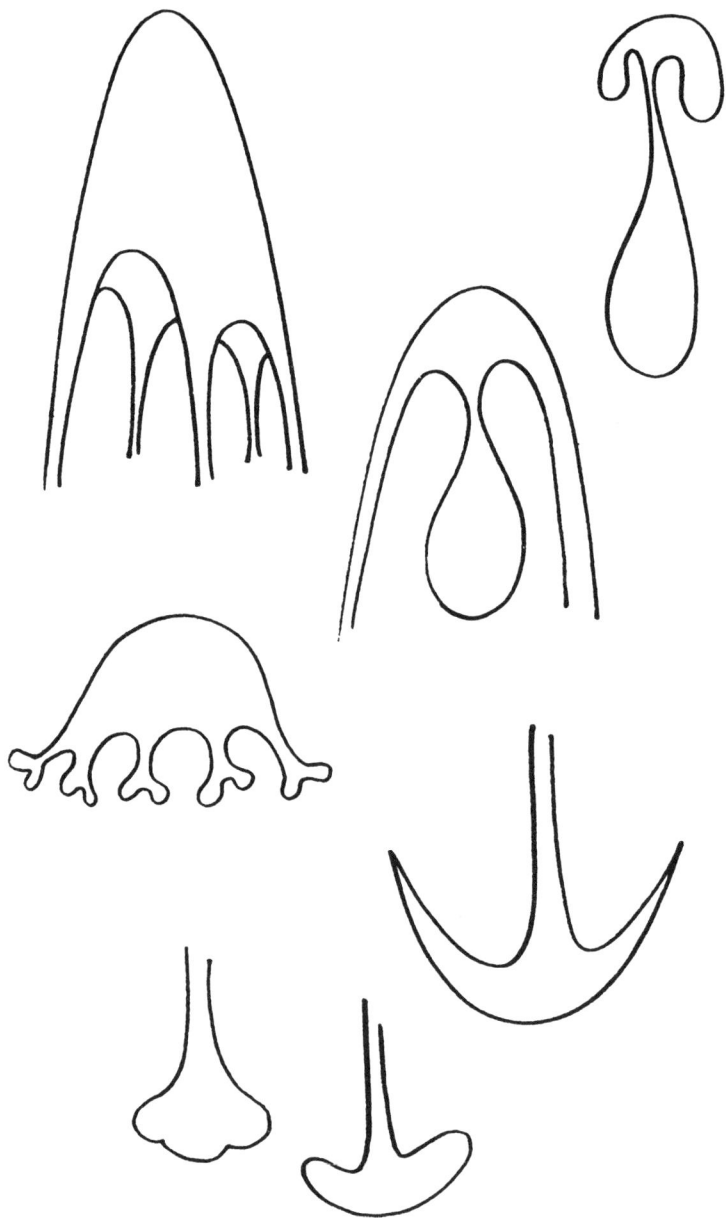

Studies of shapes in liquids that seek to understand the dynamics and nature of the resulting forms.

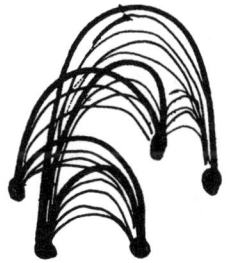

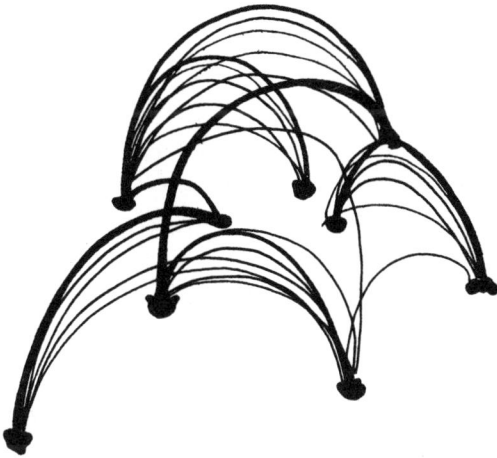

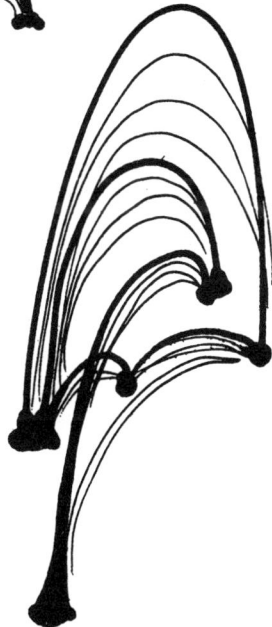

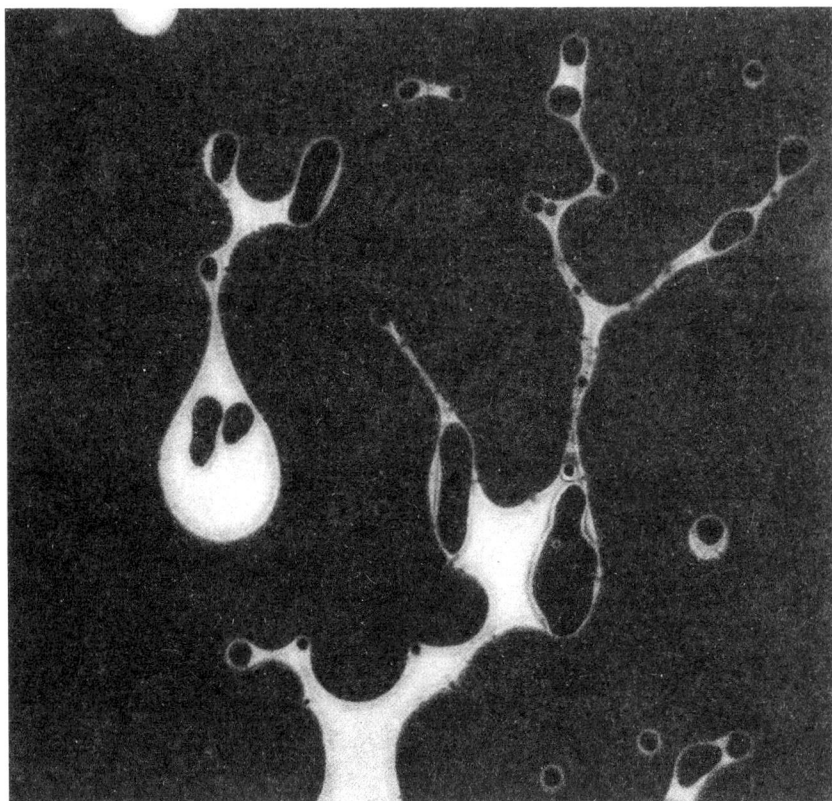

Natural forms of association between two liquids of different densities (water and oil) at a time of transition towards demulsification. Bromographic images by Tonino Petrocelli.

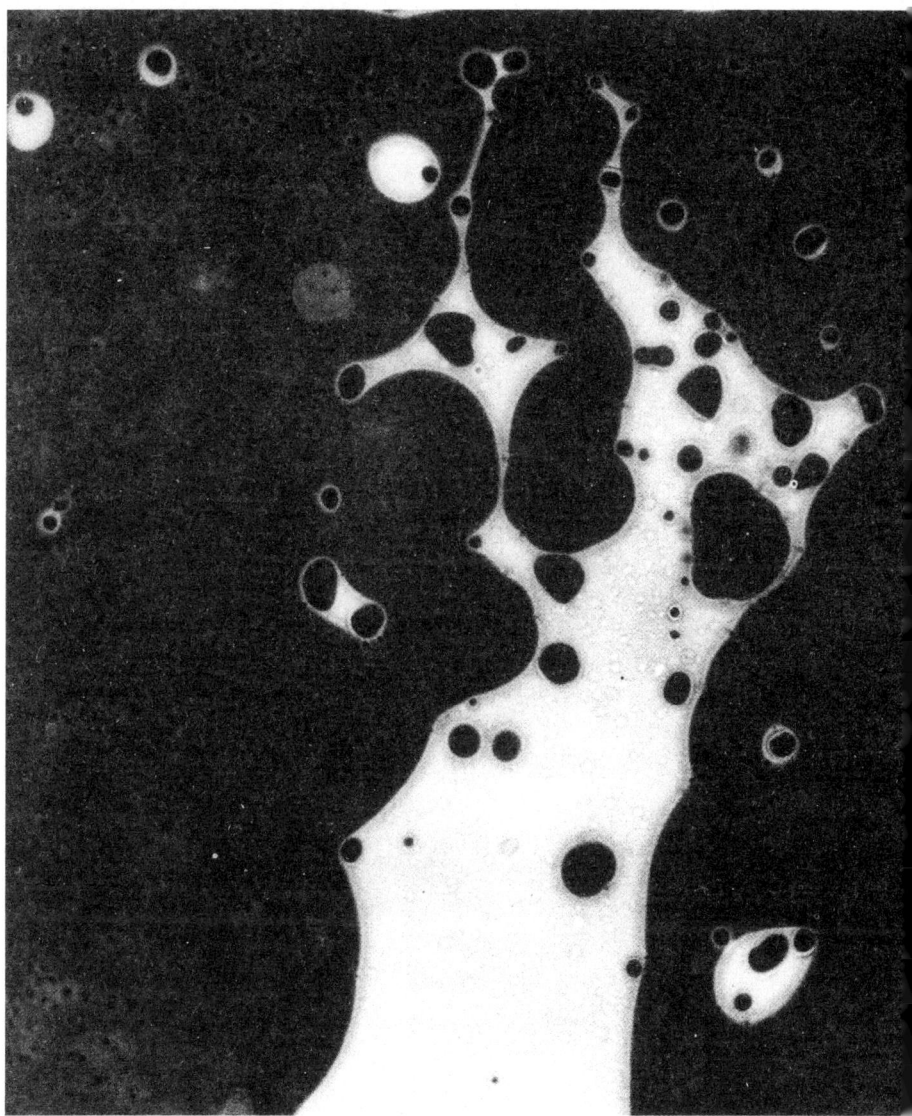

The relationship between an object's material and shape must always be taken into consideration because research into the behavior of materials can lead to better, more precise design solutions. In the case of a vase, the logical shape is that of a droplet or, in other words, a flask. A Murano glass vase by Fulvio Bianconi.

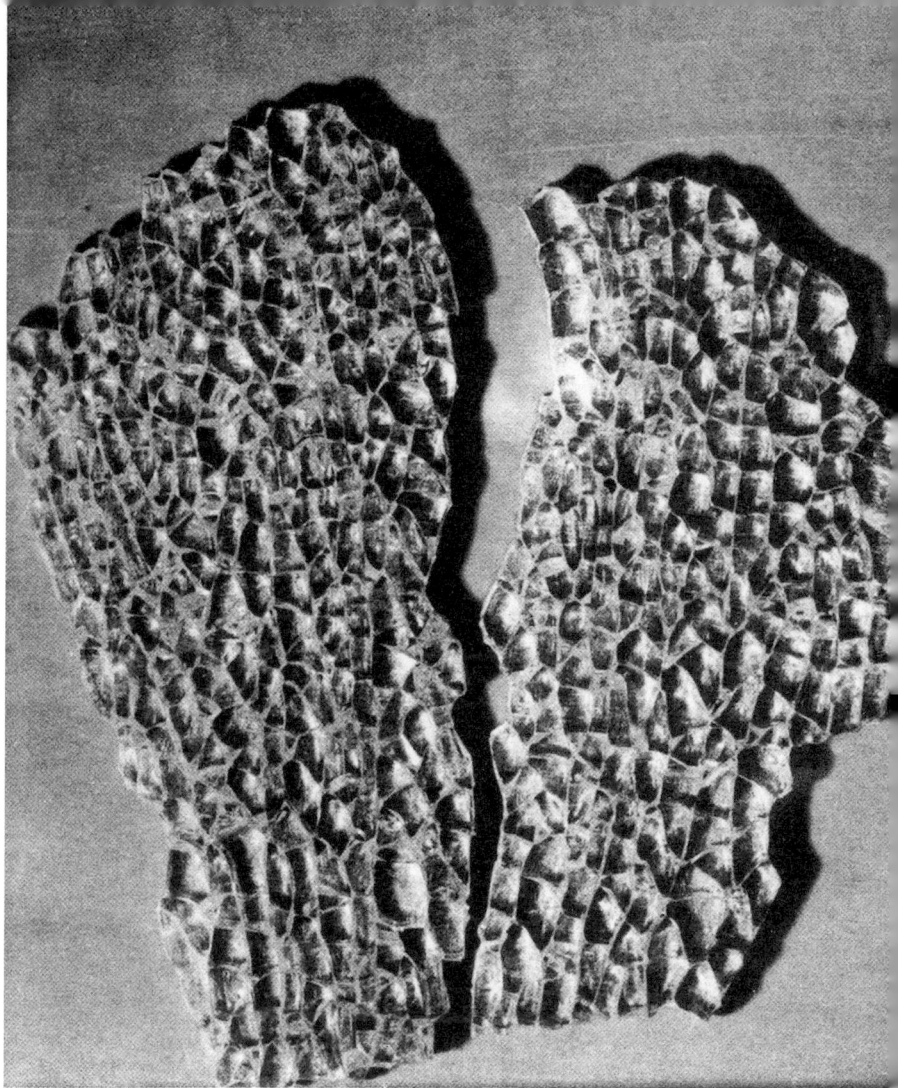

In these shards of safety glass shattered by a blow one can observe both textures and shapes.

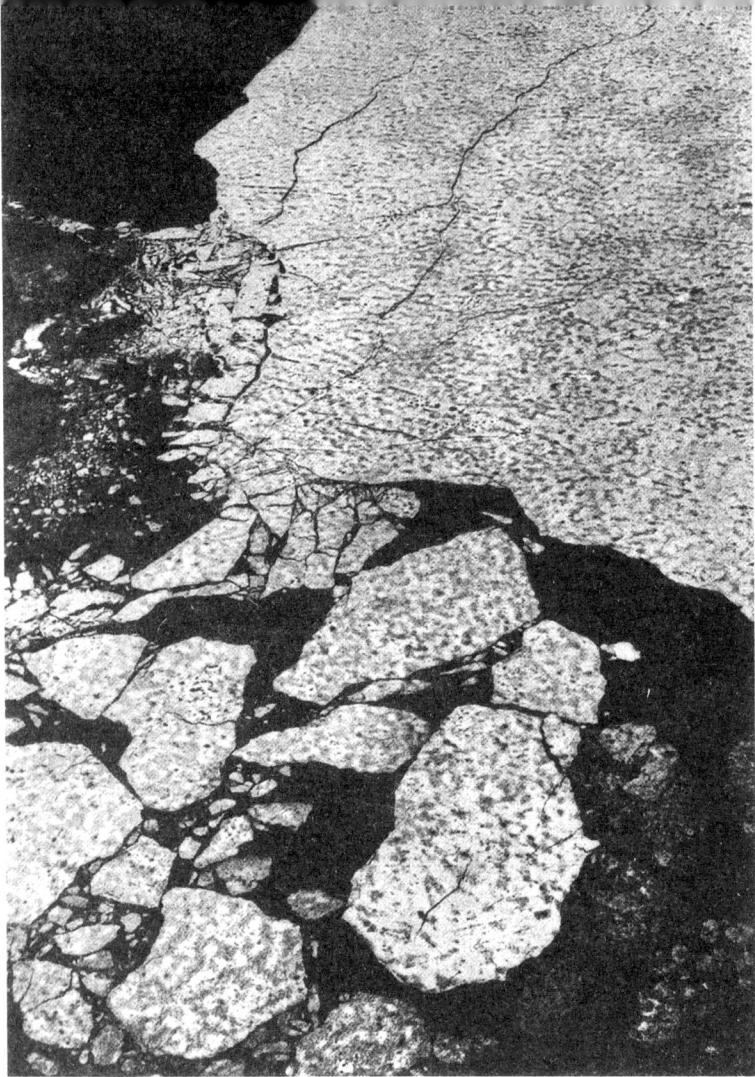

Ice breaking up on Lake Inari in Lapland, Finland. Mario de Biasi, photographer.

An exercise involving textures and spontaneous shapes obtained by abrading plastic transparencies for purposes of projection (5 × 5 cm). Carpenter Center for Visual Arts, Cambridge, USA.

The crystallization of salts used as a photographic negative for the study of texture, natural shapes, and light.

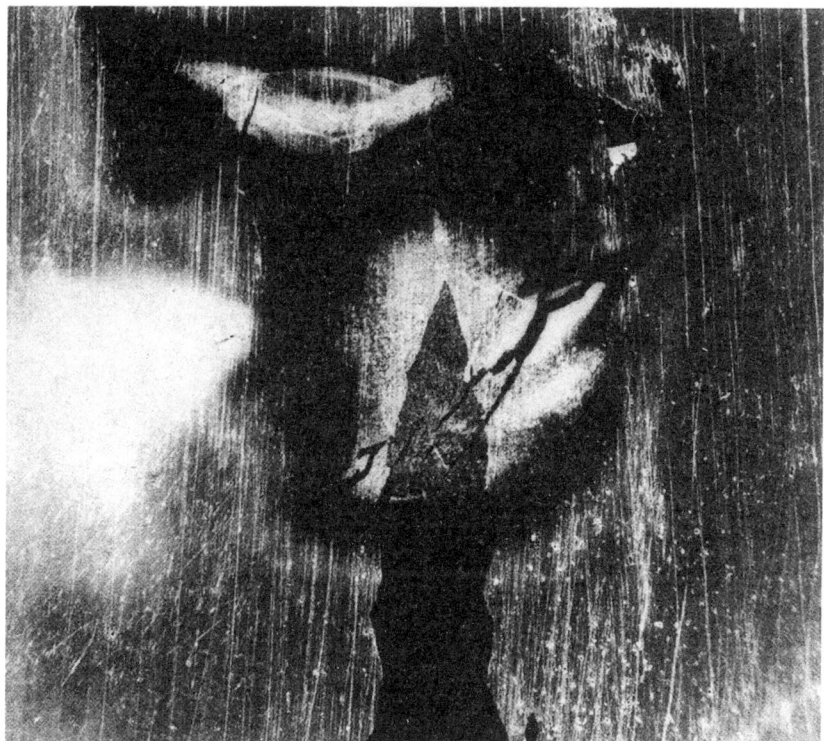

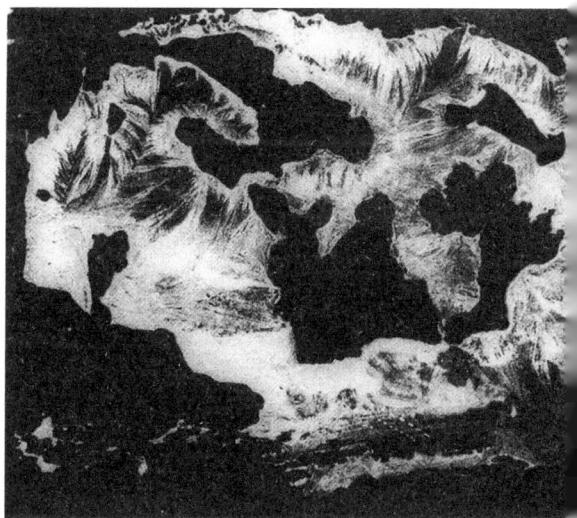

233

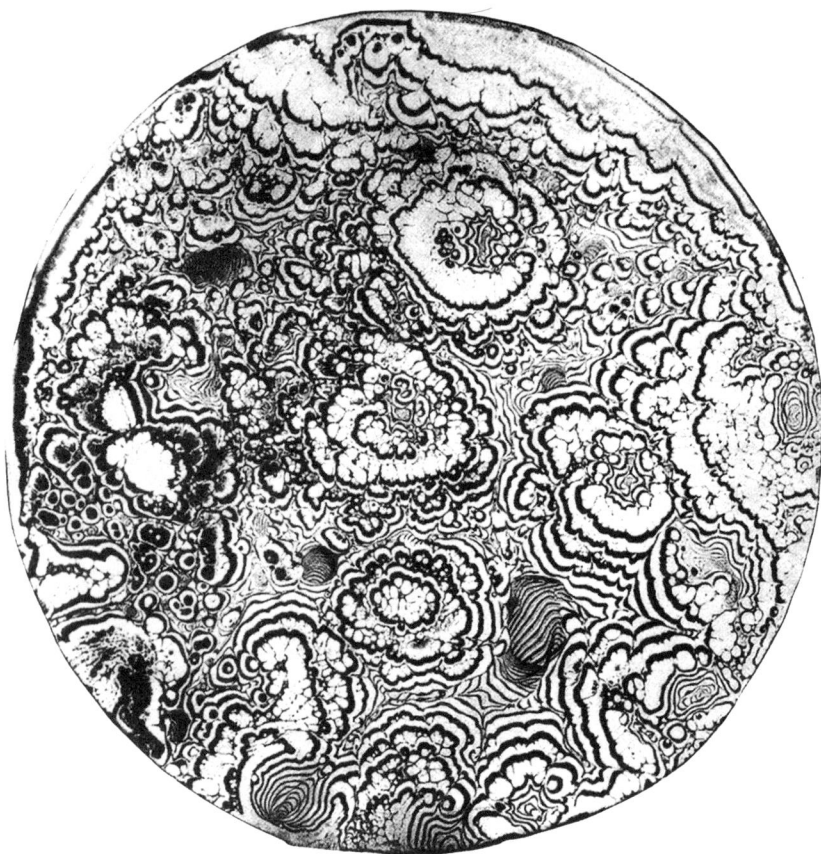

The progress of oxidation on a titanium disk.

The development of lines of contact between titanium, tungsten, and zirconium plates and corrosive solutions are rendered visible in electrochemical and metallurgical research labs. This allows for interpretation of the lines that form over time much like the concentric rings of a tree trunk.

The oxidation lines can be etched into the surface of the metal plate by applying alternating current (with a frequency of 50 hertz) with the resulting image reflecting the state of rest or turbulence of the liquid solution.

The designs vary depending upon the frequency of the alternating current, the angle of immersion of the plate, the shape of the metal plate, the microgeometry of the metal surface, the presence or absence of obstacles or nonconductive materials, the properties of the liquids (viscosity, surface tension, etc.), and other factors.

The images were produced by Pietro Pedeferri in the laboratories of the Milan Polytechnic.

A blow up showing the varying dynamics of a liquid surface.

The image of a vortex.

Different aspects of oxidation reflecting the dynamics of a liquid surface.

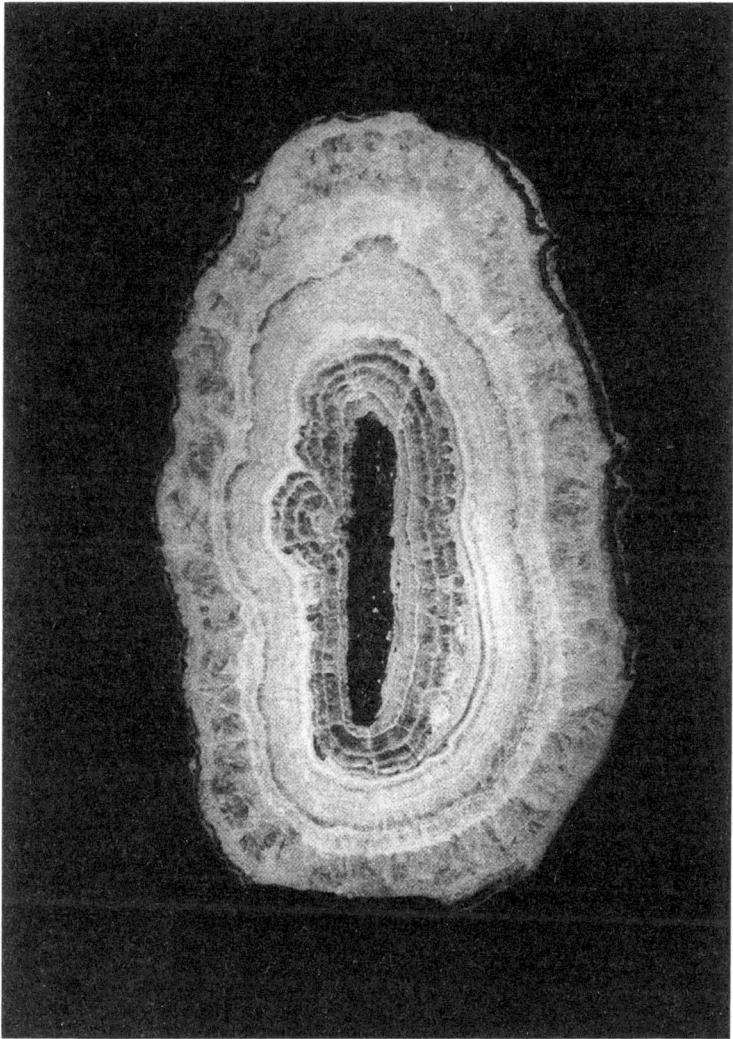

We encounter the same images in cross-sections of certain minerals. They assume the same shapes even if their temporality differs. Oxidation on a metal surface occurs quickly; the formation of a mineral very slowly.

Shapes created by sandblasting a sheet of plywood. Sandblasting
abrades the softer portions while placing harder portions in relief. From
Prof. Robert Preusser's visual design course at MIT; Nishan Bichajain,
photographer.[113]

Interconnected breakage patterns in ordinary glass. From Prof. Robert Preusser's visual design course at MIT.

Configurations generated by pressing transparent mastic between two 5 × 5 cm slides and then projecting and printing the image like an ordinary photographic negative. Different degrees of plasticity result from varying the position of the light during projection.

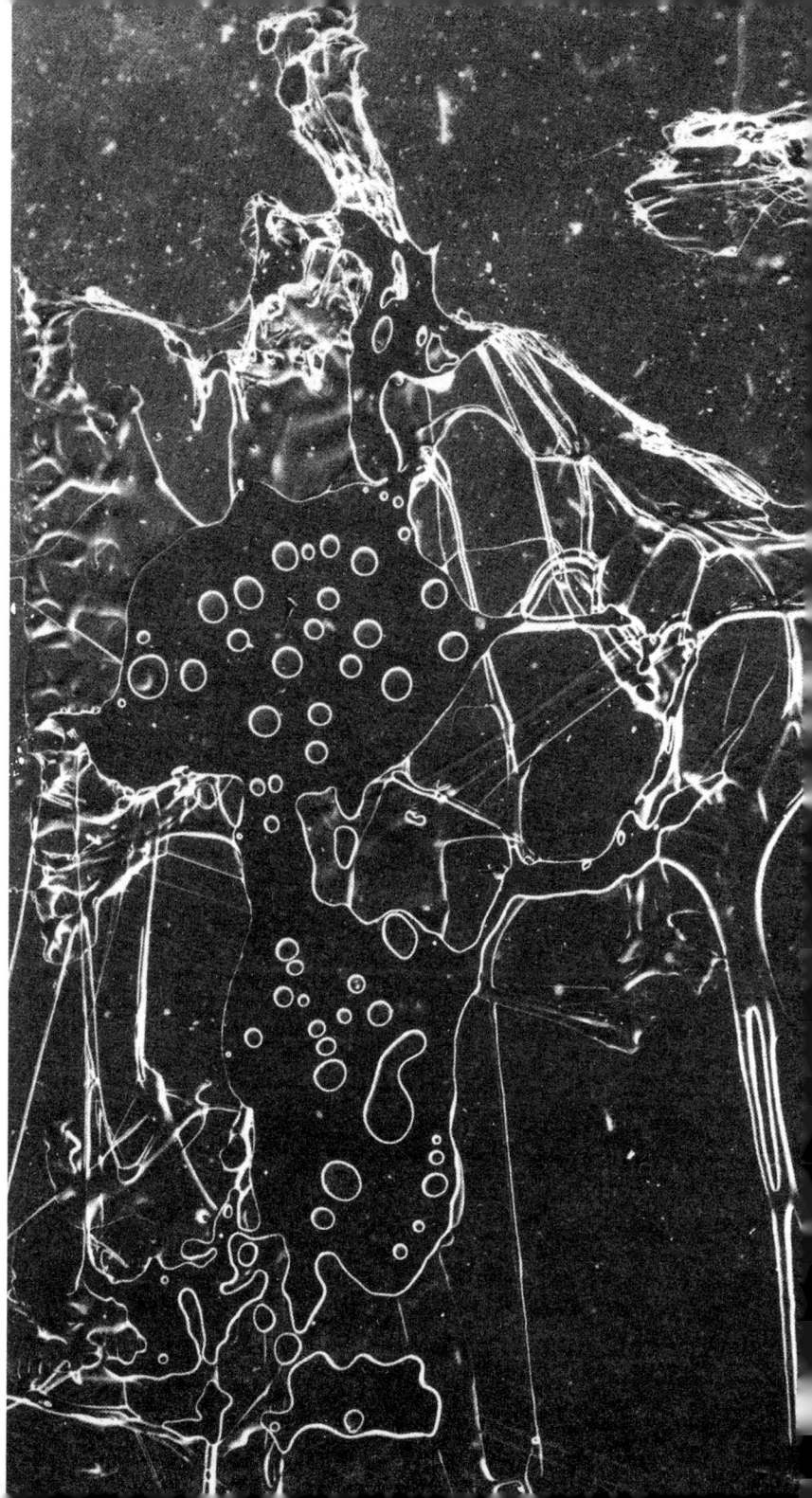

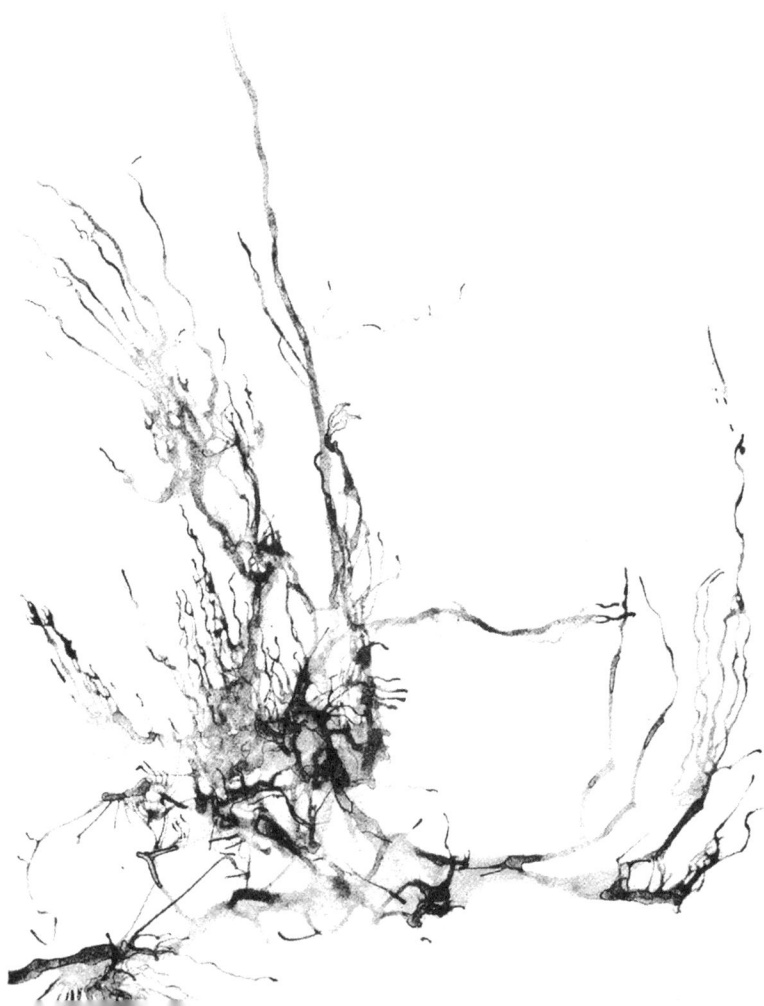

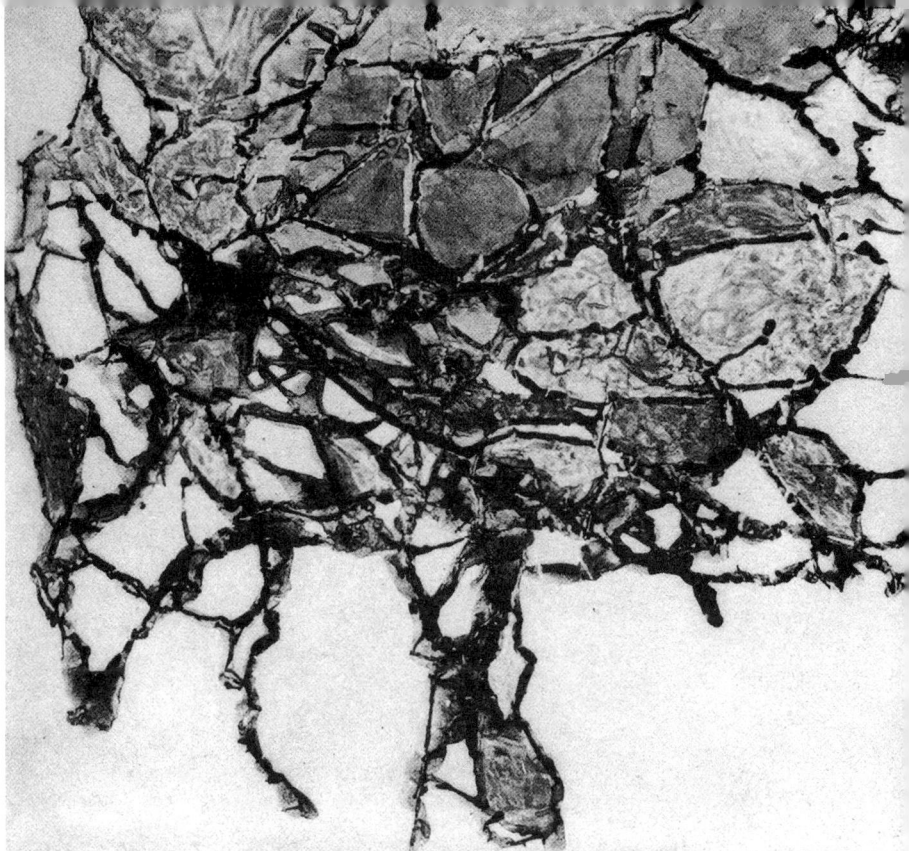

How do forms that aren't geometric, of the sort we defined as organic, take shape? How best to investigate and understand their nature? I don't believe that drawing is the answer. To reproduce a tree root or an electrical discharge accurately and with the utmost precision by means of a pencil drawing means nothing. We have a better chance of achieving understanding when we recreate these forms ourselves, so that they reveal themselves with the same naturalness with which a river reveals its shape in the process of becoming a natural landscape.

The vertical figure on the left was created by blowing drops of diluted ink across a flat paper surface.

The horizontal figure above was made by pouring diluted ink onto the highest outcroppings of a large, crumpled sheet of paper in order to create a simulation of an uneven landscape. The ink remains light where it flowed and dark where it lingered. Once the sheet is flattened out, the resulting shapes can be established on the basis of color zones.

243

An organic shape created with diluted ink and mixed techniques (i.e., not drawn).

The same set of shapes reinterpreted by a Xerox machine. Every now and then, it's a good idea to try out new techniques to explore mutations. Carpenter Center for Visual Arts, Cambridge, USA.

One of the defining characteristics of these organic forms is branching, which continues until the material runs out. Exercises in branching with two or more branches can be carried out. Above is an example of two-way branching into eight branches; three-way branching into five branches is on display below.

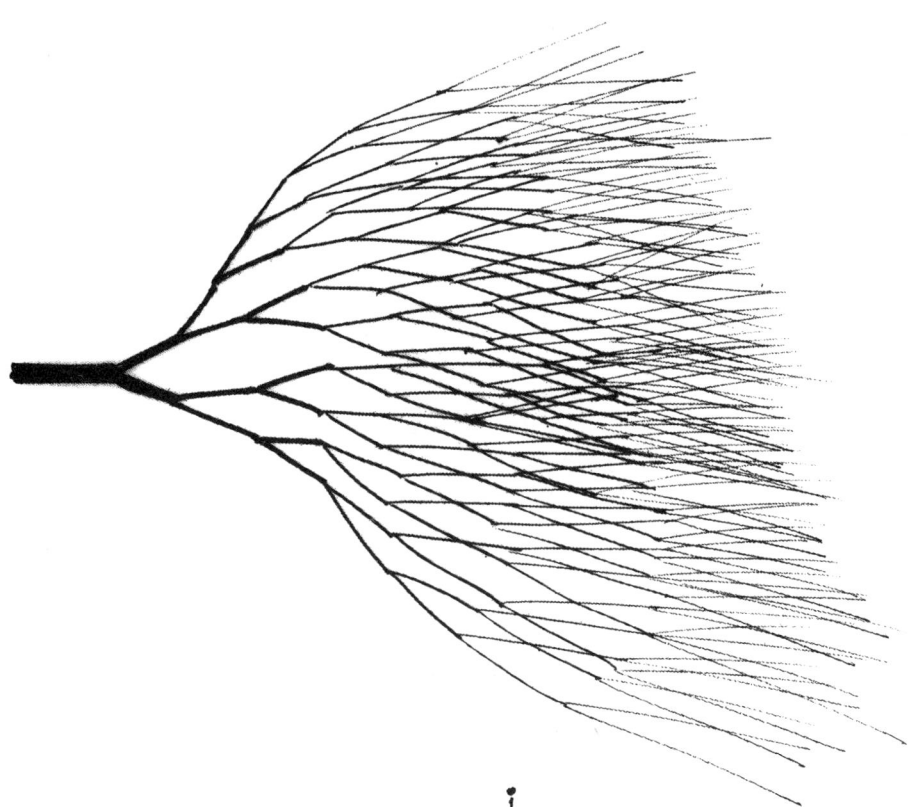

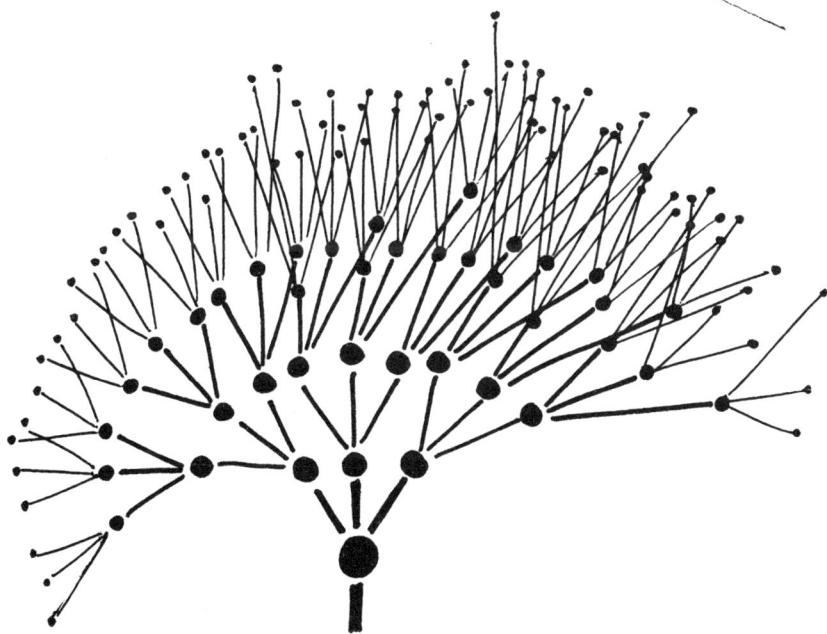

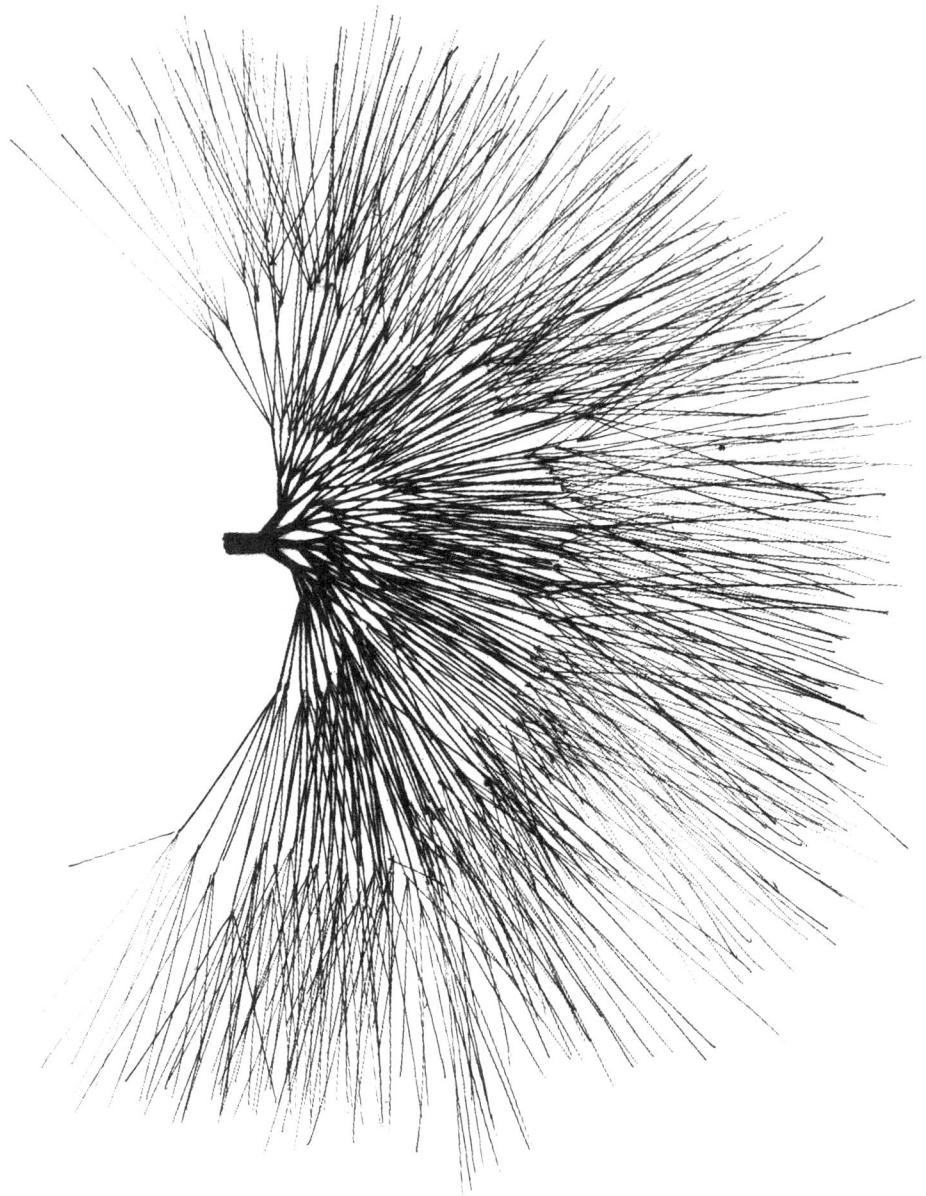

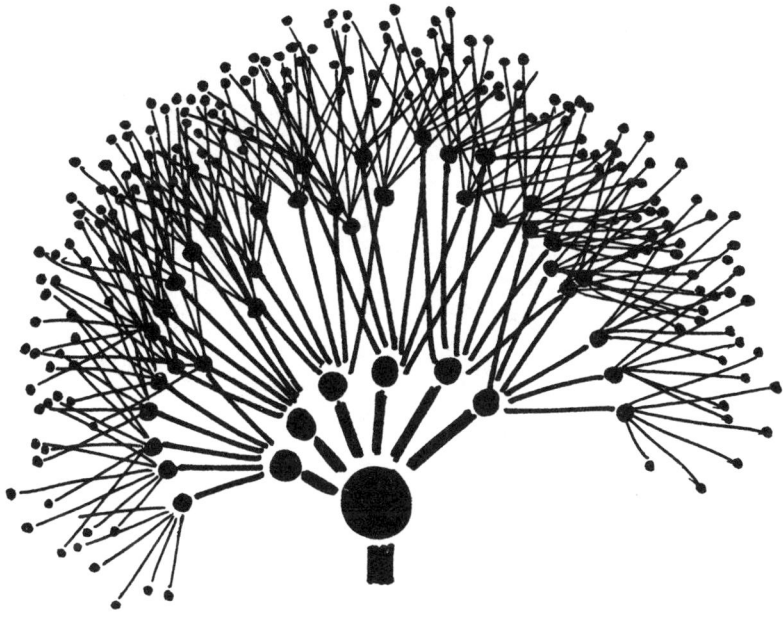

Six-way branching out of four branches, five way branching out of five, and four-way branching out of six.

An instance of branching in which a consistent branching angle is visible.
Aldo Codoni, photographer.

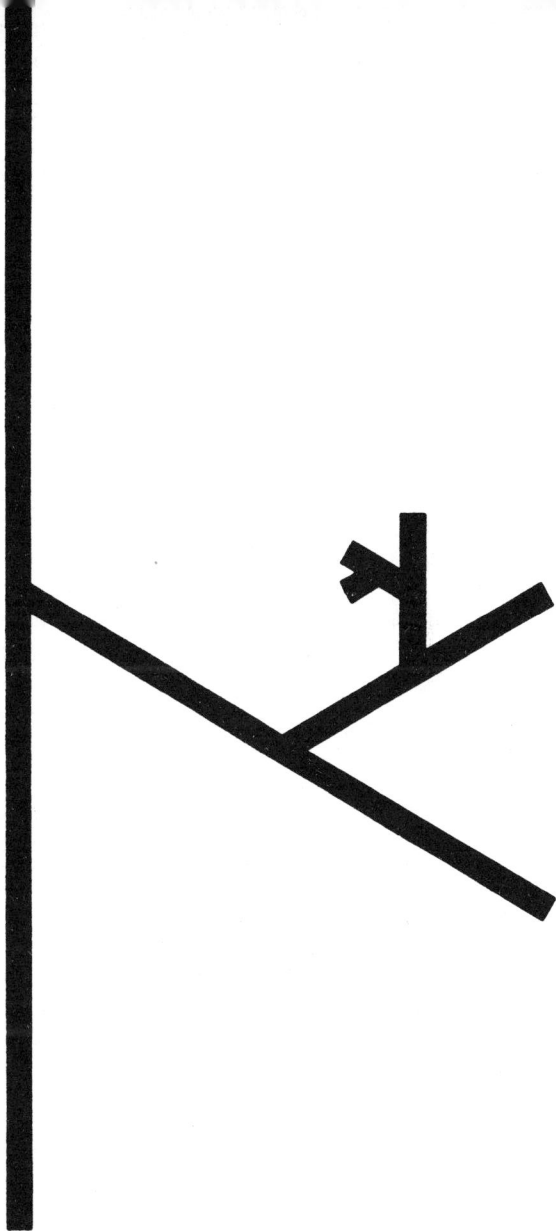

A drawing by Max Bill from 1942. Halfway up the large vertical mark, a series of segments branch out whose angles are consistent, with a gradual reduction in segment length.

After looking into the nature of textures and forms in all of their expressions (including organic forms), I believe we can move on to examining structures: that is, those constructions—from the Latin *struere*: to build—that are generated by means of the repetition of identical or similar forms in close proximity to one another, whether in two or three dimensions.

In the present context, the defining characteristic of a structure is that of modulating a space, endowing that space with formal unity, and facilitating the work of the designer who, by addressing the module's core question, ensures the entire system's cohesion. The standard example of a modulated structure is a beehive; but such structures can also be found in the plant and mineral kingdoms. More recently, structuralism has demonstrated that structures permeate every human activity, from language to politics. Here we will be dealing exclusively with structures generated by shapes and, consequently, with questions of modules and submodules, connections between modules, joints and nodes, and shapes internal to modules.

How many elementary structures exist from which all other structures can be derived by altering dimensions and angles? How can modules and submodules or the diagonals that cut through one or more modules fill out these structures? What are coherent shapes and coherent objects according to a given formal principle? What is the best way to test a structure's conformity to a model?

Let us, therefore, consider structures generated by means of the accumulation of forms.

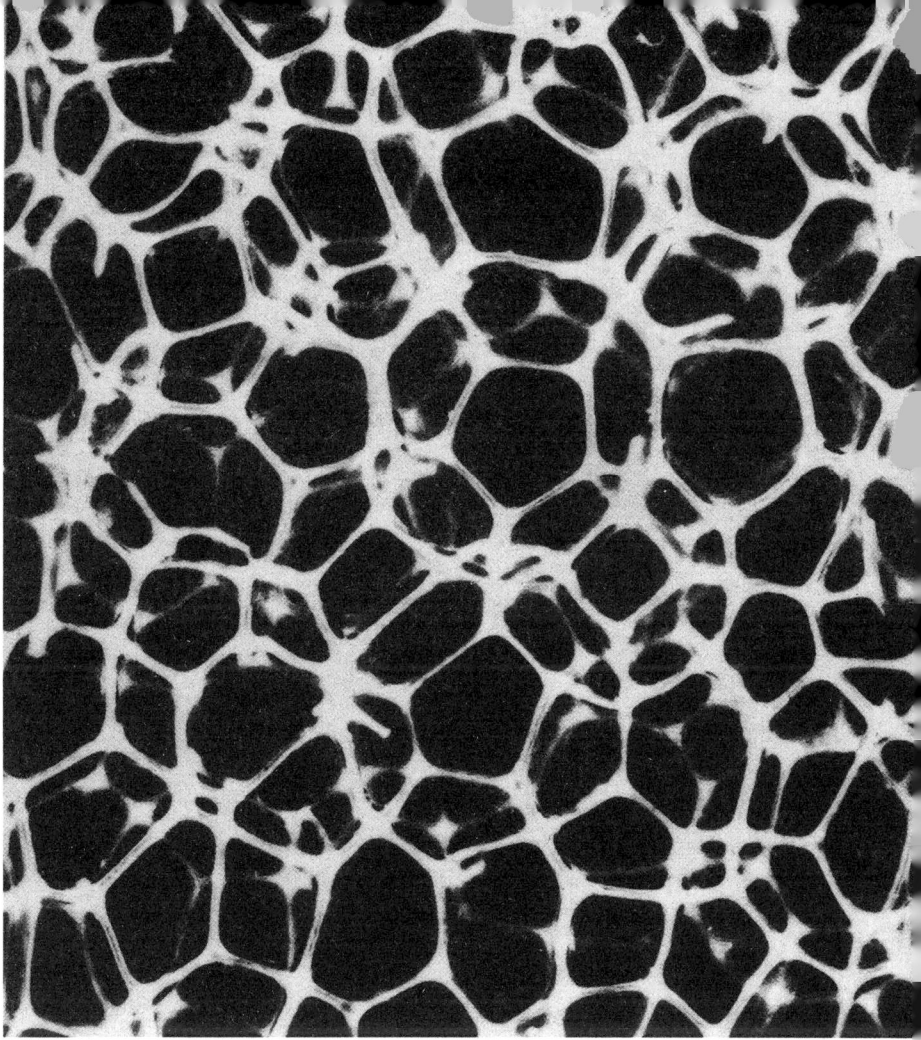

A photographic enlargement of the cell structure of a synthetic sponge. From an advanced industrial design course in Venice. Sartorelli Mattiuzzo, photographer.

In addition to semantic values, these signs, common among preschool-aged children, primitive adults, and prehistoric men, show a natural predisposition to organize and structure images.

The structure of a dragonfly's wing.

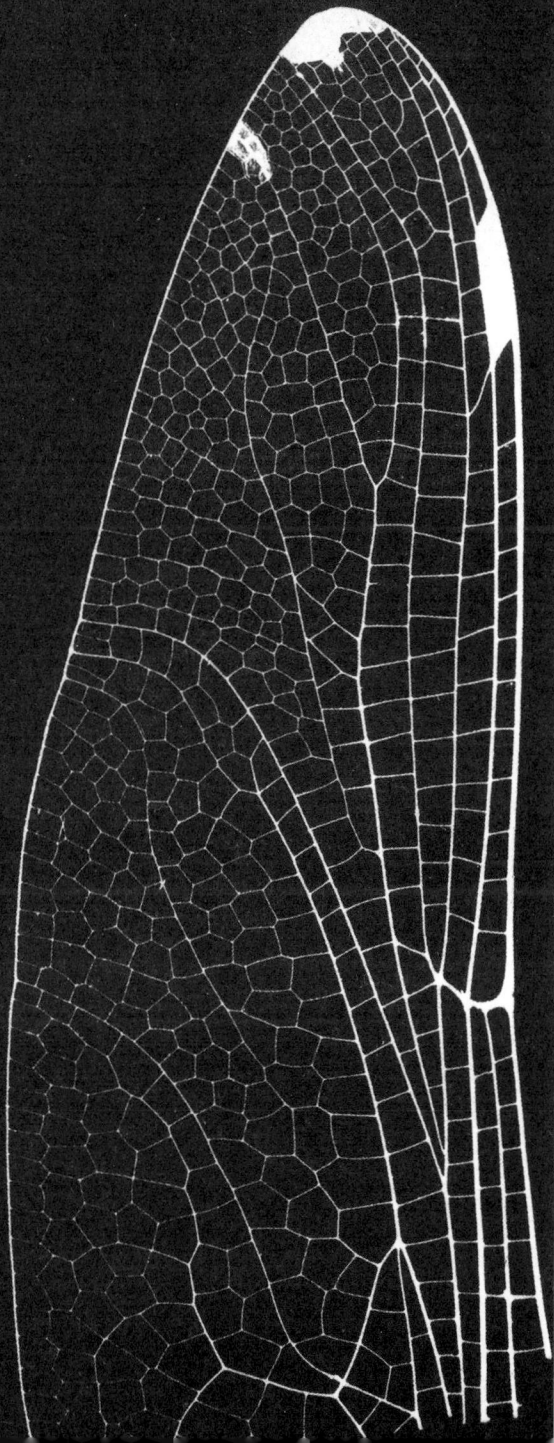

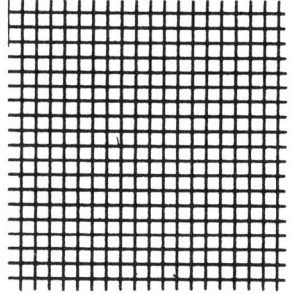

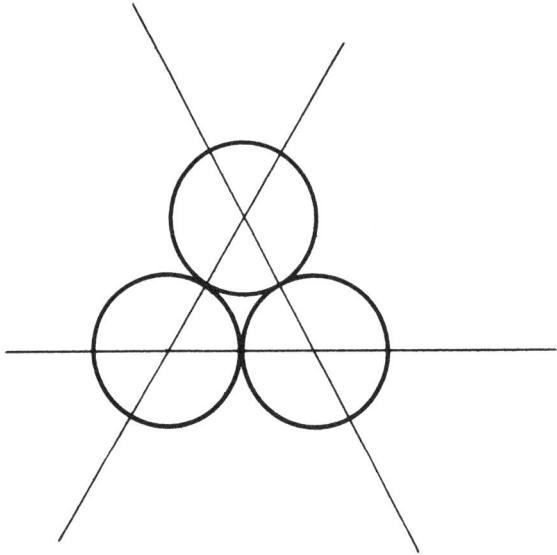

There exist three basic shapes. But the accumulation of these three shapes generates only two types of elementary structures: squares and equilateral triangles. The maximum packing of disks on a surface has the structure of an equilateral triangle. We can experiment on sheets printed with triangular and square lattices to see what other shapes can be found that are rigorously bound within such grids.

Hexagons in a triangular structure.

257

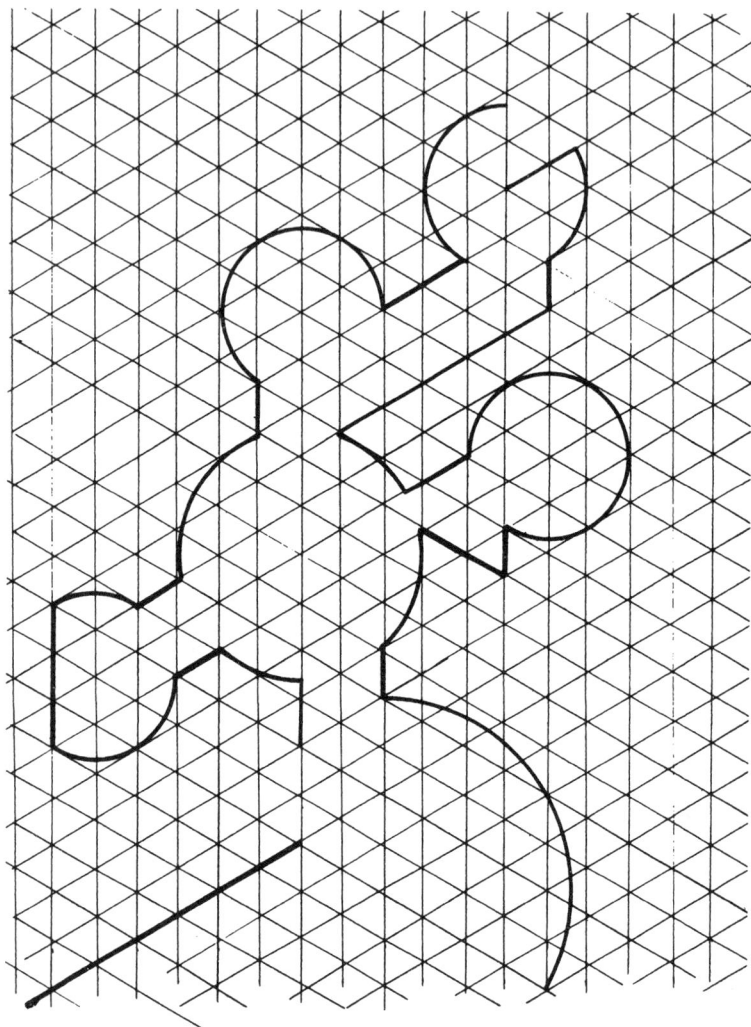

A tracing made up of straight lines and arcs of a circle, following the nodal points of a triangular structure. Carpenter Center for Visual Arts, Cambridge, USA.

A composition in black and gray based on triangular structures.
Carpenter Center for Visual Arts, Cambridge, USA.

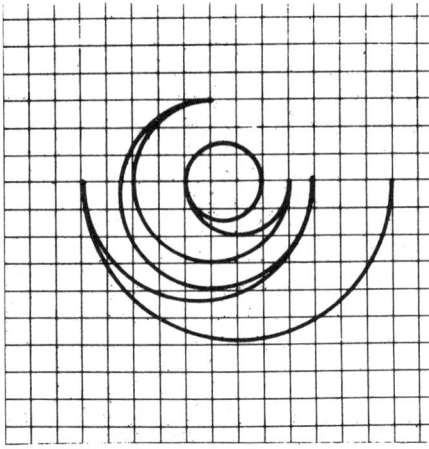

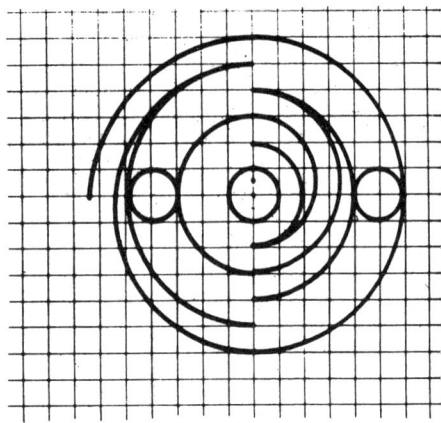

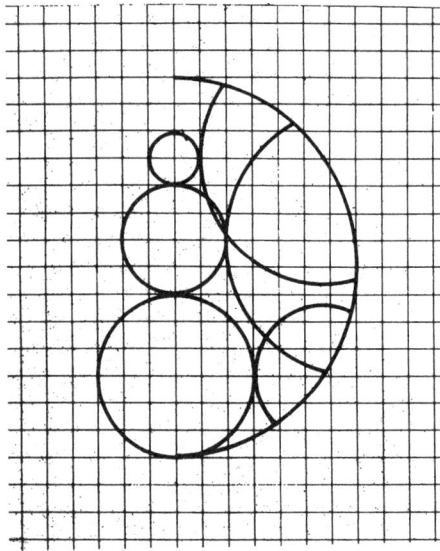

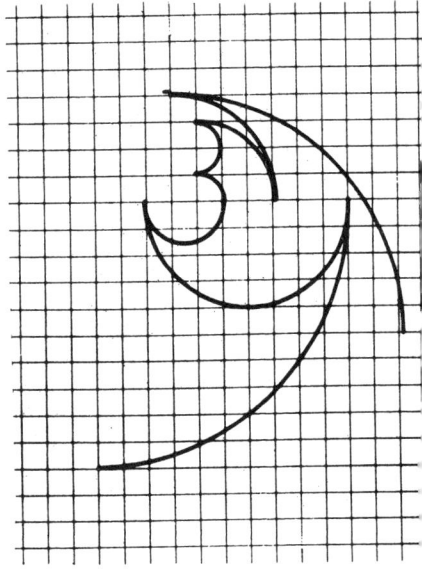

Circular paths in square structures.

Composition of circles and squares in a square structure. Carpenter
Center for Visual Arts, Cambridge, USA.

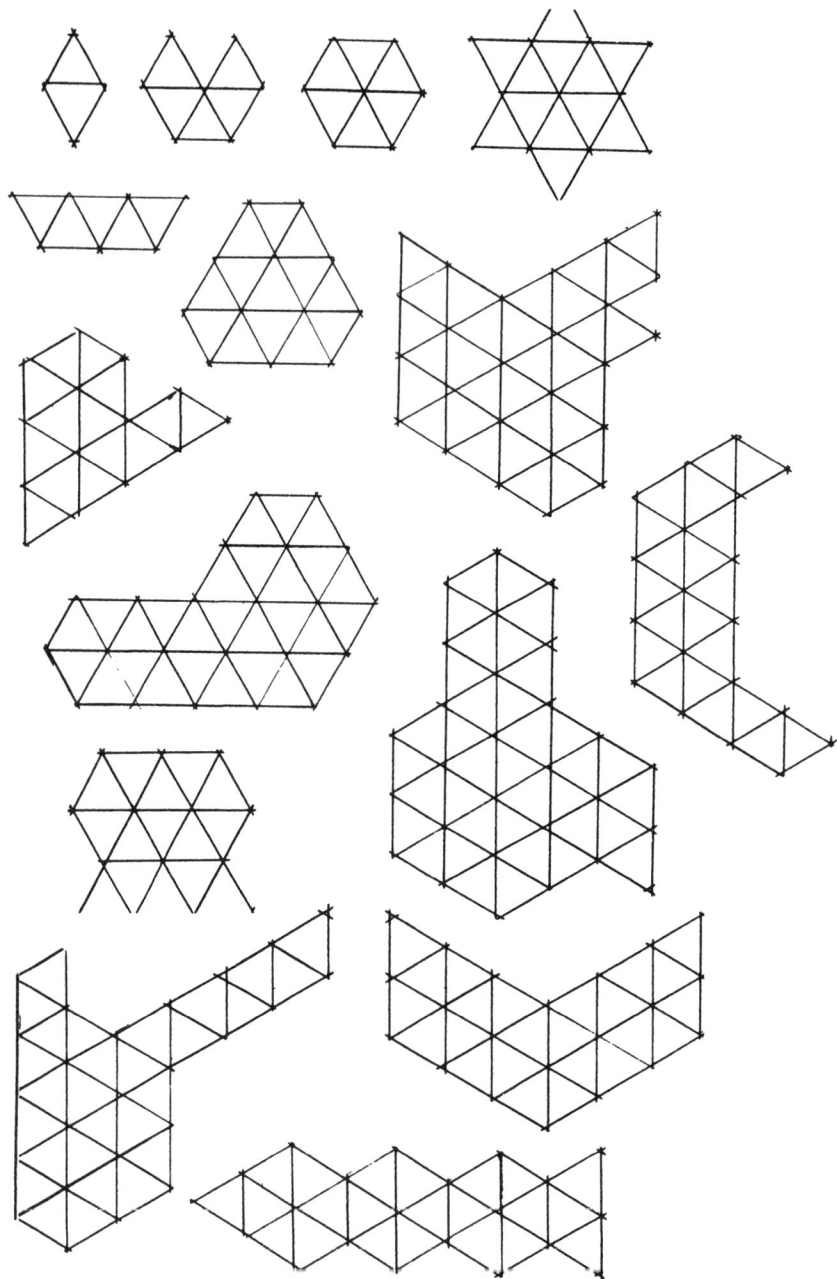

Coherent two-dimensional shapes derived from triangular structures. "Coherent" means that a shape that can be decomposed into many shapes that are identical or share the same character. These coherent forms can be derived from any type of geometric or organic structure.

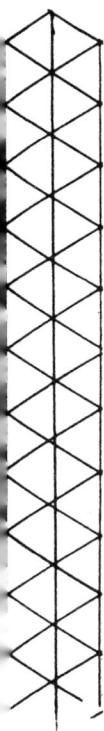
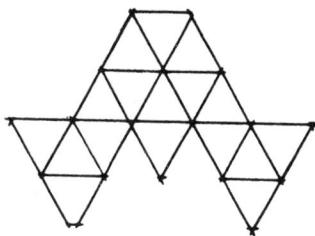
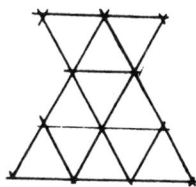
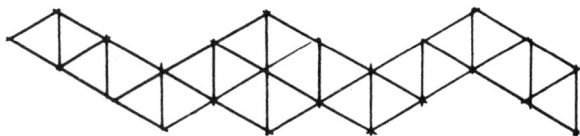
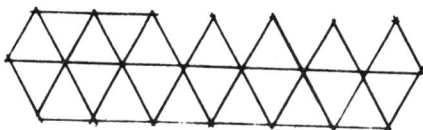
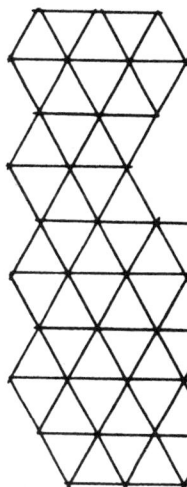
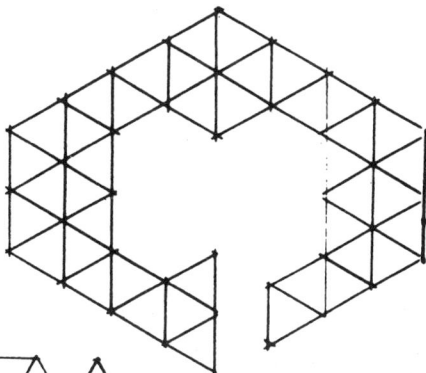
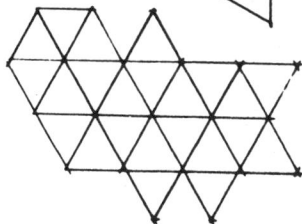

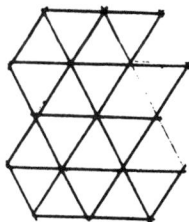
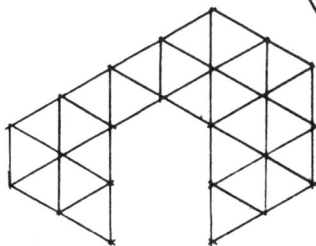

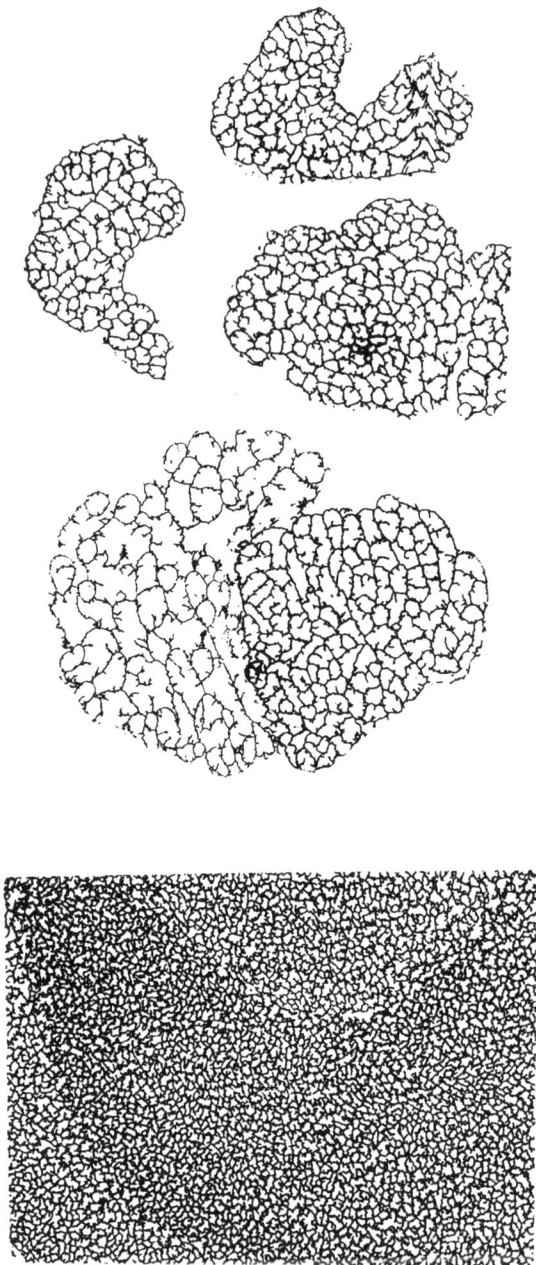

Coherent forms derived from an organic structure. In this case, the decomposition of complex forms into elementary shapes does not yield precisely identical forms (as in the case of geometric structures), but instead similar forms that share the same character.

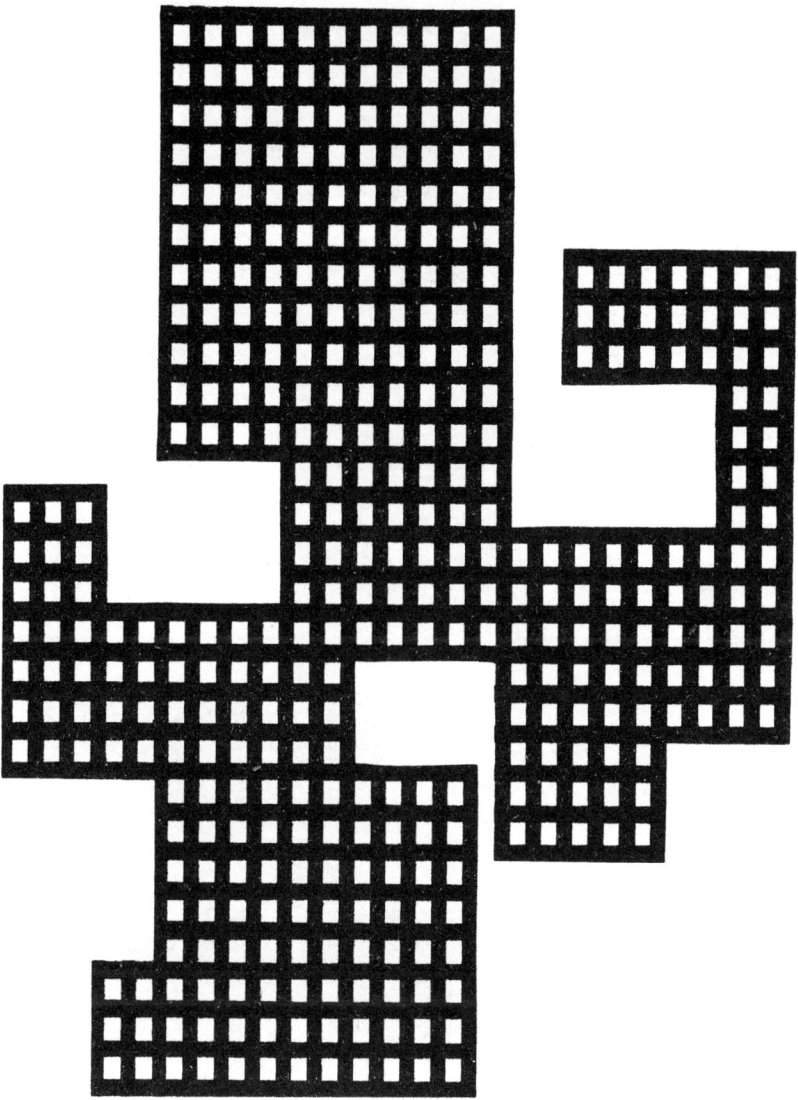

Coherent shapes generated in a rectangular structure.

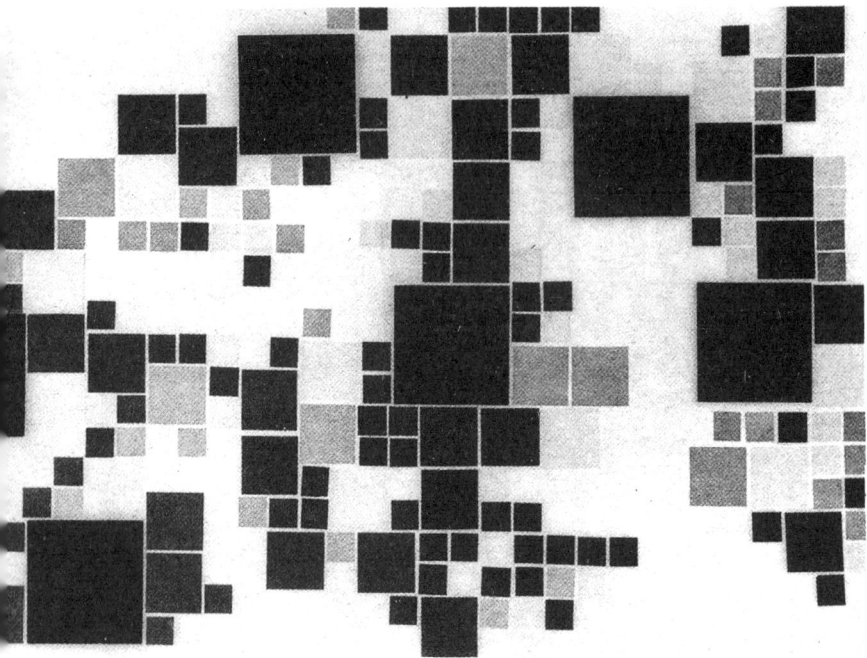

Above: a composition of modules and submodules in a square structure. Below: a composition of modules, submodules, and triangles derived from the diagonal of the square. Carpenter Center for Visual Arts, Cambridge, USA

266

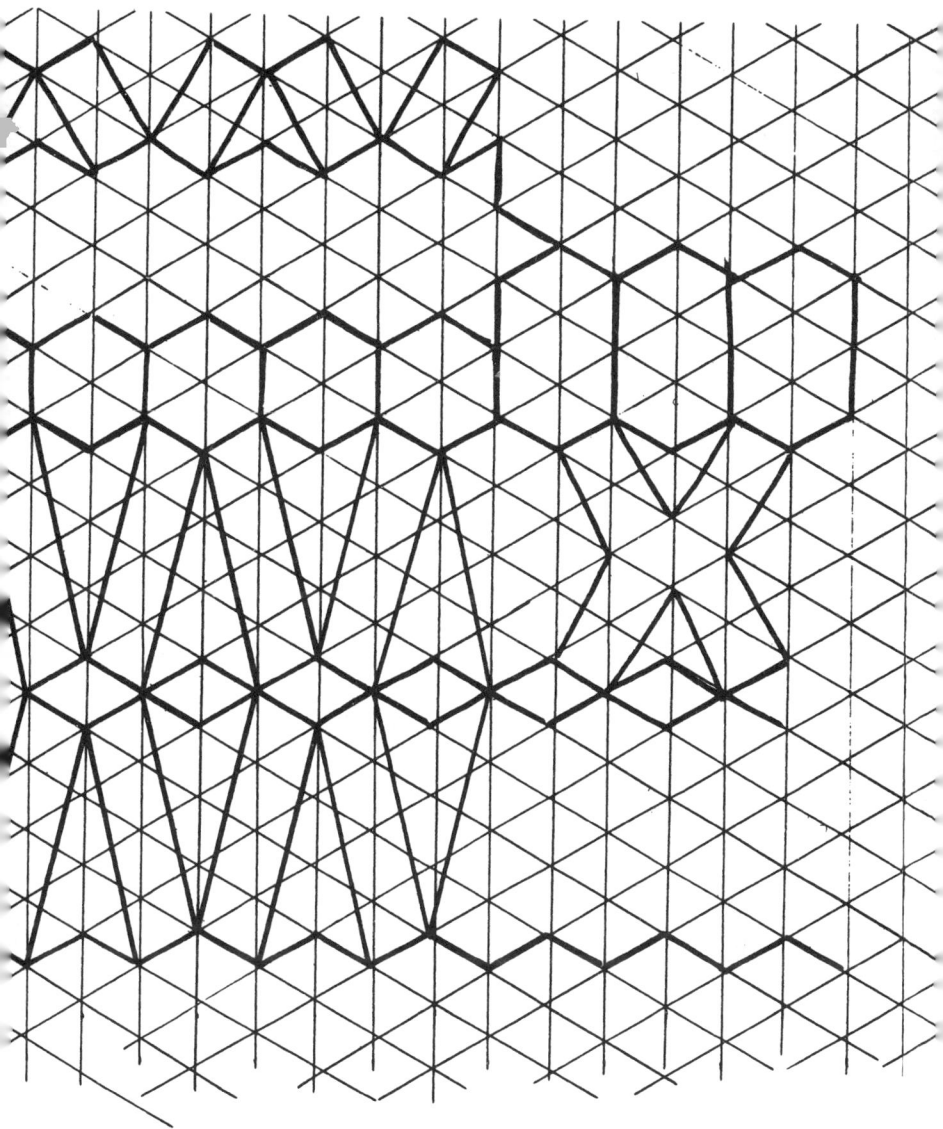

Complex structures within elementary structures. Even as one retains the nodes of the structure as a point of reference, additional structures and modules can be found, especially by using the diagonals that traverse a group of modules as the sides of additional modules.

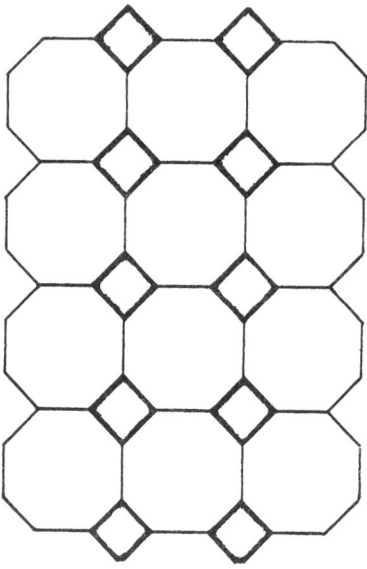

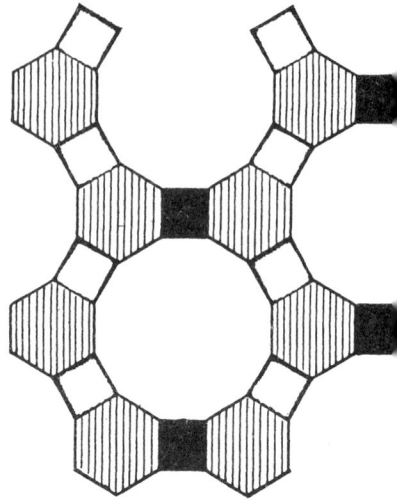

Complex structures made out of base elements.

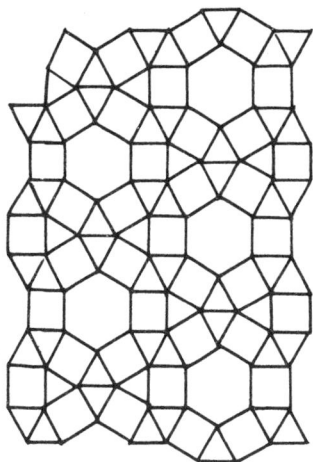

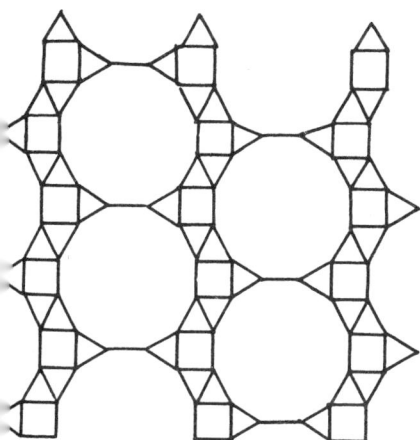
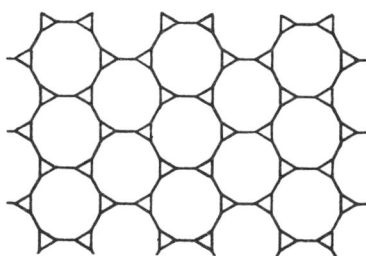
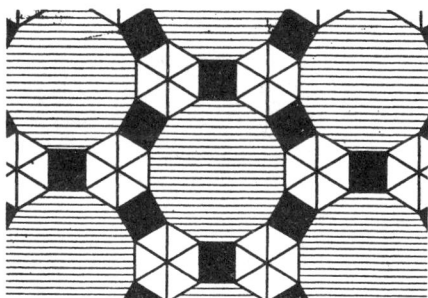

269

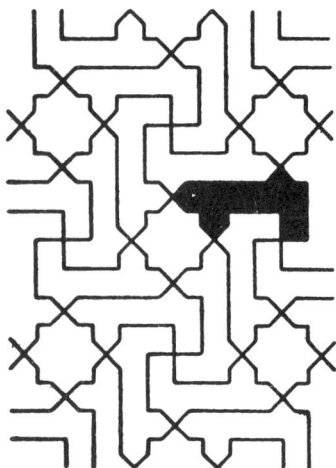

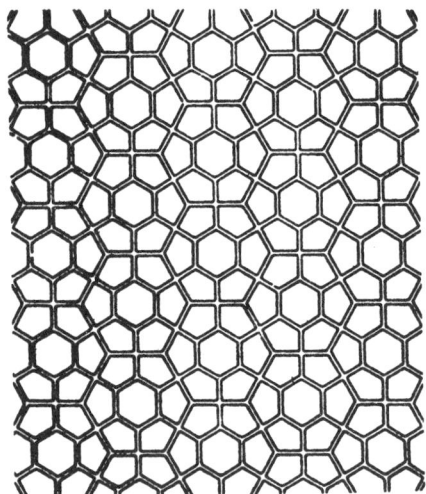

Complex structures of Arab, Egyptian, and Chinese origin.

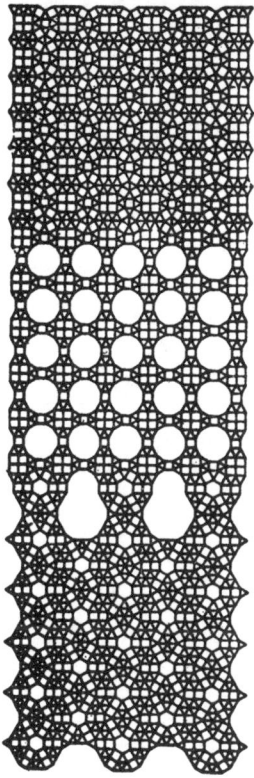

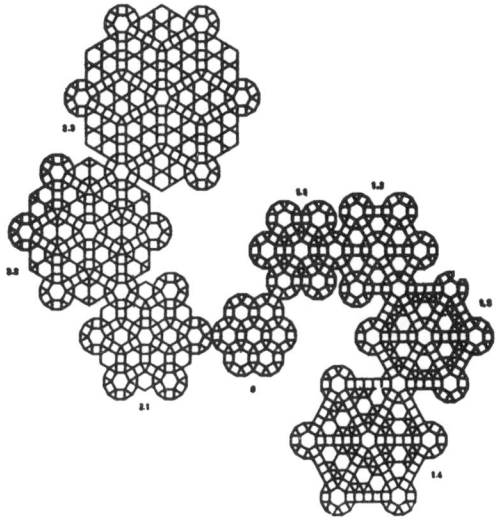

Studies of connections between varied grid structures. Ulm School.

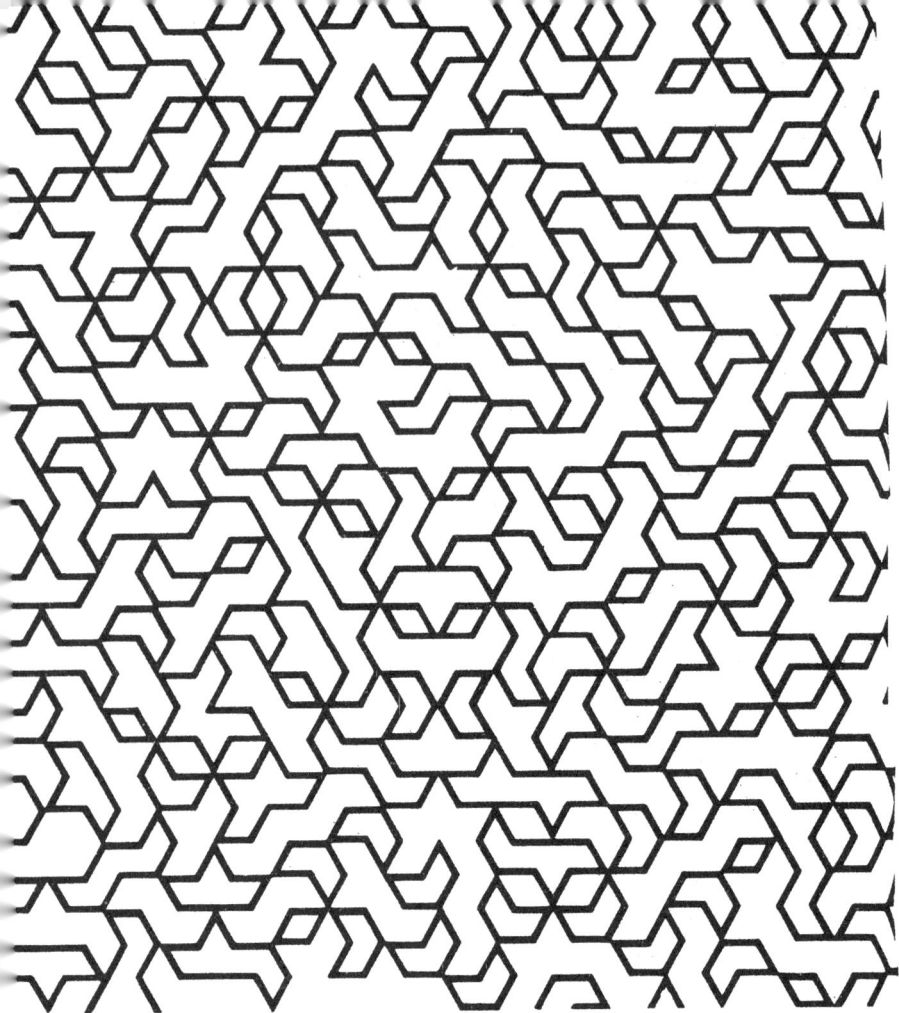

Structural variations on a triangular grid by Pino Tovaglia.[114]

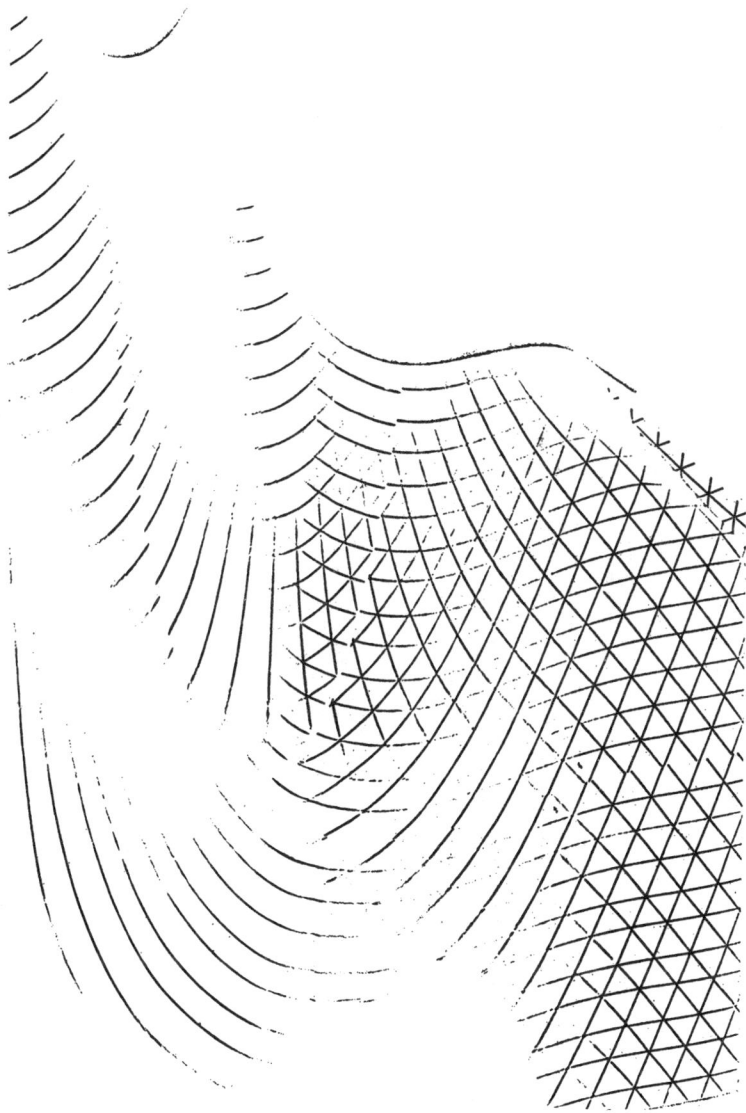

The deformation of a triangular structure, obtained by rotating a regular grid on the platen glass of a photocopy machine during the exposure.

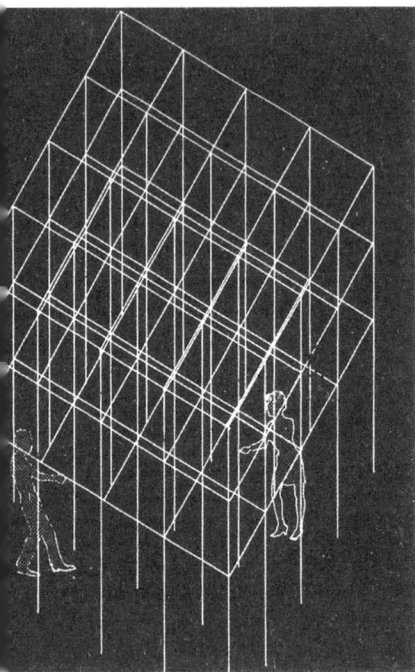

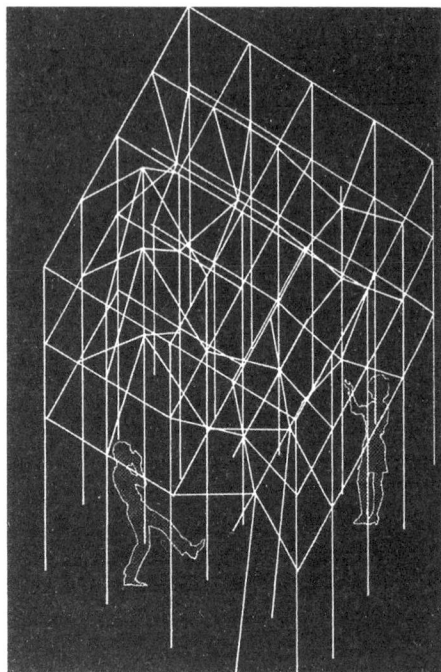

A deformable structure built in a cubic space out of elastic threads actuated by electric motors. The threads were colored with fluorescent paint and illuminated with ultraviolet light in a dark environment to render the phenomenon more visible. Gianni Colombo, *Elastic Space*, 1964–67.[115]

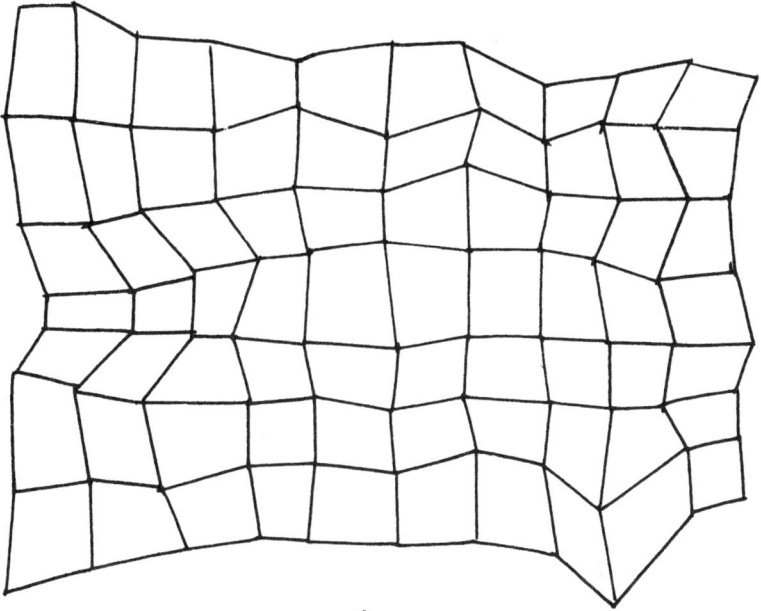

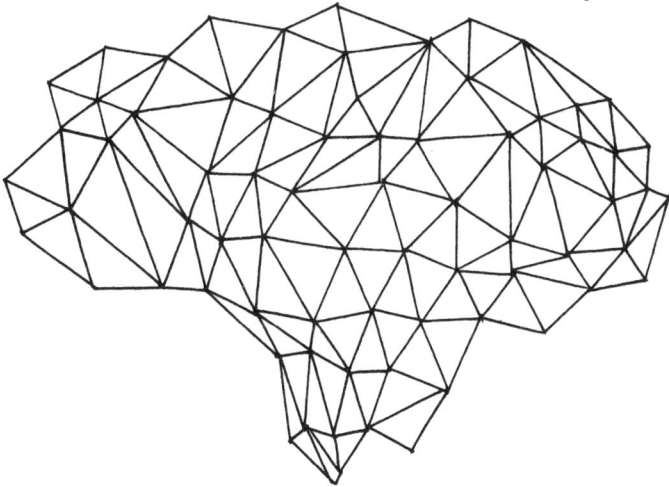

The deformation of a two-dimensional structure based on a square (above) and triangular (below) module. It's possible to alter two-dimensional structures with even greater precision by tracing a structure on a rubber sheet and then photographing distortions.

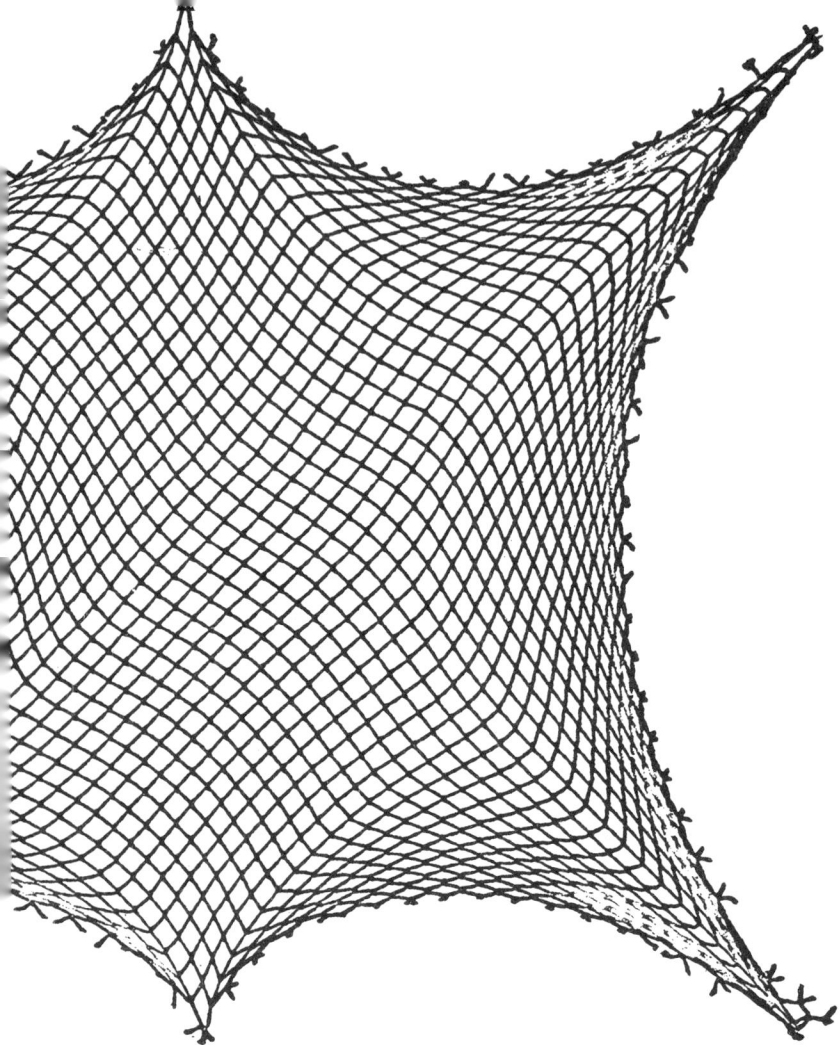

Two-dimensional deformations obtained by stretching a square clastic mesh. Elementary square or rectangular shapes are stretched by pinning a mesh onto a flat surface (as upholsterers do when stretching fabric over a wooden frame). Much as in nature, the tension lines that emerge as one deforms the original structure reveals new shapes. This exercise illustrates how an apparently irregular shape is actually the result of the deformation of a regular structure along certain tension lines. (Munari, 1970.)

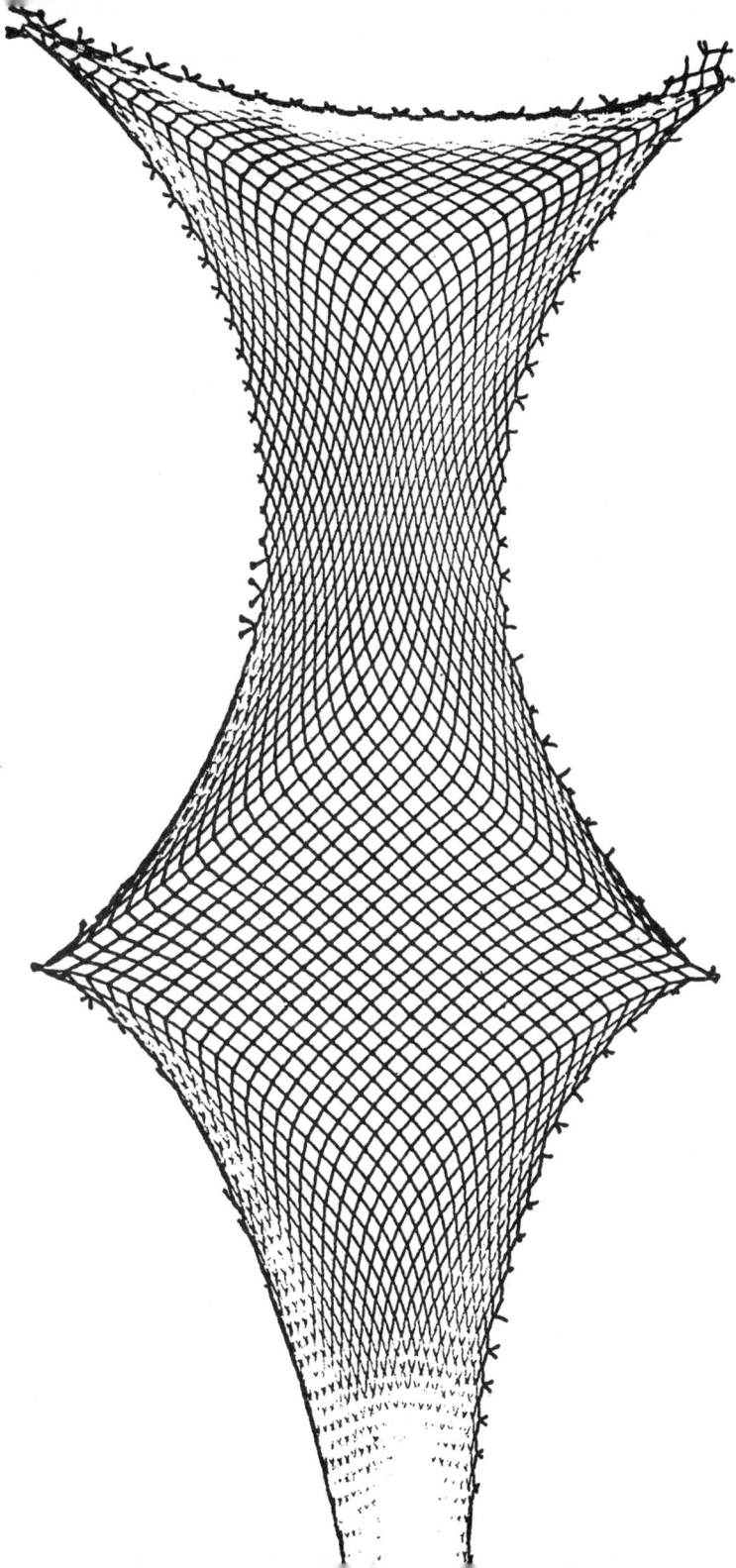

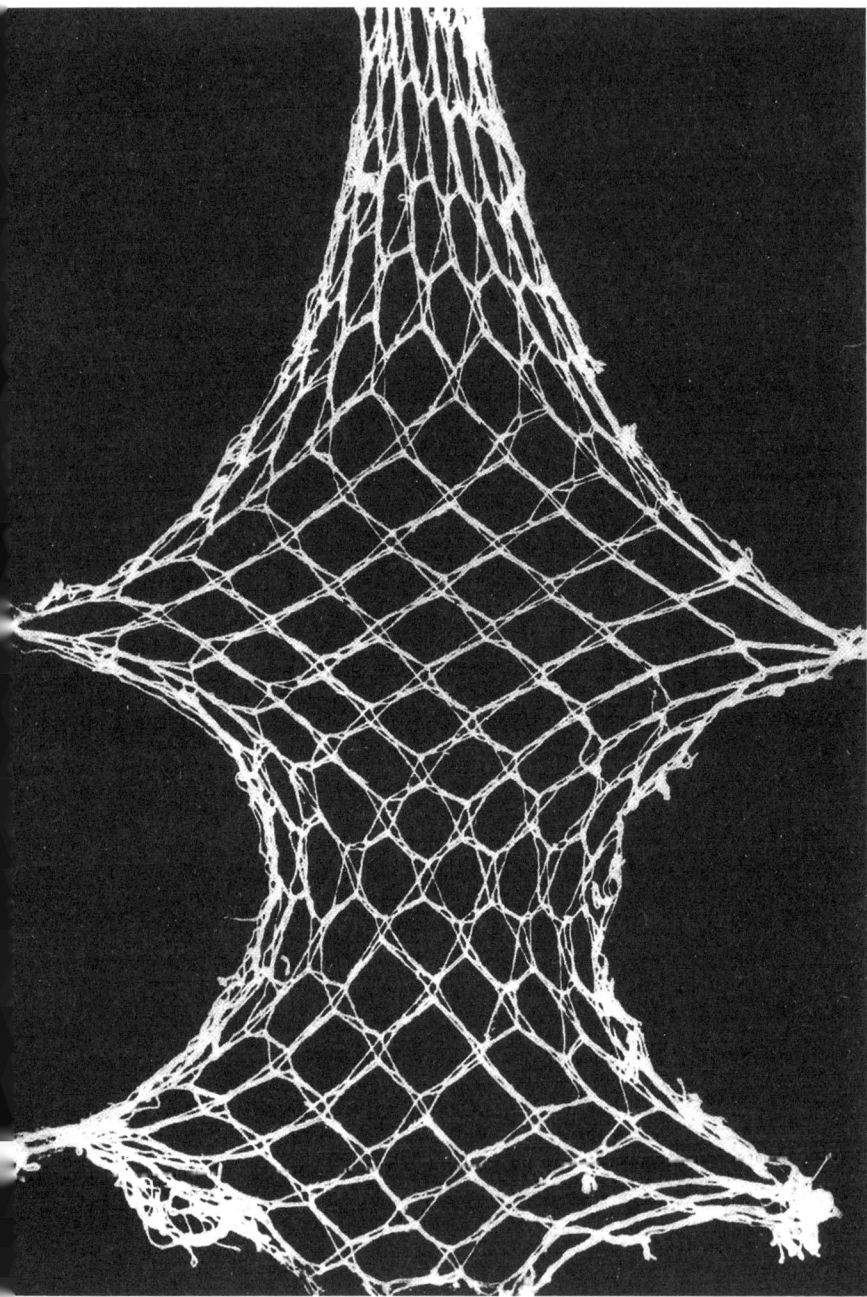

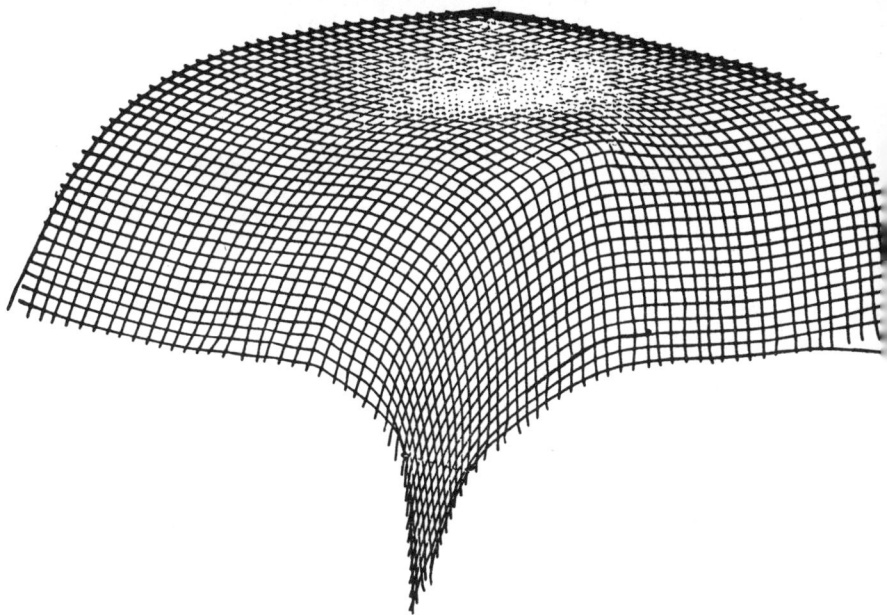

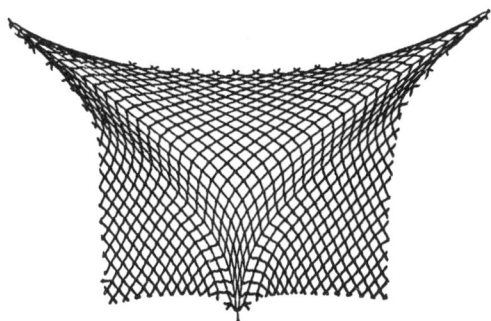

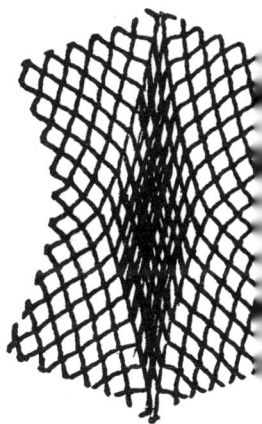

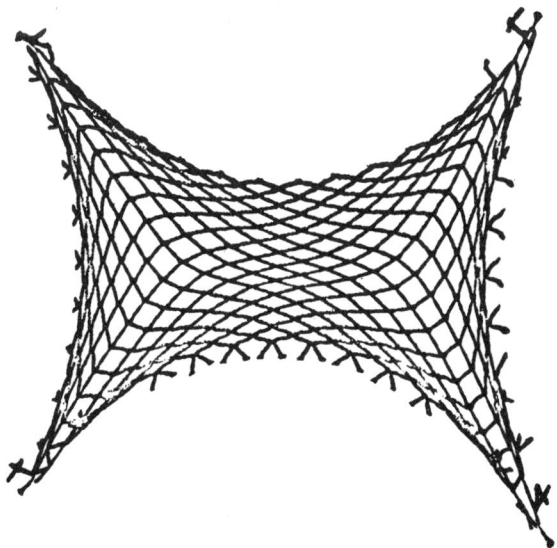

Extending modules and submodules from two to three dimensions while using the same proportions and right angles. Carpenter Center for Visual Arts, Cambridge, USA.

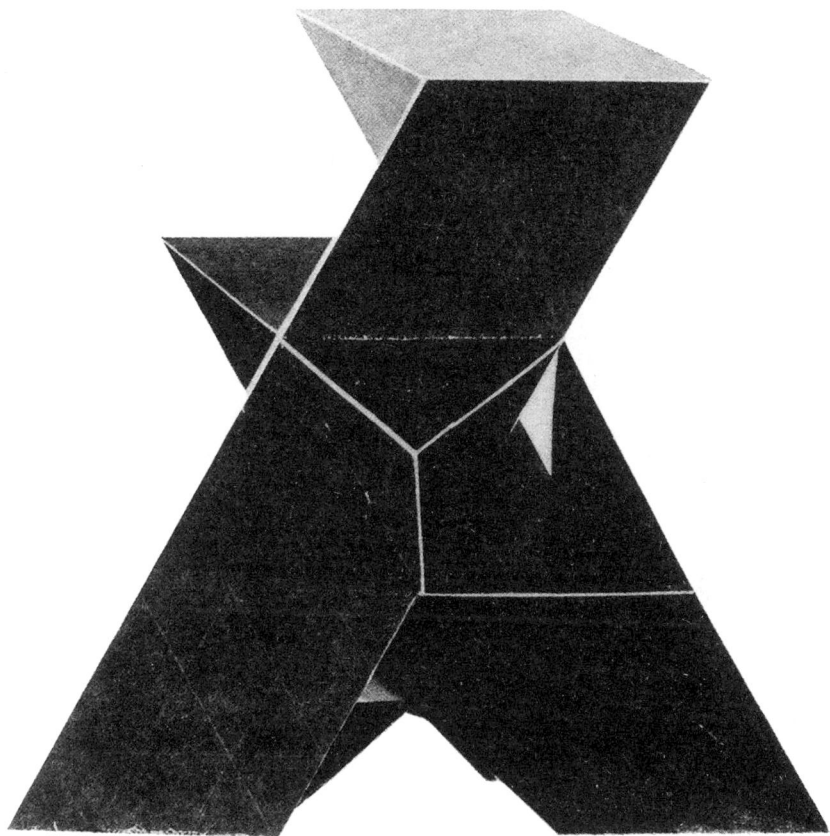

A three-dimensional object built out of equilateral triangles, which is to say, that is tetrahedral in nature. Carpenter Center for Visual Arts, Cambridge, USA.

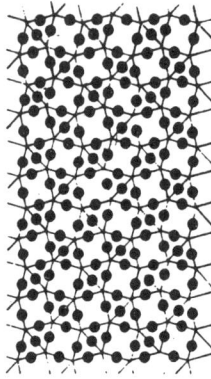

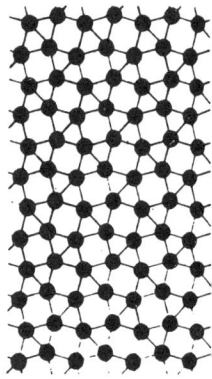

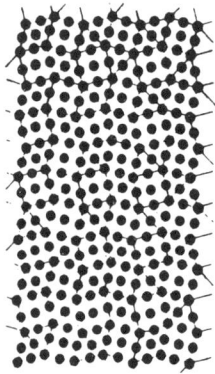

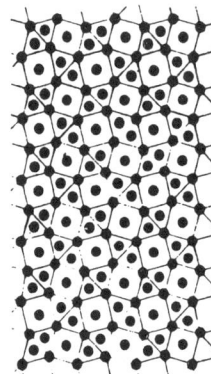

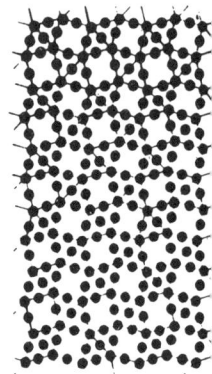

Examples of textures generated by distributing points of varying diameters on a single grid or two-dimensional structure. The problem has multiple applications in the design of perforated sheets, textiles, and other decorative domains. Ulm School.

A bas relief built around a set of modulated elements that have been arranged in random fashion. The result is a three-dimensional structure whose full areas imply regularity and whose voids imply irregularity. Bruno Caraceni, *Labyrinth Structure*, 1967.[116]

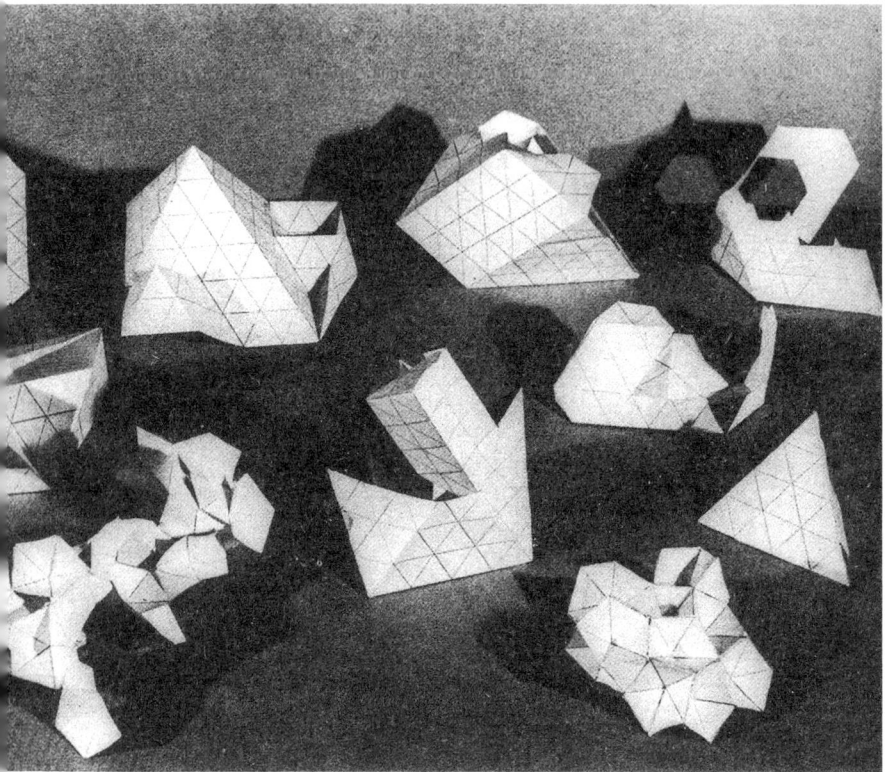

Coherent three-dimensional objects made from paper sheets gridded with equilateral triangles that have been cut along the grid and folded at the same angle as the structure's base triangle. Carpenter Center for Visual Arts, Cambridge, USA.

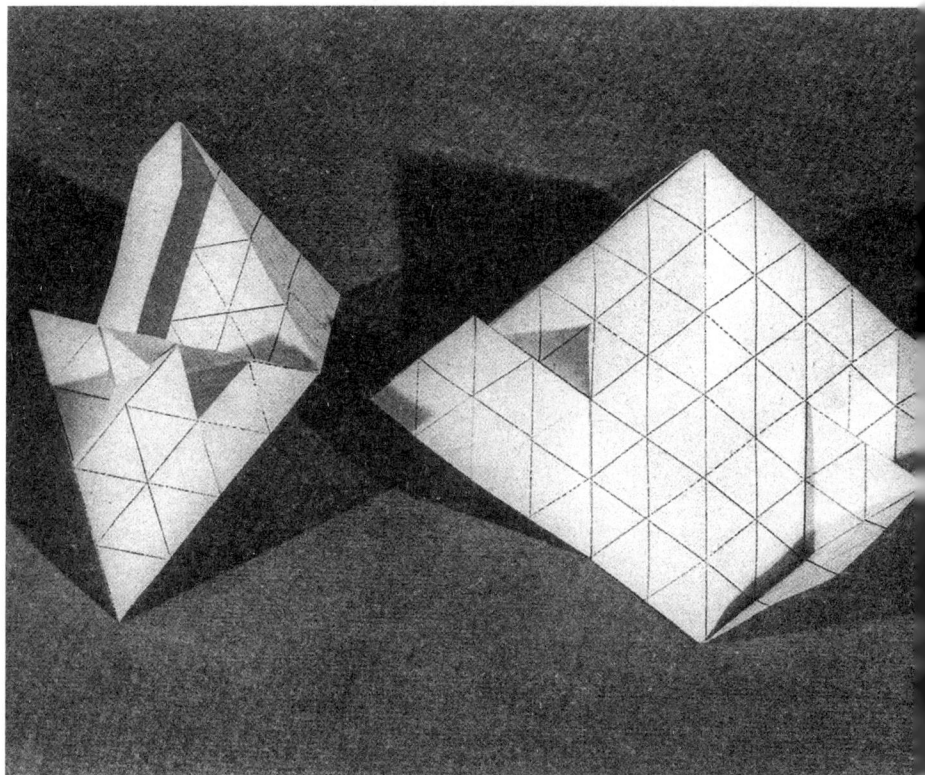

285

Three-dimensional constructions built atop a two-dimensional triangular grid. Each height measurement is equal to the side of the module or a multiple thereof. Carpenter Center for Visual Arts, Cambridge, USA.

A three-dimensional construction atop a two-dimensional square grid that also references diagonals. In this case as well, the heights mirror the proportions of the modules. Carpenter Center for Visual Arts, Cambridge, USA.

287

Three-dimensional constructions made from two-dimensional materials by means of cuts and folds determined as a function of geometric principles. Hiromitsu Kawai, Institute of Design, Milan Polytechnic.[117]

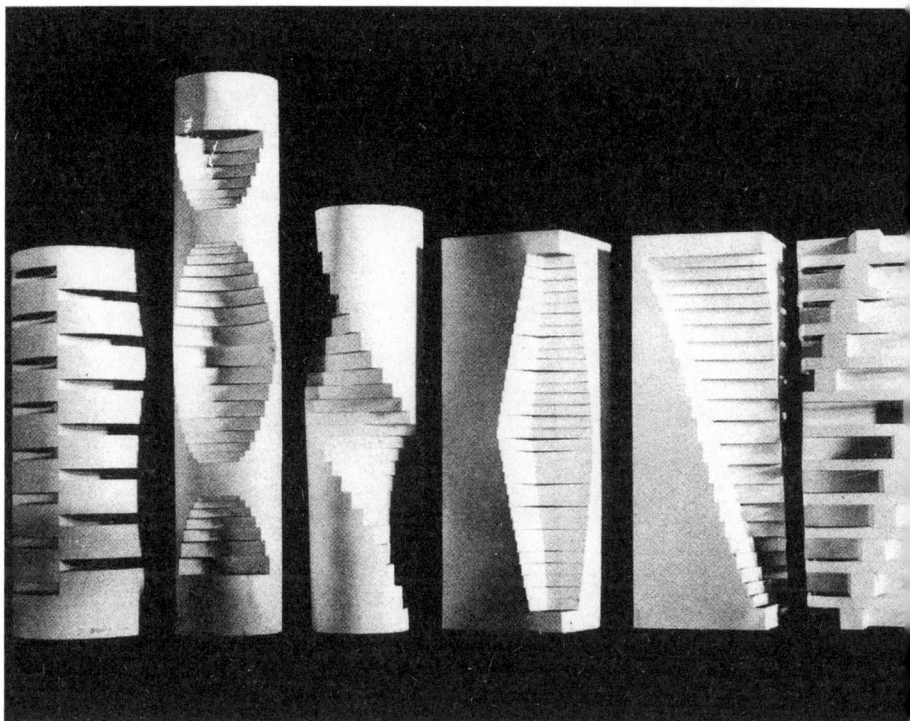

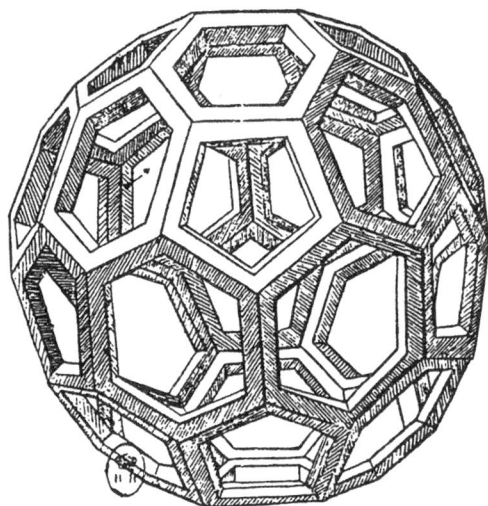

Buckminster Fuller's famous Montreal Expo 1967 geodesic dome. The structural principles are the same as those found in Leonardo's polyhedra and the design of soccer balls.

A student at the Carpenter Center building a three-dimensional structure based on equilateral triangles. A very fragile material has been selected to better test the structure's stability.

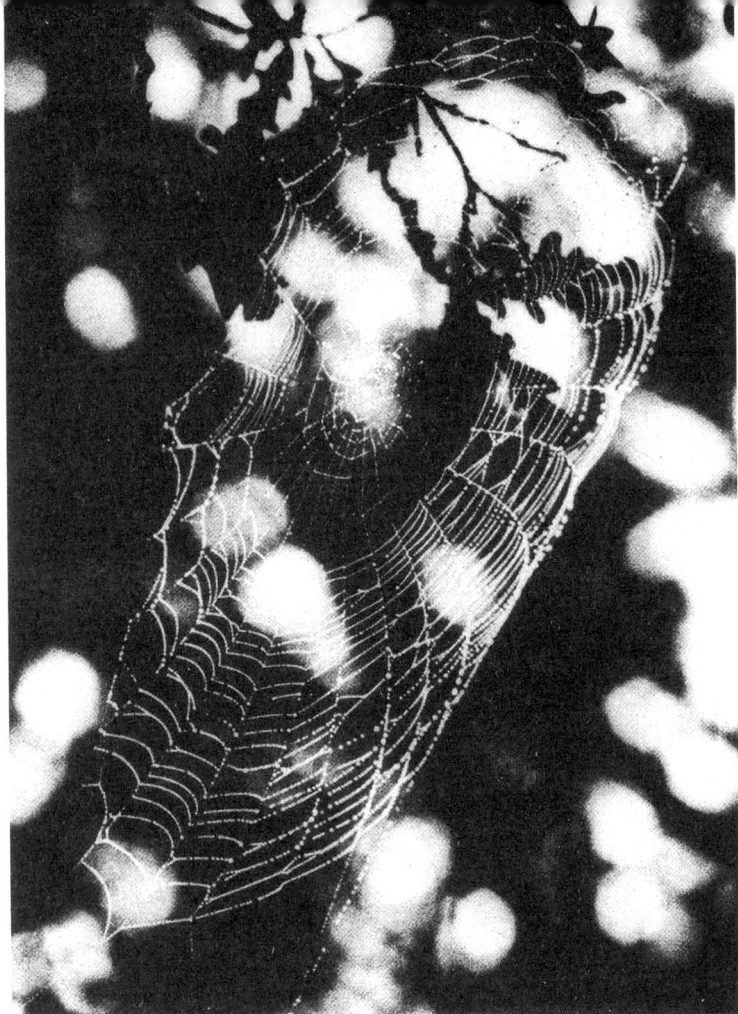

Unlike ground-supported structures, suspended structures invite a variety of solutions. A hanging structure is always lighter than one anchored in the ground because gravity works in its favor. A hanging structure is designed and assembled upside down: it starts from the top instead of the base. Mario de Biasi, photographer.

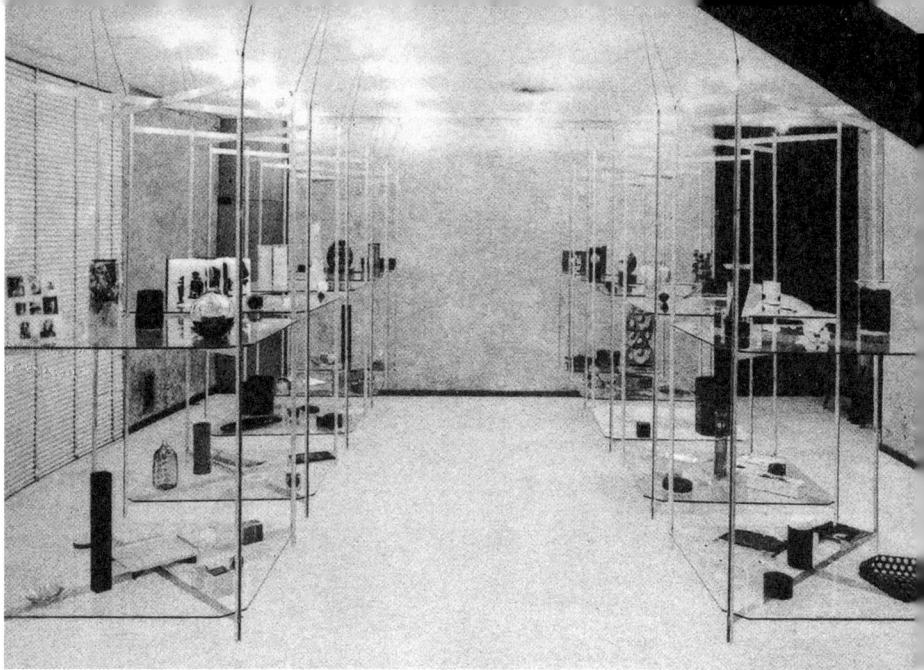

A suspended structure for exhibiting objects based on a square module made out of aluminum and glass. When disassembled, the entire exhibition takes up almost no space. Bruno Munari for Danese. Clari, photographer.

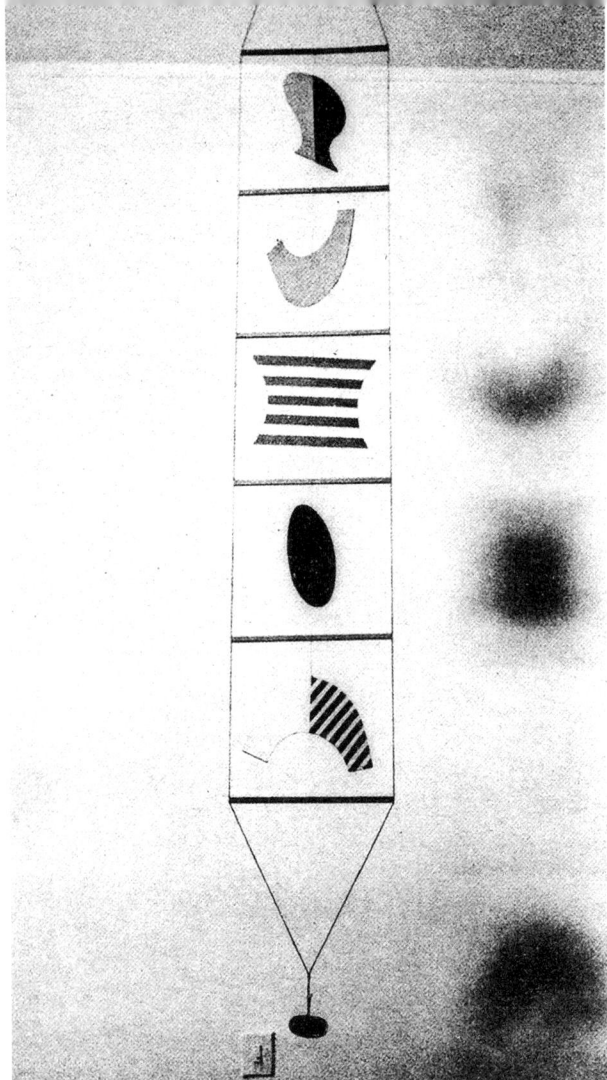

A hanging structure with rotating elements installed within its modules.
Bruno Munari, *Useless Machine,* 1934.

A modulated cubical space with elements slotted into the modules for purposes of experimenting with light and volume. Carpenter Center for Visual Arts, Cambridge, USA.

Modules and submodules in the continuous façade of the Procuratie Palace in Piazza San Marco, Venice. These modules possess not just a structural function but also a significant decorative function, limited, however, to the façade's two-dimensionality. Ugo Mulas, photographer.

Modules and submodules in contemporary architecture. In this case, the module is three-dimensional but structures the entire internal space of the building as well. Ugo Mulas, photographer.

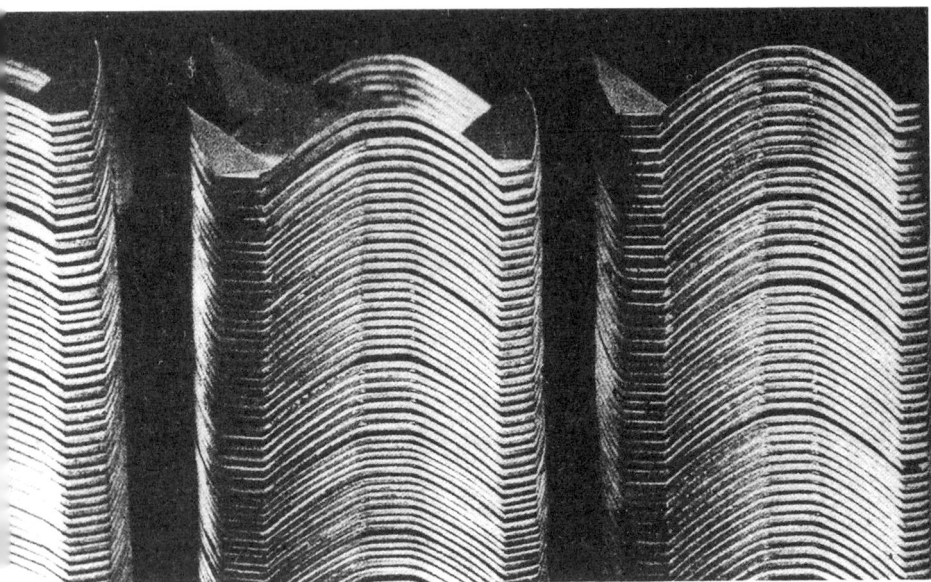

The simple and orderly accumulation of identical shapes creates an aggregate shape defined by its base component. These photographs by Mimmo
Castellano document the stacking of identical metallic forms. Some are
perfectly superimposed, others less so. By carefully studying the base
components, considering the spatial structure of accumulation—think of a
corncob as an accumulation of kernels or a beehive as an accumulation
of cells—and the rules of symmetry, complex forms can be designed that
reflect this same principle.

The accumulation of a single component in the shape of an elongated trapezoid. Made of cardboard, each unit is conjoined to its neighbor by means of metal pins. The overall shape can vary as desired. Installation design by Enzo Mari for an exhibition of design objects produced by Bruno Danese, 1965.

299

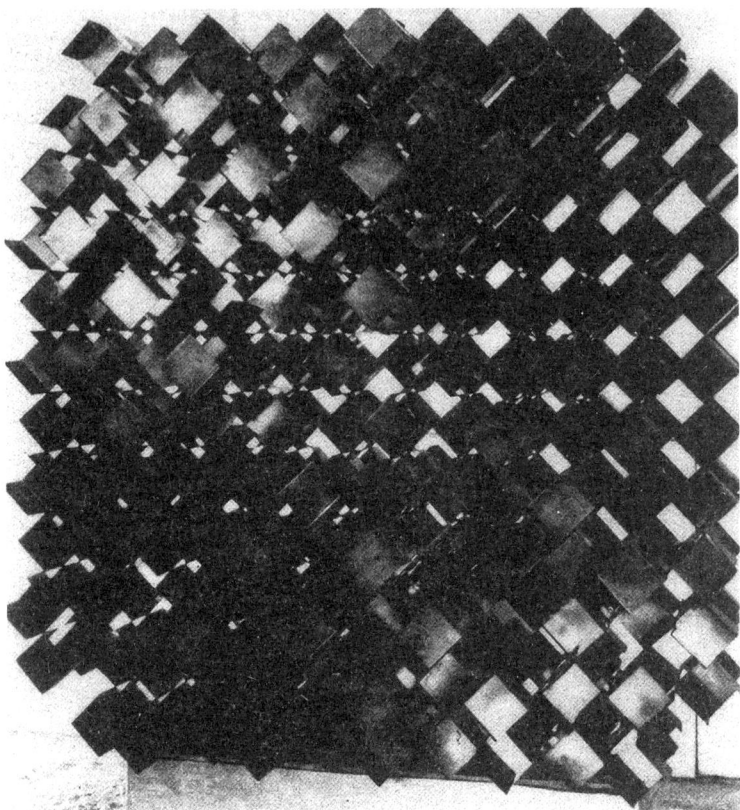

A metallic structure made up of cubes with one open side. The cubes have been welded together at their vertices. Work by Colombo Manuelli.

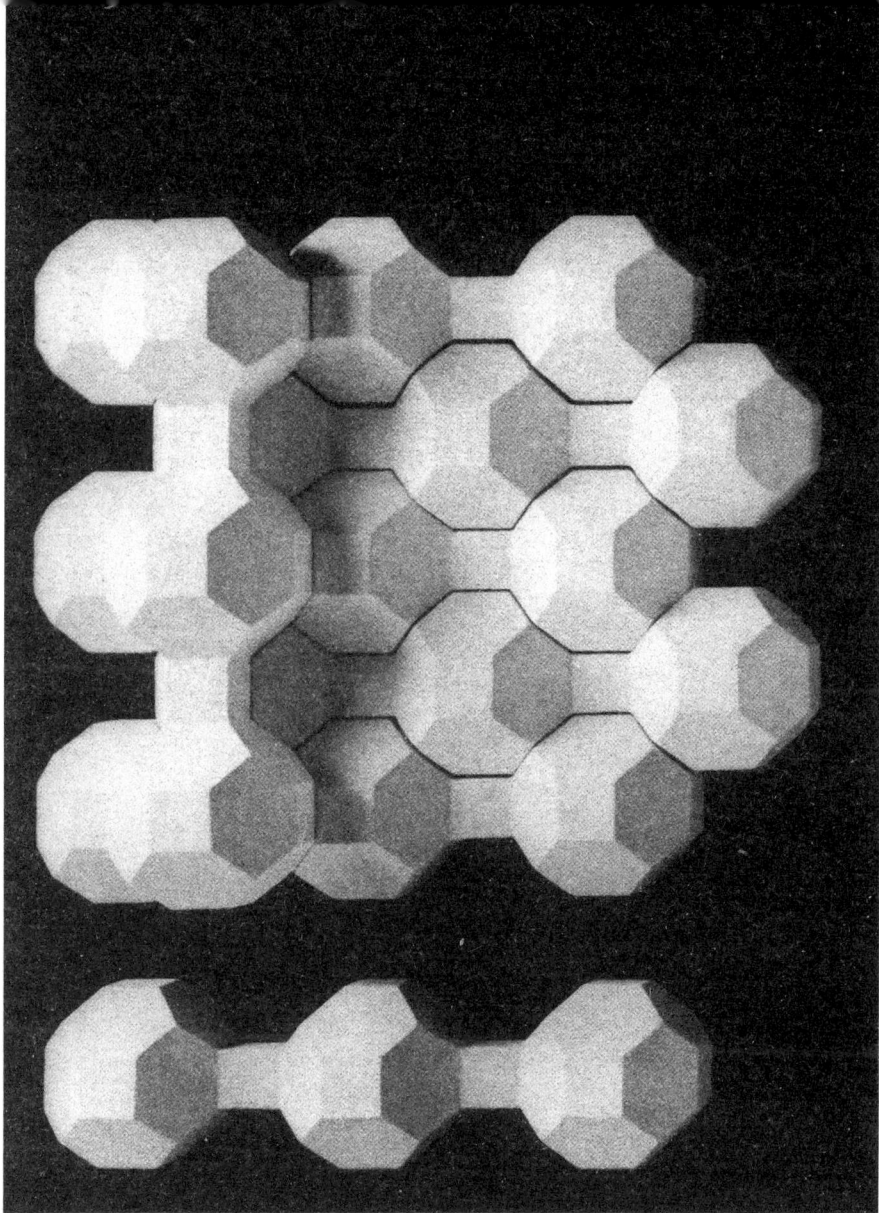

The multiplication of a modulated component. Ulm School.

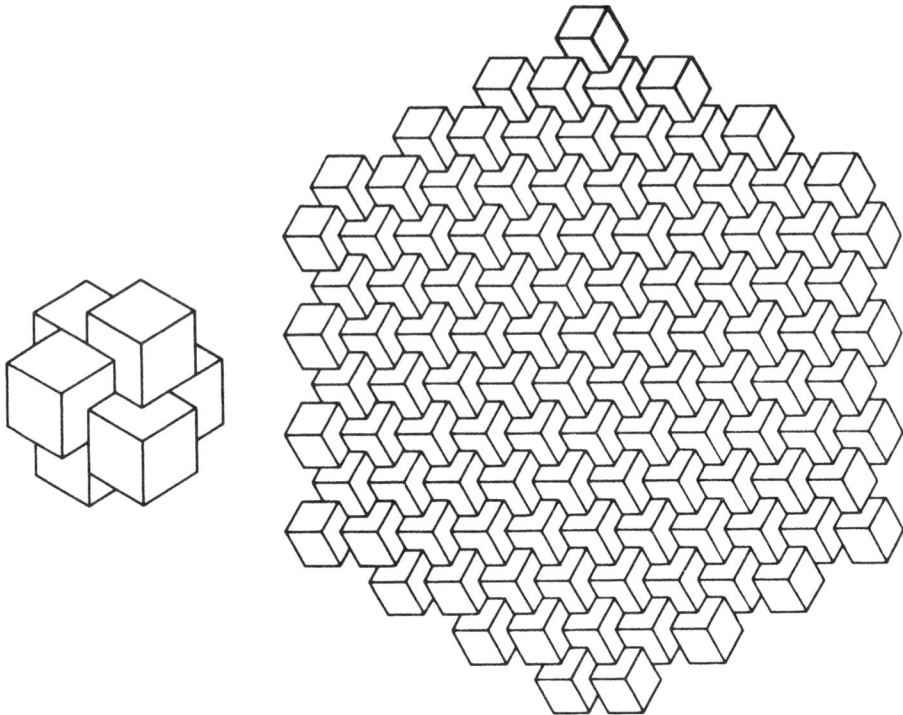

Two Dutch designers, Jan Slothouber and William Graatsma, developed a series of components for cubic structures. "In developing these projects," they write, "we have formulated some principles for orthogonal spatial constructions, based on the study of models precisely devised to characterize a structure by means of the accumulation of identical components. From an unlimited number of possibilities, constructions that are the most elementary from a mathematical point of view are the ones selected. Although they closely resemble one another, they are, nevertheless, entirely different."[118] The designers are currently extending these studies by working on practical objects based on forms derived from these same combinations.

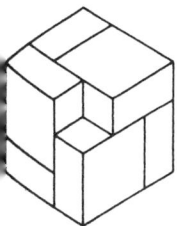

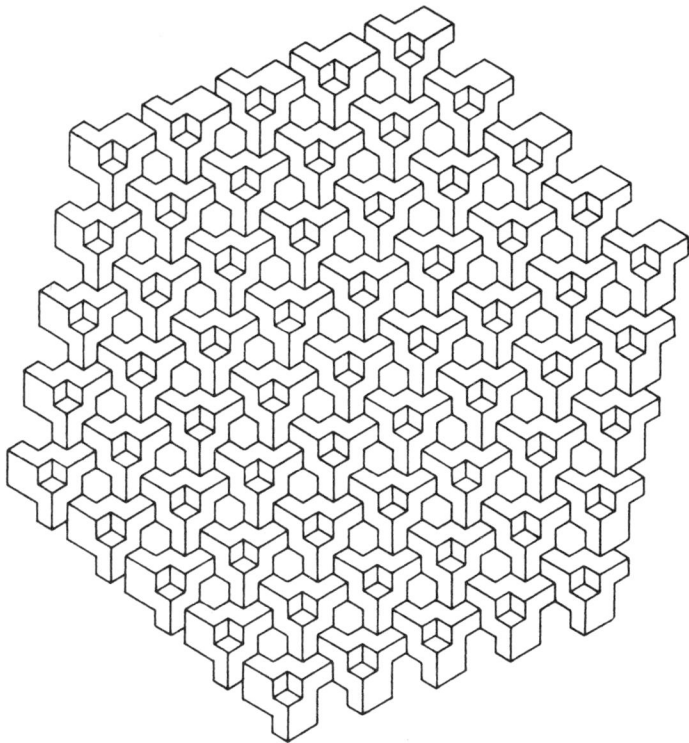

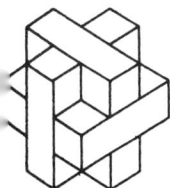

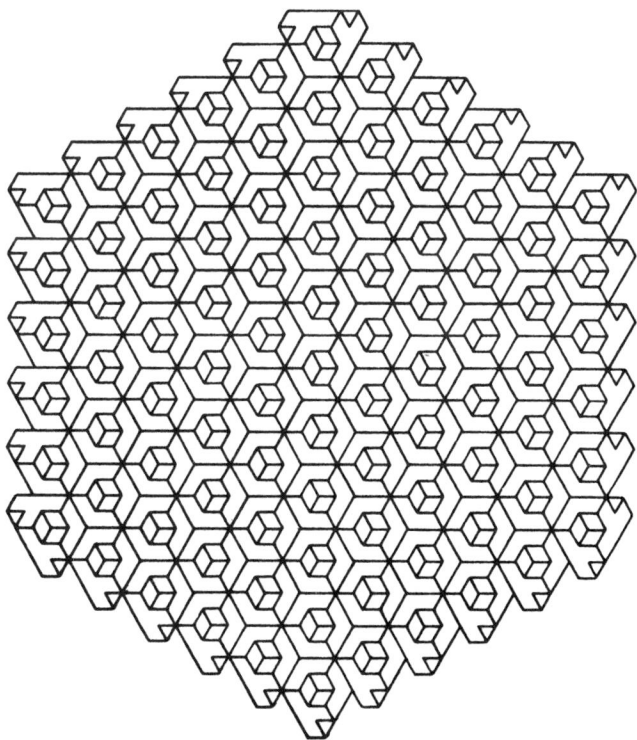

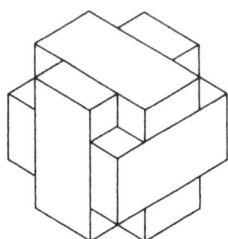
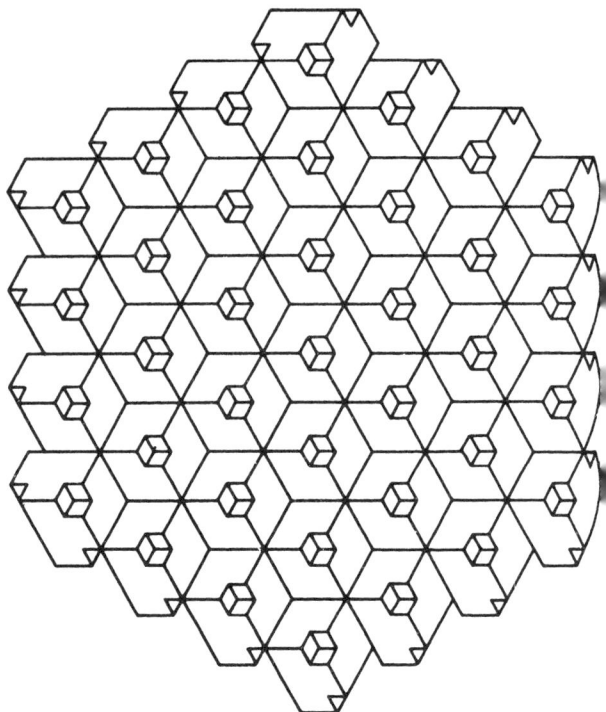
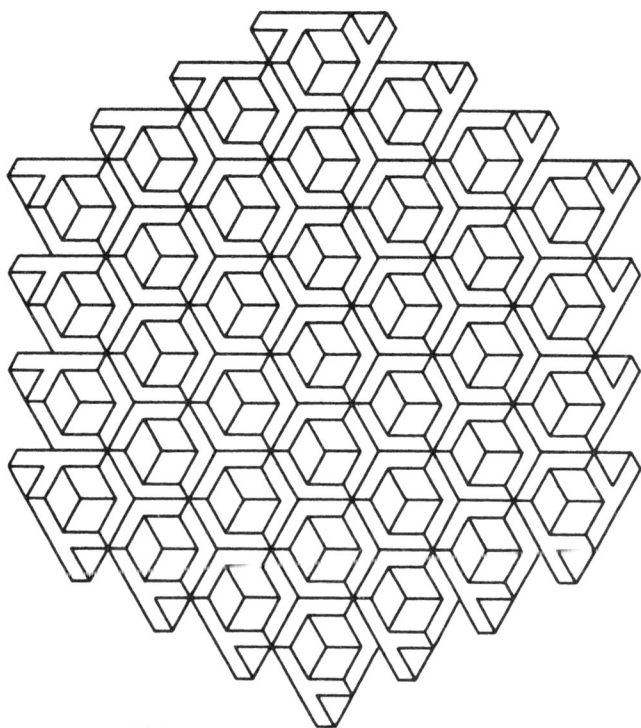
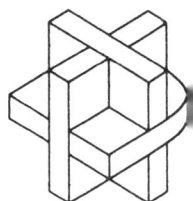

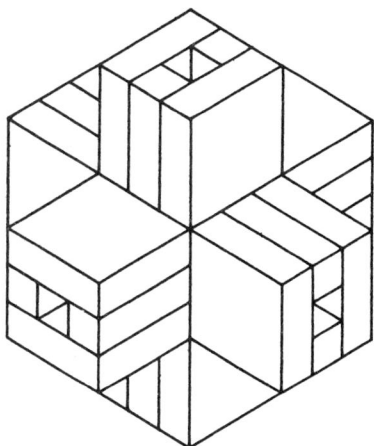

Other base elements.

A modular element made from an extremely fragile material.

The multidirectional repetition of a single element. From the studio of Richard Filipowski at MIT.[119]

306

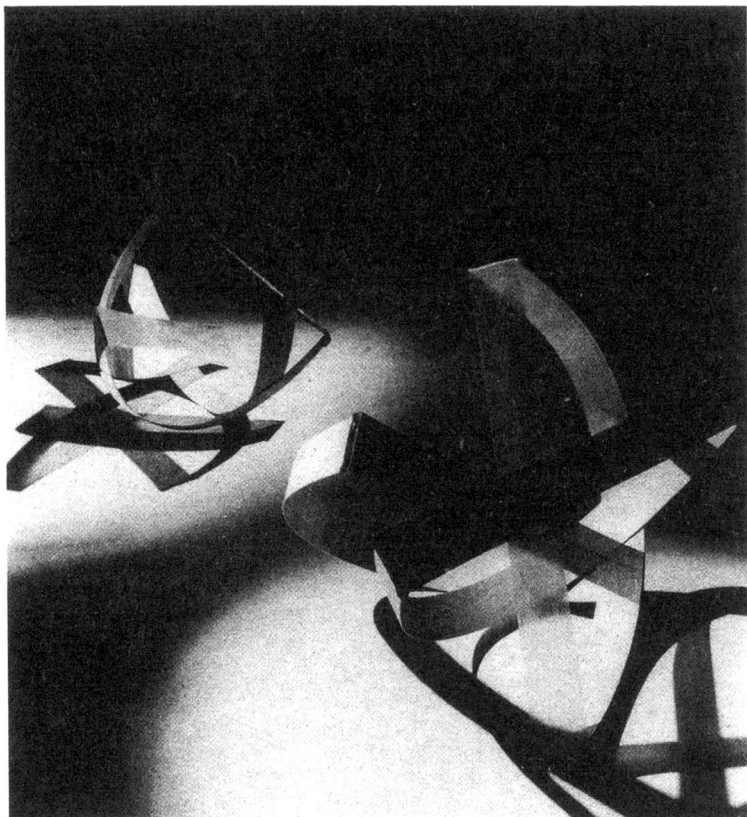

Modular elements in a tensile structure made from poplar and plastic strips.

A tensile structure. From Richard Filipowski's form and design studio at MIT; student work by Preston Pollock.

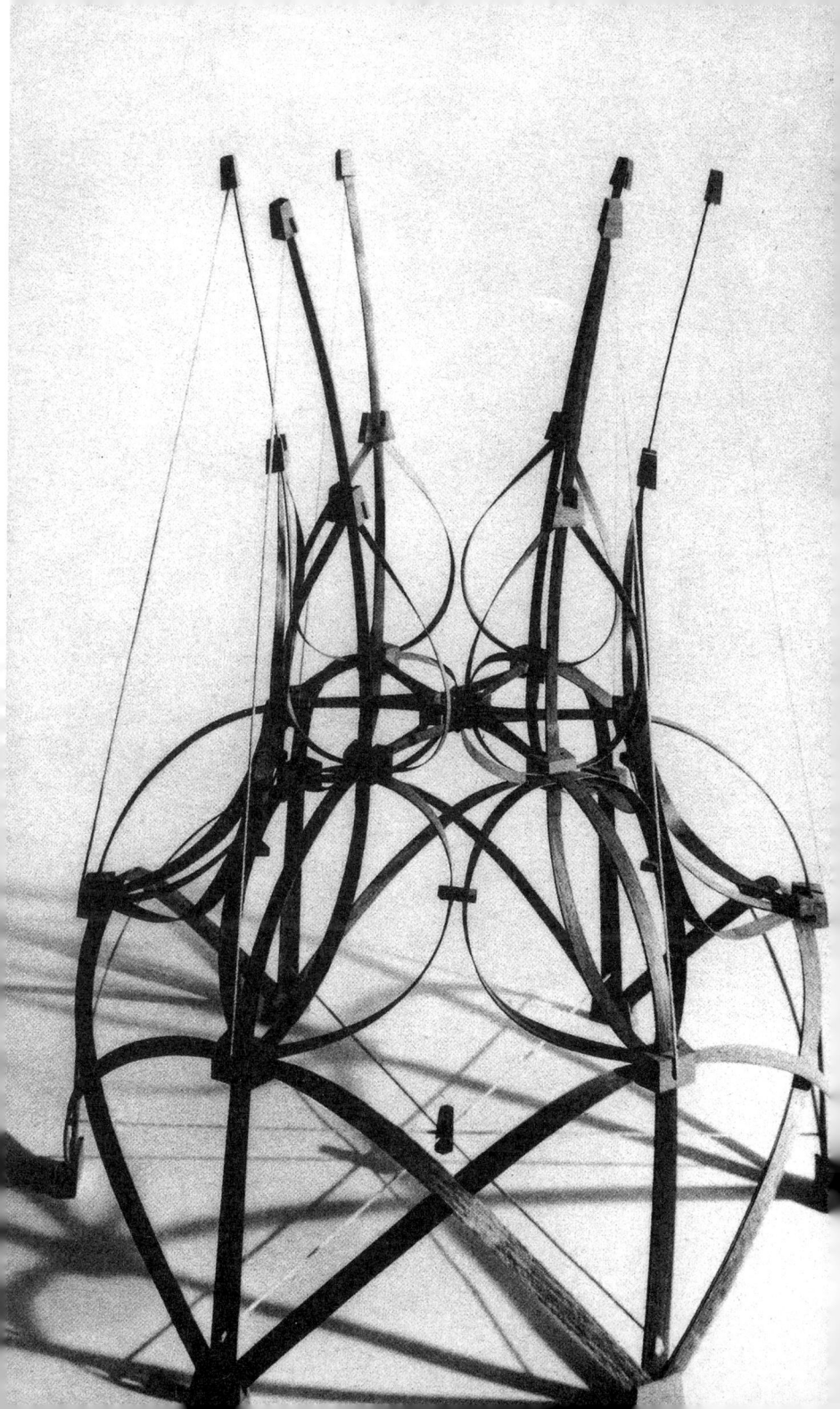

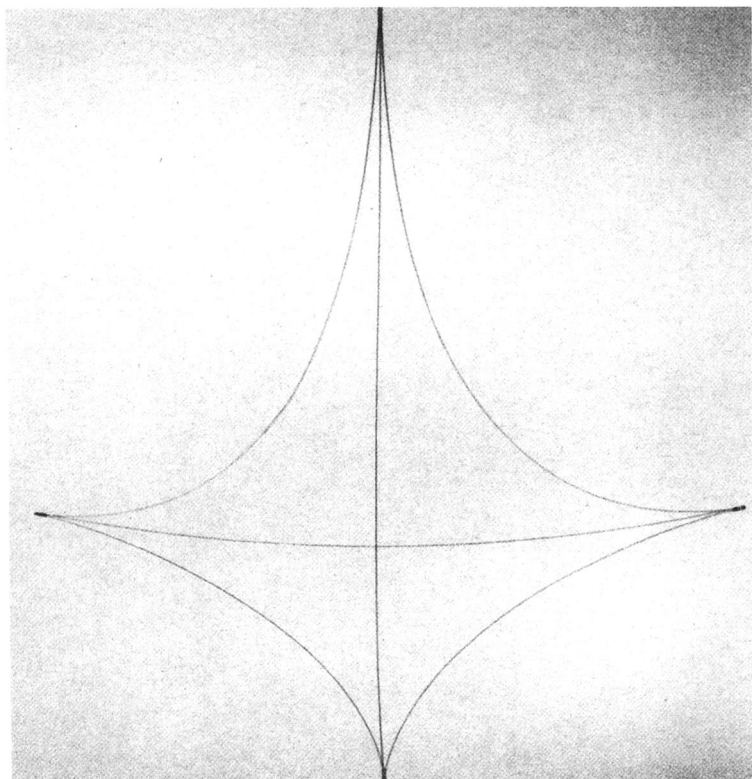

Flexy

Flexy is an aesthetic object produced in an unlimited production run by Edizioni Danese. Created to test out certain intuitions by interacting with a model designed for this very purpose, it exemplifies design research.

Flexy should be considered a flexible module with topological characteristics. Six stainless steel wires, each one meter long, are fixed at four points in three-dimensional space corresponding to four vertices of a tetrahedron (6 wires = 12 ends, 3 ends × 4 vertices = 12 ends).

Three wires extend out of each vertex of the tetrahedron. Since the wires are flexible, they don't form straight lines but instead curves in accordance with the laws of elasticity and gravity. When all four vertices are placed on the ground, Flexy arranges its wires into harmonious curves. However its four vertices are arranged, Flexy adapts, forming elegant curves both in two and three dimensions.

310

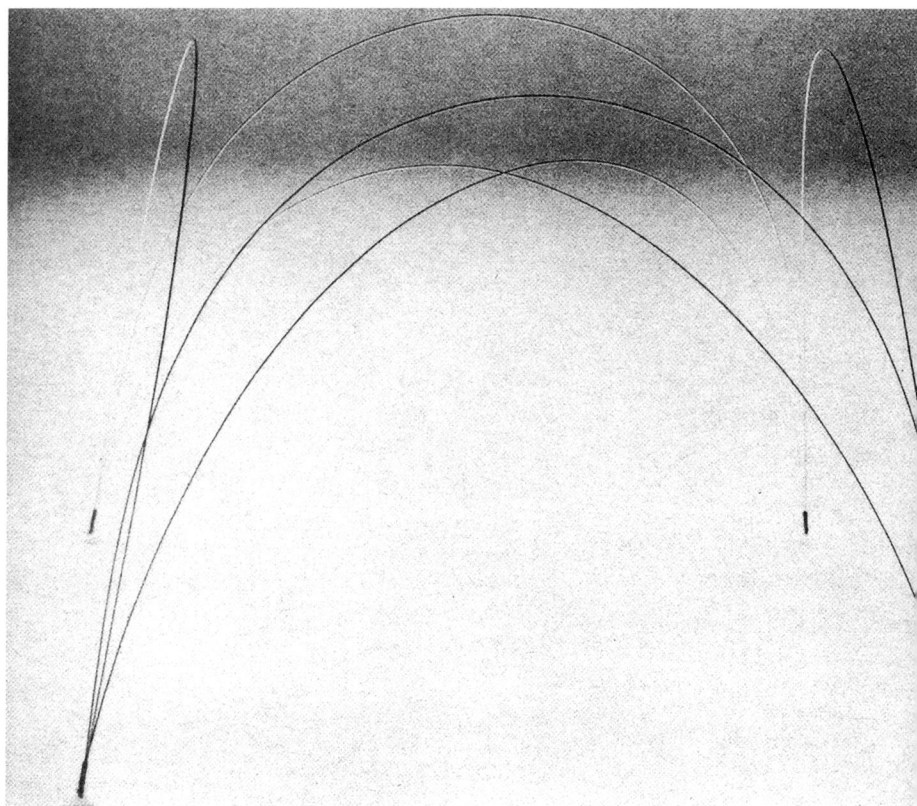

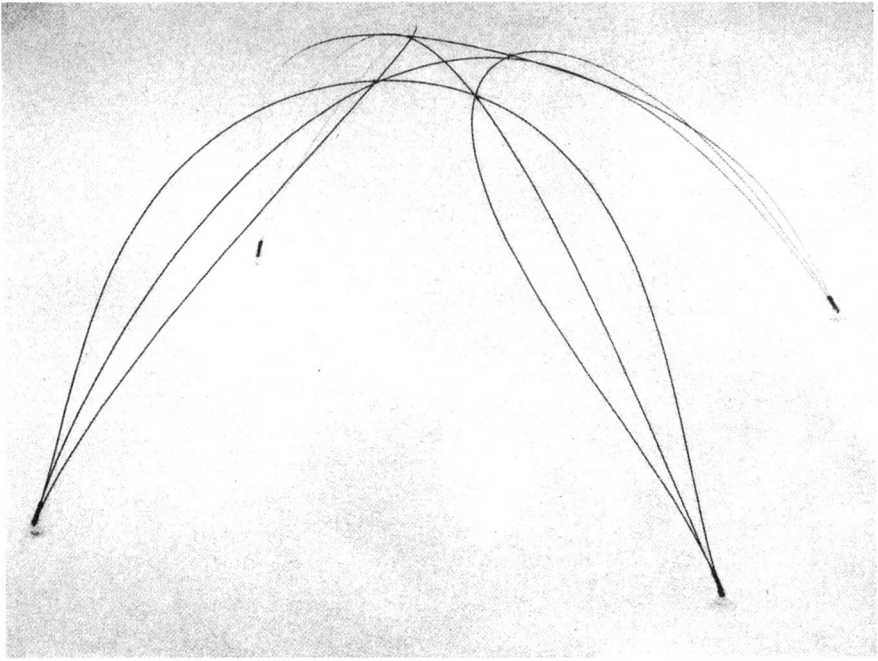

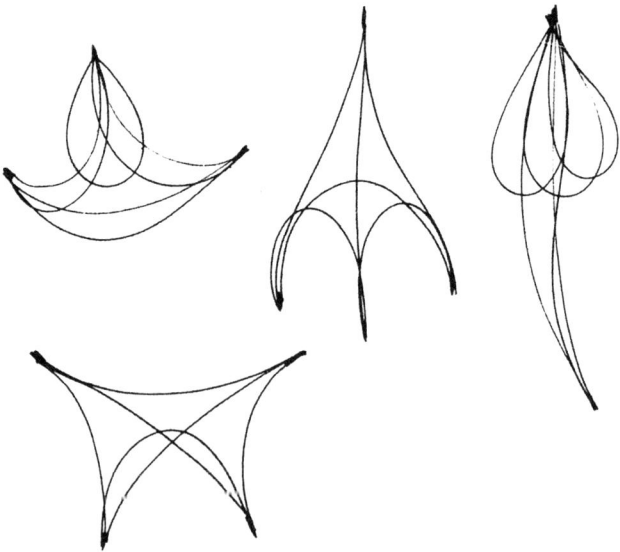

312

The object, thus, doesn't assume a single shape or a predefined stance; rather it assumes *all shapes*: both those discovered by means of experimentation and those not yet discovered. Thanks to the complexity of the information it relays to the user who is manipulating and modifying it, Flexy stands out with respect to static aesthetic objects that are able to convey only a single unit of information.

Once they have achieved a proper understanding of working procedures, designers can explore new modes of visual communication by creating experimental models by means of the most disparate techniques and materials.

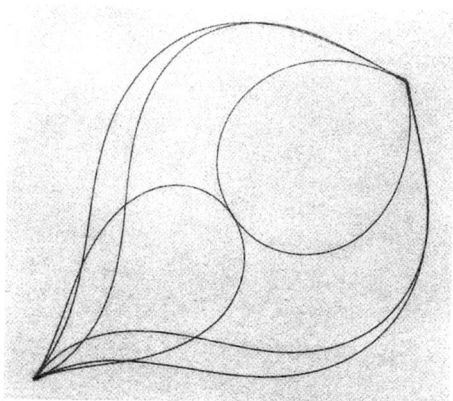

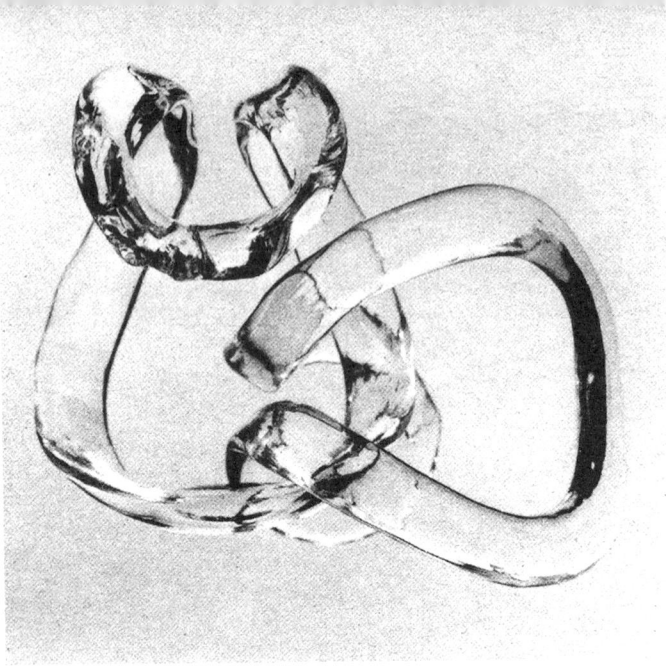

This is a module best defined as organic in origin because it takes into account the nature of the material from which it is made: in this case, glass. Its hook-shape allows for the creation of a variety of concatenated shapes. Angelo Mangiarotti, designer.[120]

Enzo Mari, *Structure* 795, 1965. In his notes on thematic variations, Mari states that both visible and invisible natural phenomena are always organized in large series of identical particles that coalesce into modular structures that assume varying elementary patterns until they give rise to new modular units. These new units, in turn, restructure themselves, slightly altering the initial pattern. The components follow the pattern as faithfully as possible at every stage. When two or more different orders of particles intersect randomly, however, each set changes just enough to reestablish the initial equilibrium. Such variations can be called "thematic" and account for the slight differences between particles belonging to the same set. They constitute their individuality. Considerations of aesthetics shouldn't disregard this fact. Mari's research in this domain began in 1953.[121]

316

An aerial view of some Montreal Expo 67 pavilions. The way in which the repetition of a given module with variations renders a construction visually and structurally distinctive is clear.

Model of a set design for Swiss Italian Television's show Lavori in corso.[122] The design pairs together two cubic modules that share an overall measurement of 2.1 meters. One module measures thirty centimeters; the other seventy centimeters $(3 \times 7 = 21, 7 \times 3 = 21)$. Monotony is avoided by recourse to combinations that add up to less than two meters and ten centimeters. The support surfaces fulfill various practical needs and, by altering the combinations, the overall layout can be adapted to suit new requirements. An approach of this kind could lead to the development of simple modules for interior furnishings.

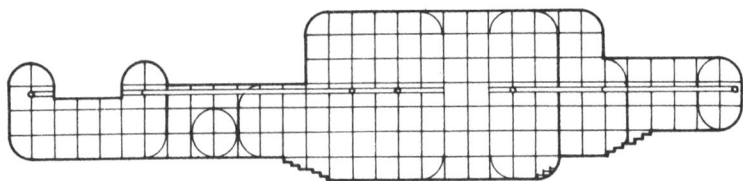

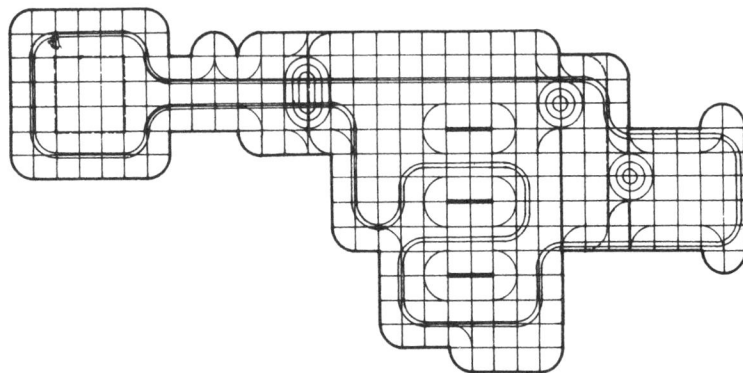
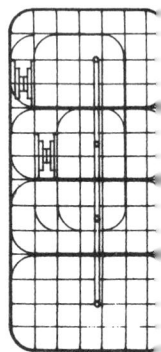

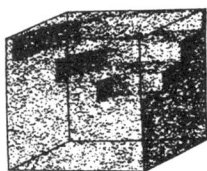
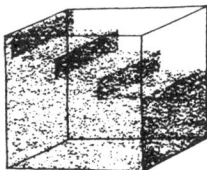
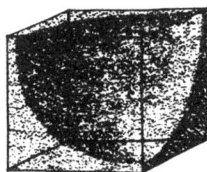

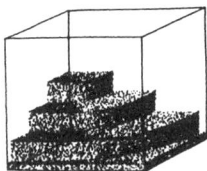
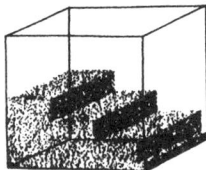
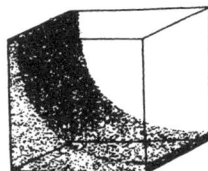

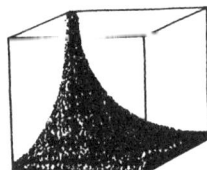

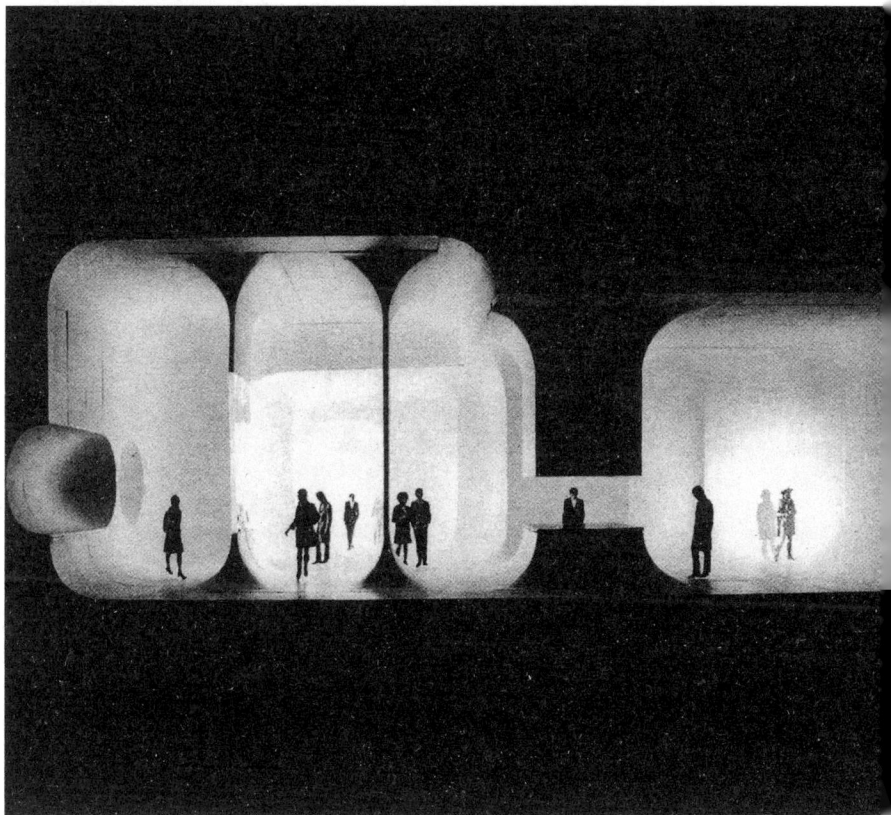

Mimmo Castellano, project for the Italian pavilion at Osaka Expo 1970.[123]
An example of interior architecture built around seven modular elements
that interconnect flat surfaces, determining both the transitions between
different levels and the exhibition spaces. This sort of experimental modular architecture provides solutions for every variety of usable space while
maintaining an exemplary formal coherence.

An exercise in symmetry based on the repetition of a module whose position is repeatedly shifted. School of Ulm; Tomas Davies, student.

Vittorio Mascalchi, studies of the structure of two- to three-dimensional modular elements.[124] By joining together six quarters of a disc, a cube can be generated with geometric characteristics unlike those of a standard cube. The object is made from transparent perspex to highlight its overall shape, 1967.

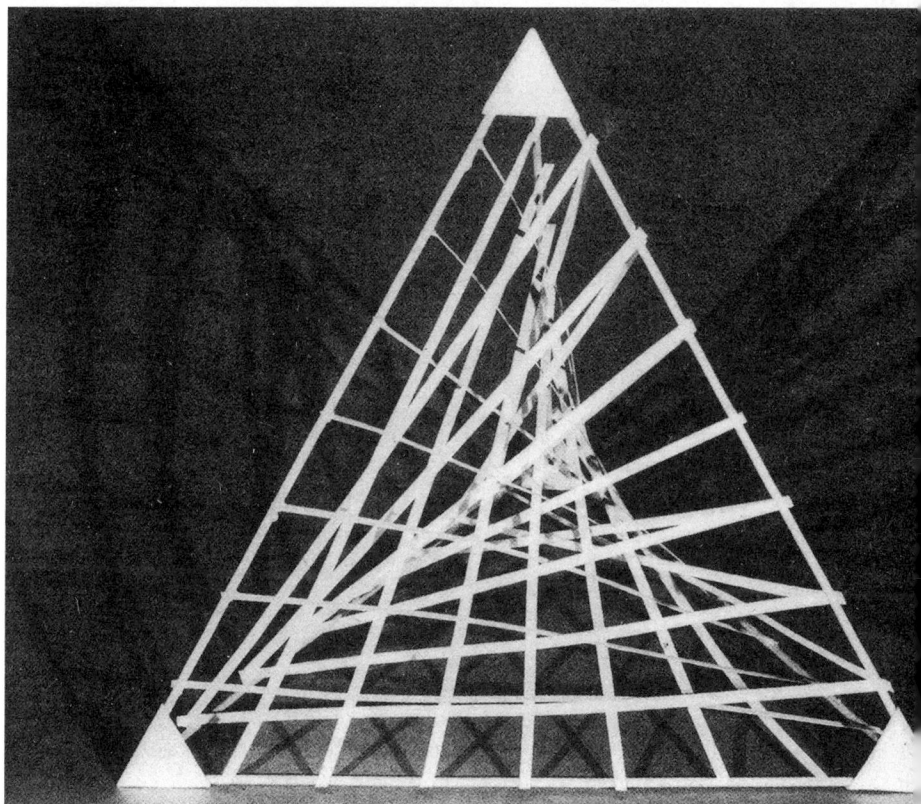

One of numerous possible structures that can be inscribed within a tetra-hedral module. A larger structure composed out of such modules gives rise to a complex structure that can vary depending on the way in which the modules themselves are assembled.

A detail of a modulated space. Ugo La Pietra and Alberto Seassaro, architects (1966).[125]

In Japanese architecture, which is always rigidly modular yet infinitely varied, organic nature is always present alongside geometrical modules. It's the same equilibrium that inhabitants of the metallic modules of industrial architecture seek to restore by hanging vases of Tradescantia Zebrina Pendula (referred to in dialect as *miseria*) in their living spaces.[126]

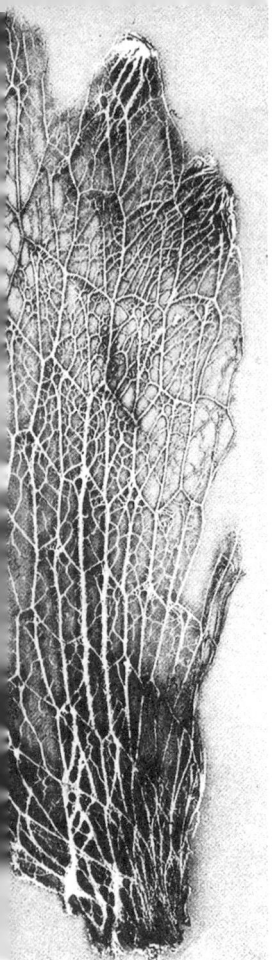

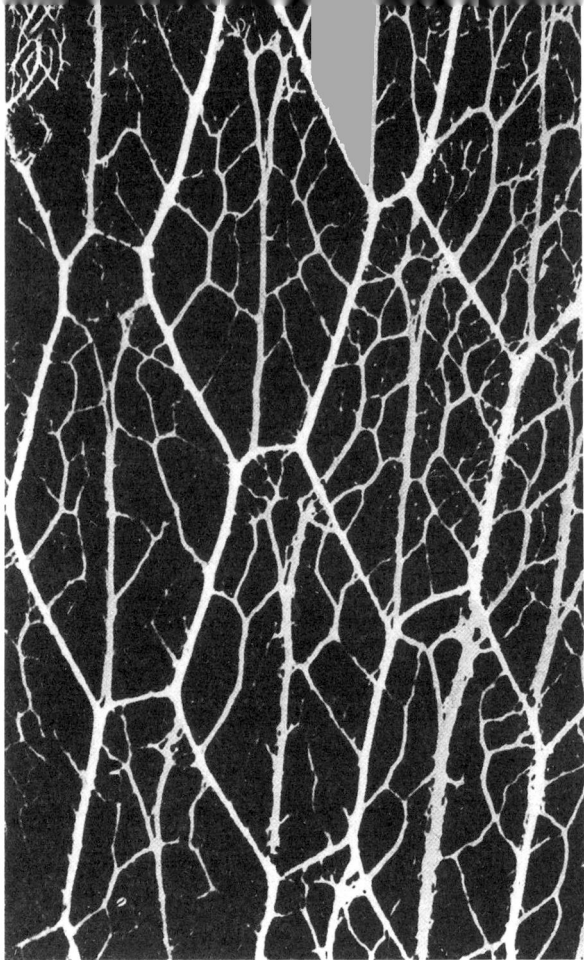

The ribbing in a prickly pear leaf is made up of deformed hexagons within which a second module develops due to the vital needs of the plant itself. Another structure grows within each hexagonal module, slightly different in the case of each module. For a forceful case study of variations within modules that serve an aesthetic and (perhaps also) psychological purpose, consider the facade of the Church of San Martino in Lucca. Gianni Berengo Gardin, photographer.

Modules devised to compose a structure can also be designed as interlocking assemblies. In such cases, however many the possible variations,
the mode of interlocking must be calculated with care to achieve a
well-integrated whole. This is one of the founding principles for the
much-celebrated mass production of objects with an aesthetic function:
such objects needn't be reproductions of "one-offs" but instead should be
modular in design so as to allow for large numbers of variations despite
being mass produced.[127]

Angelo Bozzola's "operational modules" (1970) are composed of identical parts that can each be lodged within one another by the person interacting with them.[128]

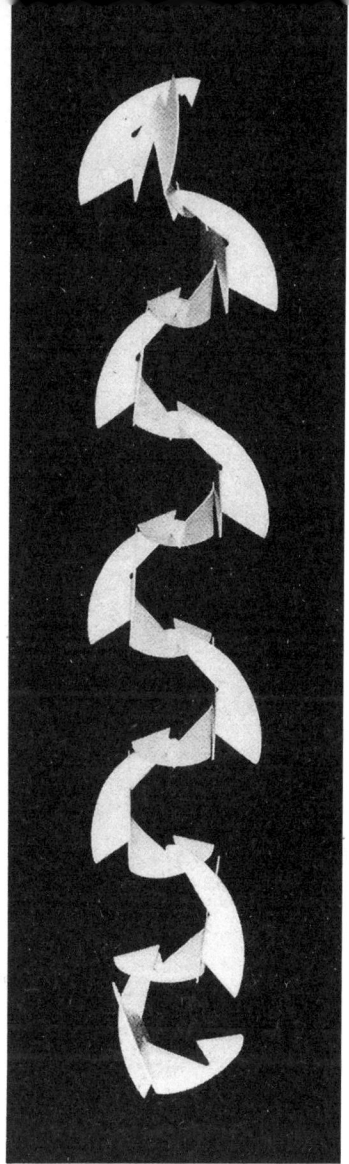

A surface modulated to form an interlocking module. Ulm School.

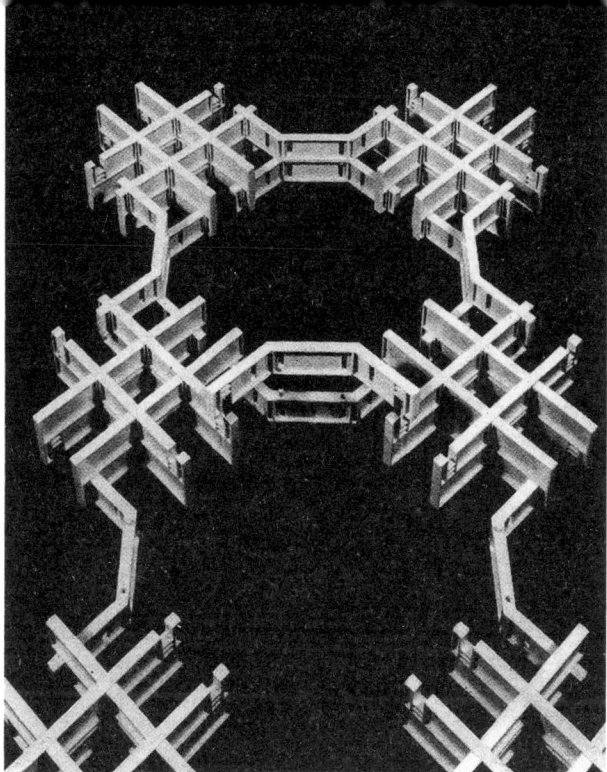

A Gratik Structure for the creation of non-opaque partition walls. The two basic components, one flat and one angular, are made of plastic which also makes it possible to deploy the structure outdoors.

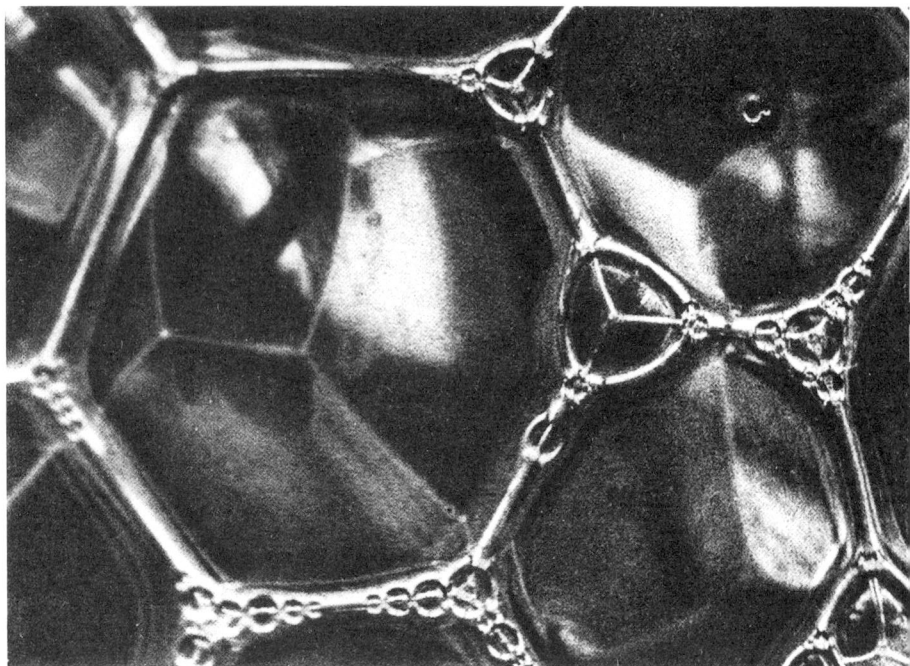

Studies of how foams and soap bubbles aggregate. From the Advanced Course in Industrial Design, Venice. P. Campagnol and P. Vian, photographers.

The accumulation of modular structural elements raises the issue of connections between the modules, joints, and nodes. These nodes or joints can be of various types depending on their purpose. There exist very simple right-angled joints. Others are designed to accommodate the vertices of equilateral triangles. Others still can accommodate any angle. Some joints take into consideration only points of attachment, while others allow for continuous lines of attachment between planes. Experimentation can be conducted in all materials.

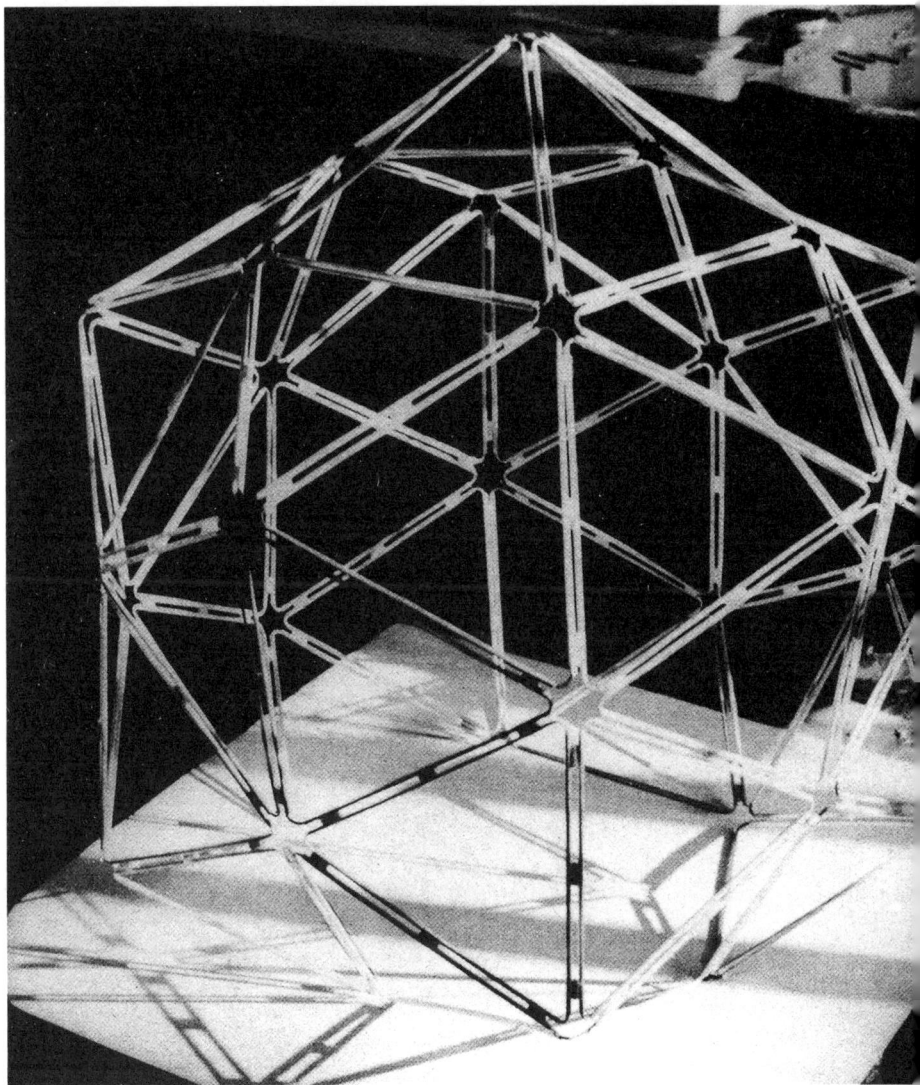

A model of a large structure composed of pyramids with a pentagonal base made out of drinking straws held together with adhesive tape. The joints consist in portions of U-shaped bent wire inserted into the straws. Even when built in this manner, the model was able to support a weight of five kilograms. Designer Rinaldo Donzelli.[129]

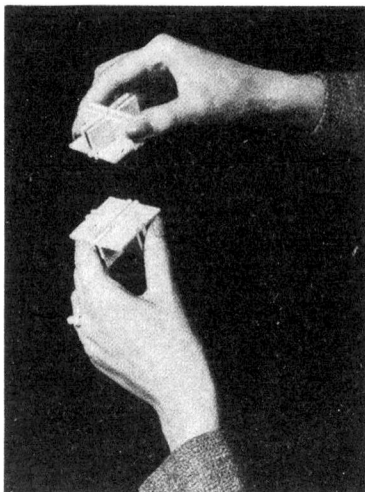

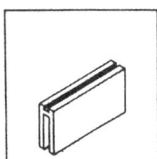

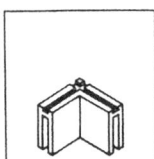

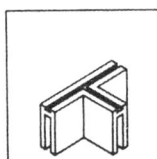

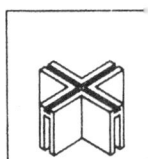

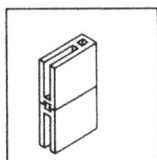

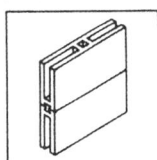

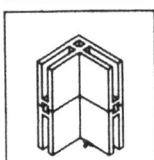

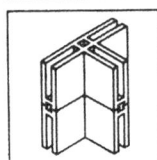

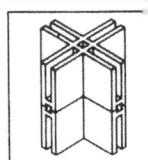

Interconnecting joints that employ dovetail interlocking. These plastic joints conjoin a structure made up of planes rather than tubes. The planes in question can be made of glass, wood, or plastic; all must possess the same thickness.

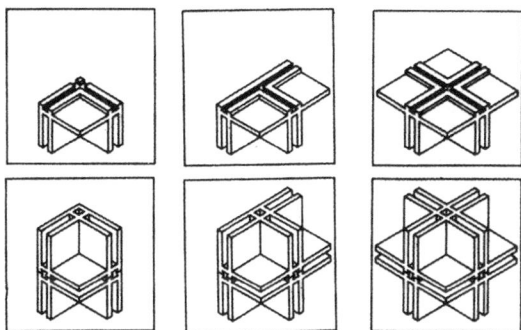

Reasonably tall constructions can be assembled in this manner, particularly in the case of exhibition spaces and store windows. The drawings document some of the thirteen elements that make up the system. Hans Staeger and Manfred Malzacher, raum-technik-system, 1964.[130]

The CUB 8 joint system devised by Angelo Mangiarotti (1967). This type of plastic joint, made from PVC, is linear: unlike joints designed to connect tubular modular components, it connects planes instead of points. There are two core components: a distinctive edge profile and an extrusion that snaps in along the edges of the entire panel, joining two panels at a time. The illustrations above illustrate the limit cases for open and closed volumes.[131]

An interior space developed and interconnected using CUB 8 linear joints.

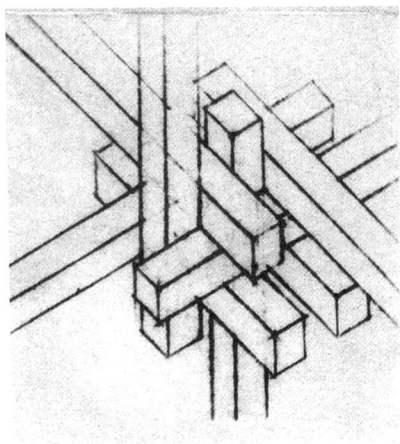

Leonardo Mosso, architect. A joint for a serial, three-dimensional wood structure made of square slats measuring 5 × 5 cm.
A building in Turin employing this system (1962).

Mero is a system composed of rods and globes with which any number of trigonal structures can be assembled. A trigonal system is defined as one that forms triangles out of three rods and three globes, and conjoins these triangles in three-dimensional space in such a way that each rod is, as a rule, part of at least two triangles. The principle of trigonal construction isn't a human invention. Rather, it is a fundamental structural principle of nature in the truest sense of the word.

Only after the discovery of certain static and mathematical relationships did it became possible to apply these principles in the field of construction. The original idea for the Mero system was that of Max Mengeringhausen in Würzburg, Germany, who envisaged applications in the domains of aeronautical and industrial construction.[132] Subsequently, Karl Otto's numerous pavilion designs for the Berlin [City of Tomorrow] exhibition brought the Mero system to the attention of the general public.[133] Many contemporary builders are oriented towards metallic constructions of this type, such as Fuller, Mannesmann, Makowski, and Fentiman.[134]

In his 1892 book *Das Fachwerk im Raume*, August Föppl (with whom Max Mengeringhausen studied) was the first to develop a theory of metallic structures. Föppl's law of spatial structure stability states that if "g" indicates the number of globes and "r" the [minimum] number of rods, a spatial structure can be defined as statically stable so long as the following equation is solved: $r = 3g - 6$. Accordingly, a triangle with $g = 3$ and $r = 3$ is the simplest stable form made of rods and globes or nodes. A tetrahedron with $g = 4$ and $r = 6$, in turn, is the simplest stable spatial structure built with triangles.

The laws for the construction of regular spatial structures (trigonal system) established by Max Mengeringhausen states that:

— Spatial structures are perfect when they are made from triangles combined in such a way that, when assembled, they form octahedra, tetrahedra, cubes, or truncated cubes (cuboctahedra).

— The side lengths of the faces of the truncated cube, the cube itself, and the tetrahedron inside the cube follow a geometric progression, each increasing by a factor of $\sqrt{2}$.

— With the length of rods from this series and the use of a universal type of globe or node, infinite other derivations can be formed in addition to the described geometric shapes.

A Center for Structural Research was founded in Würzburg, Germany, on May 5, 1968. Directed by Max Mengeringhausen, it deals with the theory and practice of spatial structures.

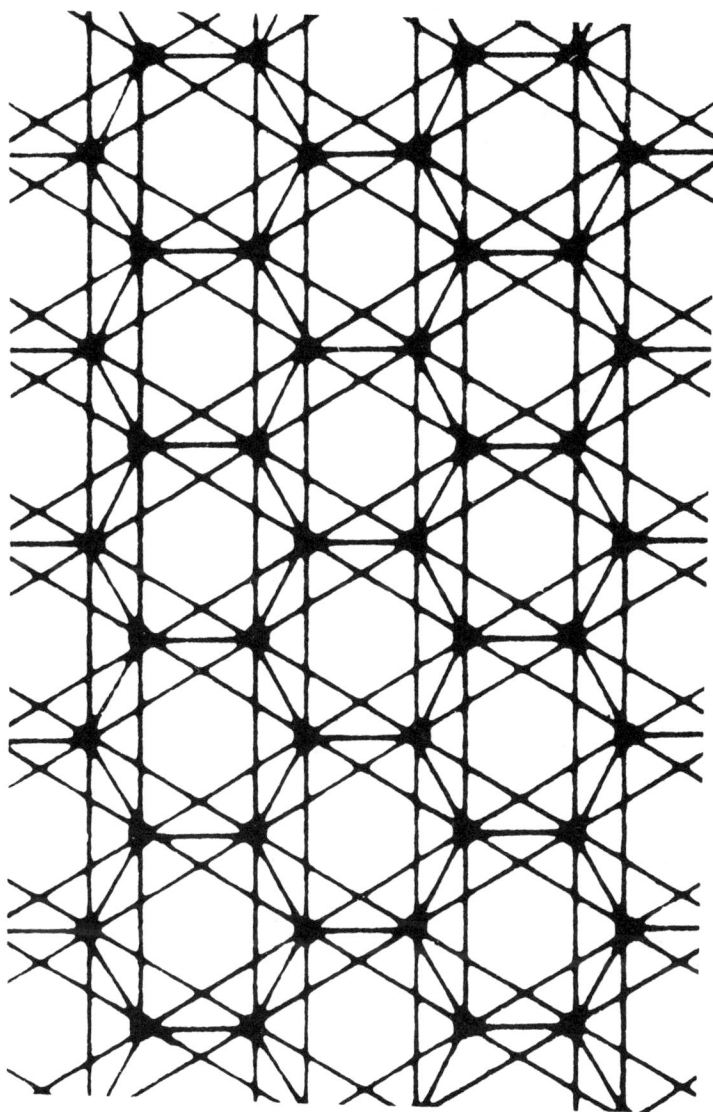

A Mero lattice.

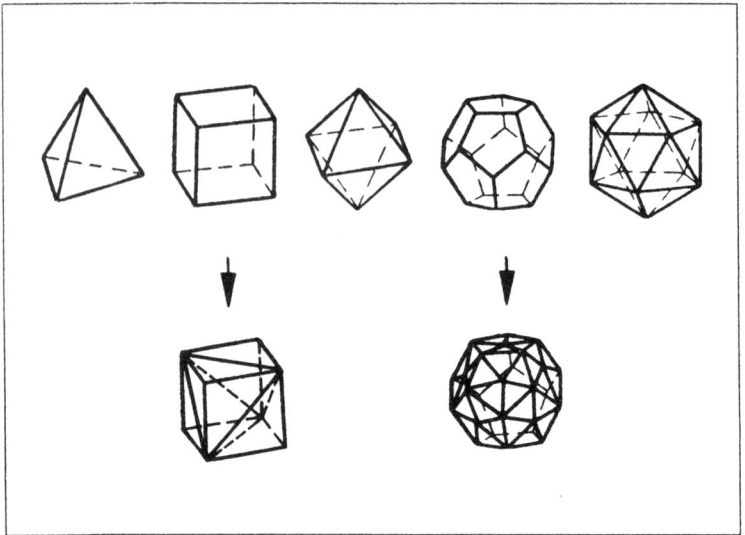

The ancient Greeks discovered the equilateral and right-angled triangle, established the rules of triangular calculation or trigonometry, and made use of regular polyhedra like the following:
the tetrahedron, with four faces
the hexahedron (cube), with six faces
the octahedron, with eight faces
the dodecahedron, with twelve faces
the icosahedron, with twenty faces.

In his theory of spatial structures, August Föppl demonstrated that of all the regular figures of the ancient Greeks, only the tetrahedron, the octahedron, and the icosahedron are completely stable structures, while the cube and the dodecahedron can be stabilized only by dividing their faces into triangles.

The universal Mero node or globe is an 18-faced polyhedron which is nearly spherical. Each face has a threaded hole oriented towards the center of the globe. The threaded holes are arranged so that, by screwing in rods of appropriate length, both tetrahedra and cubes can be constructed. An 18-faced polyhedron can be made with 24 Mero globes and 48 rods of equal length. The polyhedron will be stable if each square face has a diagonal.

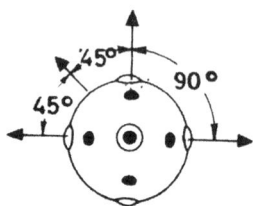

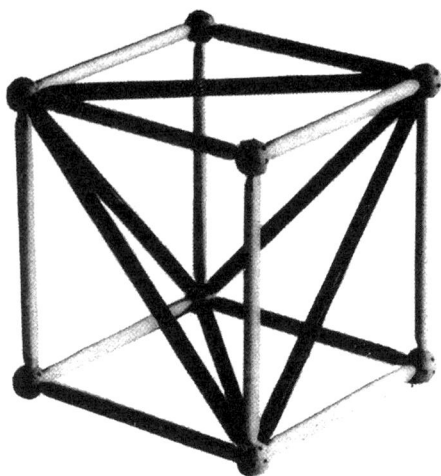

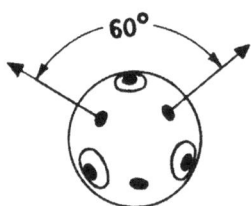

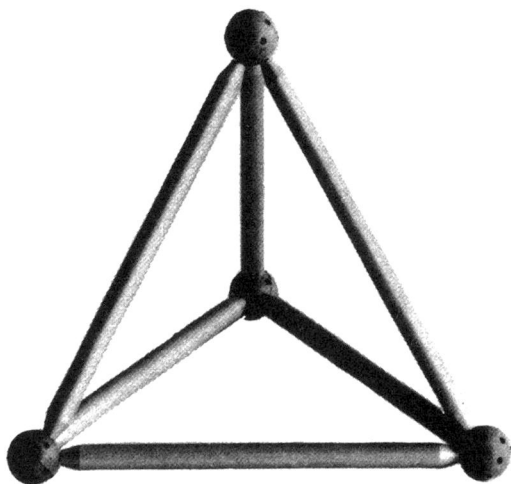

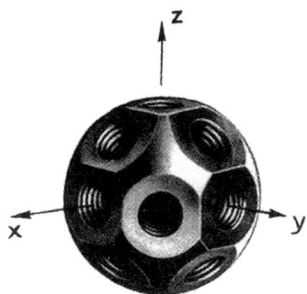

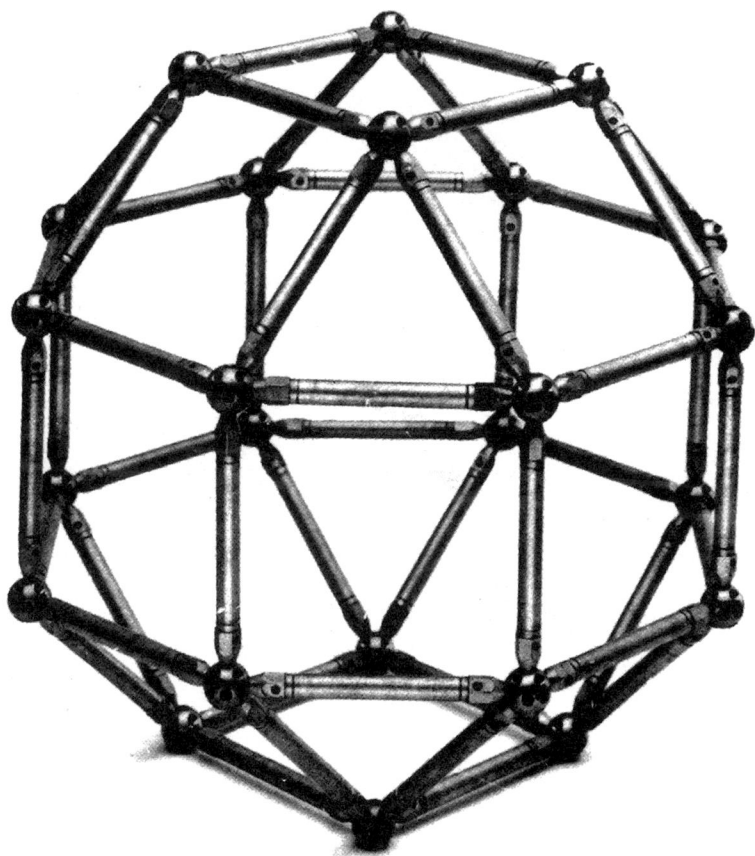

A dome akin to a hemisphere built with two different rod lengths and standard Mero nodes, made of cubes and parts of cubes. The standard rod length is 2.5 meters; the maximum internal height is 55 meters. H. Bauer, design.

A Mero structure in the shape of a tetrahedron built in Bern during the construction of the church of Saint Matthew. The photograph was taken before the roof was attached. Design by B. Peterhans, W. Frey, and A. Egger.[135]

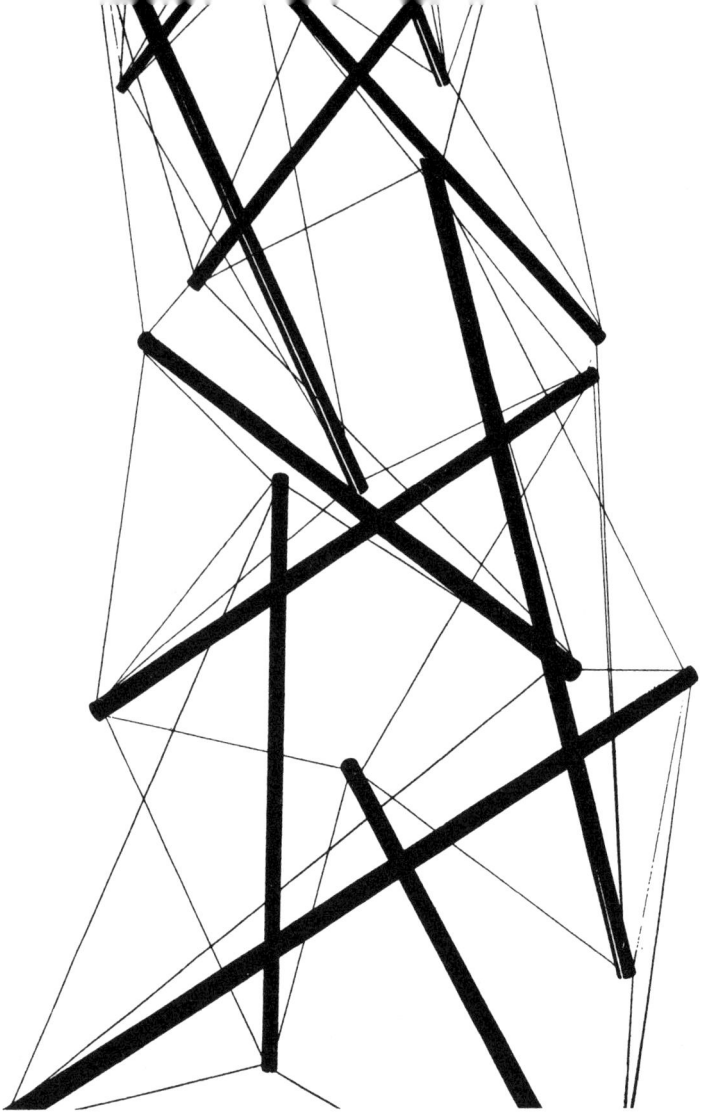

A self-supporting structure constructed with metal tubes and cables. The tubes don't touch one another. The modular element that gives this structure its shape is enclosed in a geometric solid (octahedron or icosahedron). The component tubes, under compression, correspond to internal diagonals that connect two opposing vertices. The cables correspond to the external edges and are in tension. The combination of multiple modules forms a solid structure. Kenneth Snelson, New York.[136]

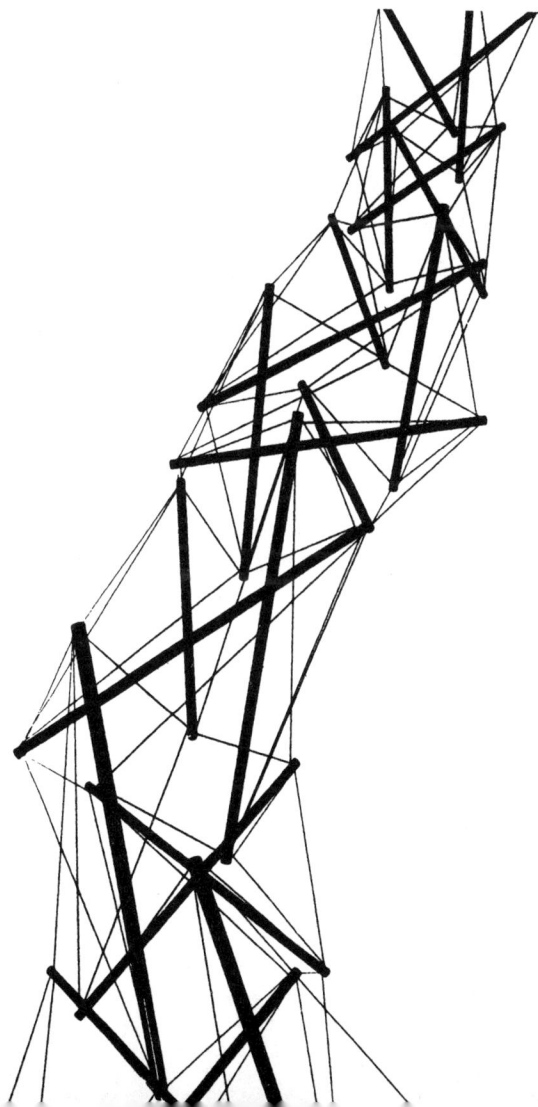

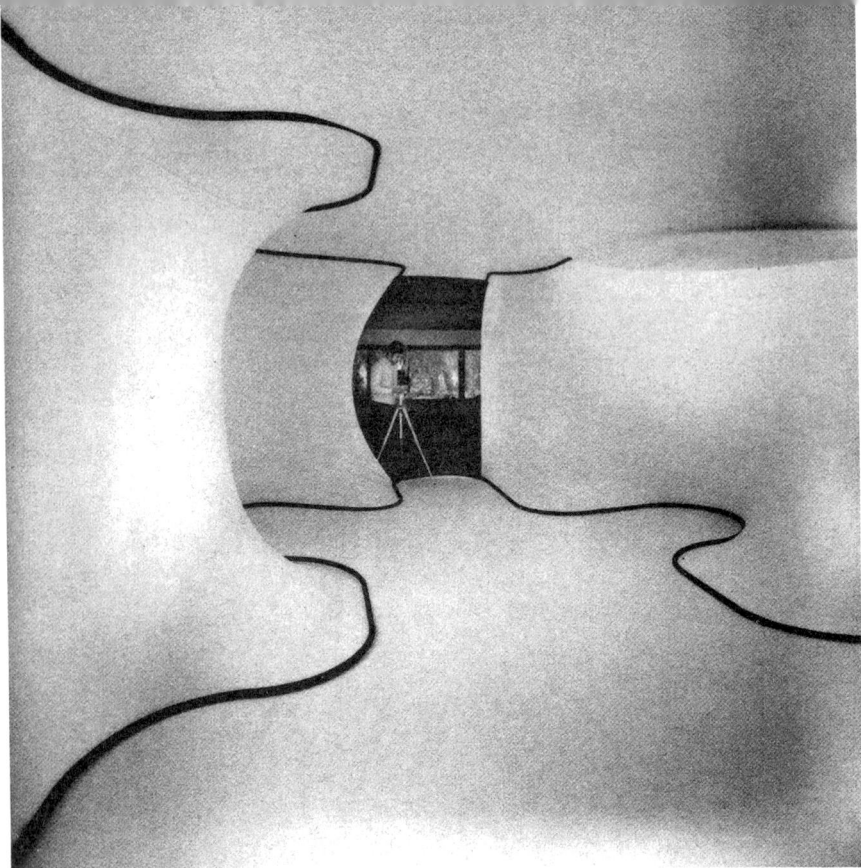

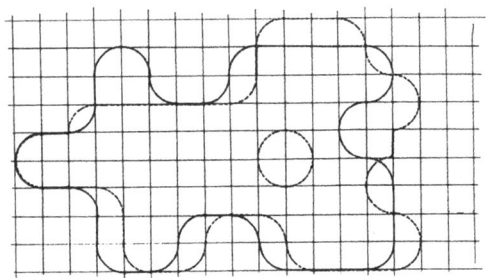

Andrea Roggia, a faculty member at the School of Design in Novara, designed this spatial environment to take advantage of the elasticity of double-knit nylon. The supporting structure is made of 32 mm diameter iron tubing and features curves modulated over a 60 cm square grid structure. The work was exhibited at the Galleria Civica d'Arte Moderna in Milan in 1968.

Simultaneous Contrasts

The rule of simultaneous contrasts is one of the most venerable in the field of visual communications. According to this rule, the proximity of two forms of contrasting nature enhances and intensifies their interaction. Such contrasts aren't limited to formal or material characteristics: they can extend to semantic contrasts as well, such as the juxtaposition of images representing a lightning bolt and a snail.

Beyond the wide range of color contrasts achieved by recourse to complementary colors, one can experiment with other kinds of contrast: between negative and positive; geometric and organic; a black cube and a light, flexible line; static and dynamic; simple and complex. The contrasts between large and small, and between fat and thin, have always amused children, while the contrast between convergent and divergent or between centripetal and centrifugal is appreciated only by connoisseurs.[137]

Contrasts between order and chaos, simple and complex, stable and unstable, static and dynamic, compact and expansive, regular and irregular, hanging and supported, crescendo and diminuendo, usual and unusual, evident and camouflaged, real and apparent are fairly easy to establish. Everyone has noticed how contrasts between empty and full, angular and rounded, narrow and wide, continuous and broken, smooth and rough, light and dark, vertical and horizontal, parallel and crossed enhance the overall design of a building. Other contrasts can be conveyed between light and heavy, precise and vague, concave and convex, opaque and transparent, solid and shapeless, uniform and mixed, natural and synthetic, tension and compression . . .

And then there are the contrasts between pure and decorative form, between anticipation and delay, between closed and open, between hollowed and protruding, between elementary and difficult, between childish and adult, between secret and public . . .

To the forever unsatisfied, I'd suggest establishing a simple contrast between a solid, parallel, dark, static, rough, opaque, closed, real, rigid, extravagant, angular, unique, and complex form with . . .

Color raises two questions for designers: how to employ precolored industrial materials and how to integrate color elements into the design of objects.

Color doesn't serve the same purpose for designers that it does for painters. Designers work hand in hand with science and industry, whereas painters are associated with craftsmanship and manual production. Designers use color objectively; painters use it subjectively.

For designers, the right colors are those inherent in the materials used to produce a given object. An object made of stainless steel has its own natural color, as does an object made of wood. In addition to being arbitrary and providing false visual information, color applied on top of the material detracts from the object's nature. Certain decorative materials, like fabrics, can infuse an environment with notes of color that support its function. For interior decoration, base hues should be neutral and color components as mobile and changeable as needed. A permanently colored environment can become tiring for those who reside there, whereas a variable chromatic environment is more agreeable.

Traditional Japanese homes may once again serve as an example: natural woods, plaster whose color derives from a special clay and straw (not artificial sources), natural straw tatami mats.

Natural materials are also used for window papers, lamps, and the metal parts of locks. Color is freely expressed in fabrics, lacquered furniture (lacquered for practical reasons), small objects, and flowers which vary according to seasons and occasions.

There's also a functional aspect to color that involves the psychology of visual communication. The color of an object in use for extended periods (e.g., a typewriter) needs to be matte and neutral to avoid reflections that can tire the eyes. When stared at for a long time, an intense color evokes its complementary color in the retina to restore a physiological equilibrium.

The color-material relationship also needs to be factored into color choices. Certain colors are unsuitable for certain materials. Even black, which might seem universal, varies across different materials. Black rubber doesn't look like black wood; black glass diverges in appearance from black metal; and so on an so forth.

An experiment illustrates the point. If one sews together various types of white fabrics (linen, terry cloth, cotton, velvet, nylon, hemp, etc.) into equal-sized squares, dyeing them all the same color, the color appears different depending on the material. Another experiment concerns the relationship between color and light. When one exposes a single color sample to different artificial and natural light sources, changes in hue become apparent.

A designer can make the right color choices by keeping all of these considerations in mind.

Artists usually develop their works using classic or well-tested techniques, so they don't require a specific methodology. They express themselves by means of familiar techniques which they manipulate using distinctive tricks, like perspective effects in painting, to forge works that abound in personal ideas. Designers, on the contrary, are obliged to employ all sorts of materials and techniques. Free from artistic preconceptions, they require methods that allow them to execute projects using appropriate materials and techniques, as well as forms that correspond to the desired function (including the desired psychological function). The objects they produce need to possess not only aesthetic qualities but also to address every facet of a product with equanimity, including its economics. Furthermore, they need to ensure that their products are comprehensible to the public.

A multitude of modes and methods of design exist. They vary among designers and domains of design practice. It goes without saying that the method by means of which one designs an object like a ballpoint pen is going to be different from that of a whaling ship. There are divergences between the methodologies developed by Archer (programming – data collection – analysis – synthesis – development – communication), Fallon (preparation – information – evaluation – creativity – selection – project), Sidal (problem definition – examination of possible designs – limits – technical analysis – optimization – calculation – prototypes – testing – final modifications), and Asimow.[138] Nevertheless, there are also constants with which we can develop an overall scheme of our own that provides guidance, a timeline for the actions we

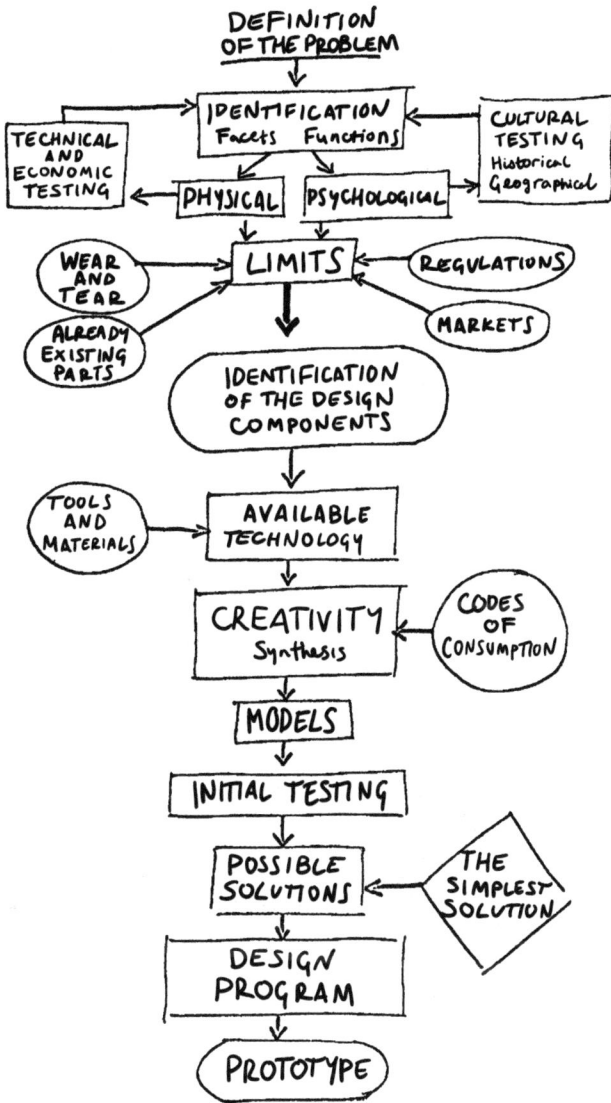

DEFINITION OF THE PROBLEM

IDENTIFICATION
Facets   Functions

TECHNICAL AND ECONOMIC TESTING

CULTURAL TESTING
Historical
Geographical

PHYSICAL   PSYCHOLOGICAL

WEAR AND TEAR

ALREADY EXISTING PARTS

LIMITS

REGULATIONS

MARKETS

IDENTIFICATION OF THE DESIGN COMPONENTS

TOOLS AND MATERIALS

AVAILABLE TECHNOLOGY

CREATIVITY
Synthesis

CODES OF CONSUMPTION

MODELS

INITIAL TESTING

POSSIBLE SOLUTIONS

THE SIMPLEST SOLUTION

DESIGN PROGRAM

PROTOTYPE

need to undertake, and a sense of the stages involved in the delivery of a prototype.

Definition of the problem. The question to be addressed can be communicated by the industry client to the designer based on a needs assessment or instead be formulated by the designer. The problem needs to be well-defined: otherwise, a rigorous definition will have to be developed. A project will find itself compromised if the starting point is incorrect.

Identification of Facets and Functions. The problem should be analyzed with respect to two main attributes: the physical and the psychological. The physical component concerns the shape of the object to be designed; the psychological component concerns the relationship between the object and its user. As regards the physical, a technical and economic evaluation needs to be carried out to establish whether the same problem has been successfully addressed in similar cases, either in whole or in part. As regards psychology, a cultural, historical, and geographical verification needs to be undertaken to see how the question has been addressed by other people in other places. Together, these two investigations may yield data that ends up modifying the definition of the problem.

Limitations. The boundaries of a given problem can be established by studying: an object's lifespan (will it be used and discarded or is it intended to last about ten years?); the need to employ prefabricated parts for reasons of economy; regulations or prohibitions regarding shapes, colors, or other features; and, finally, market requirements (black soaps don't sell well because they appear to dirty the hands). The component elements of the design components will be shaped by these constraints.

Available Technology. Every project that seeks to achieve maximum results at minimum cost needs to carefully consider the specific materials and technologies that are required.

Creativity. A designer's creativity comes into play at this juncture. The designer knows that artistic, lyrical, or fantastical sorts of creativity don't favor good design solutions because they clash with the previously examined limitations. Until a creative synthesis of all the elements has been performed, he or she doesn't know the outcome of the information gathering. An optimal synthesis is one that ensures an optimal merger of every component. Only at this point does the object take shape, assuming contours that the designer understands as "logical." Such a mode of creative practice entails *an aesthetics of logic* of the sort observable in many of nature's shapes: in shells, in plants, animals, and minerals in which the form is the result of logic.

Models. Models are the result of creative synthesis. Depending on circumstance, they may be either full-size or at scale. Models are tested by varying types of users in order to eliminate the least successful. The designer then chooses the simplest among the successful ones and moves on to define the specifications of a prototype.

ACKNOWLEDGEMENTS (WITH AN INVITATION)

A sincere thanks to everyone who accepted my invitation to enrich and update this book with photographic documentation of their work, experiments, comments, and proposals. As a result, this fourth edition has been enriched with eighteen pages of materials that are now being shared with all of Italy's design schools.

I now realize that it's indeed possible to gather together the collective labors being carried out in design schools worldwide in a single book. Should the initiative prove successful, I will be happy to act as coordinator of this informational tool and refresh its content on an annual basis.

This work may well give rise to a corpus of educational tables, models, and methods produced and shared among schools. It may also lead to a systematization of the exercises it contains that clarifies which are simple enough to be used in elementary schools and complex enough for institutions of higher learning. As such, my hope is that, together, we can enhance visual education and design awareness within society at large.

The following are some books that are of special interest to readers who wish to achieve a wider, more complete understanding of the problem sets and current and past (but still valid) techniques and methods for training designers. Here is the updated bibliography [with English editions]:

Ernst H. Gombrich, *Art and Illusion* (London: Phaidon Press, 1960).

Nikolai I. Lobachevsky, *Pangeometry*, English translation by Athanase Papadopoulos (n.p.: European Mathematical Society, 2010).

David Hilbert and S. Cohn-Vossen, *Geometry and the Imagination* (New York: Chelsea Publishing Company, 1952).

Frei Otto and Rudolf Trostel, *Tensile Structures* (Cambridge: MIT Press, 1967).

Hermann Weyl, *Symmetry* (Princeton: Princeton University Press, 1952).

Matthew Luckiesh, *Visual Illusions: Their Causes, Characteristics and Applications* (New York: Van Nostrand, 1922).

D'Arcy Thompson, *On Growth and Form* (New York: Cambridge University Press, 1961).

Hugo Steinhaus, *Mathematical Snapshots* (New York: Oxford University Press, 1950).

Donald G. Frink, *Human Mind and Electronic Brains* (London: Interscience Publishers, 1967).

Helmut Emde, *Homogene Polytope* (Munich: Verlag der Bayerischen Akademie der Wissenschaften, 1958).

K. Lothar Wolff and Robert Wolff, *Symmetry* (London: Macmillan, 1952).

Charles V. Boys, *Soap Bubbles: Their Colors and the Forces Which Mould Them* (New York: Dover Publications, 1959).

Alan Holden and Phylis Singer, *Crystals and Crystal Growing* (Cambridge: MIT Press, 1960).

Albert Einstein and Leopold Infeld, *The Evolution of Physics* (New York: Simon and Schuster, 1938).

James O. Ebert, *The Pattern of Evolution* (New York: Holt, Rinehart and Winston, 1964).

Vladimir G. Boltyanskii, *Equivalent and Equidecomposable Figures*, translated and adapted from the 1st Russian ed. (1956) by Alfred K. Henn and Charles E. Watts (Boston: Heath, 1963).

Richard L. Gregory, *Eye and Brain: The Psychology of Seeing* (New York: McGraw-Hill, 1966).

Alexander Dorner, *The Way Beyond Art; The Work of Herbert Bayer* (New York: Wittenborn Schultz, 1947).

Jeanne Bemis, *The Imagination* (New York: Harper & Row, 1965).

Pierre de Latil, *Thinking by Machine: A Study of Cybernetics* (Boston: Houghton Mifflin, 1957).

Luigi Lavagnolo, *Gli aeromotori – come si utilizza la forza del vento)* (Turin: G. Lavagnolo, 1926).

Lewis Mumford, *Art and Technics* (New York: Columbia University Press, 1952).

Abraham Moles, *Information Theory and Esthetic Perception* (Urbana: University of Illinois Press, 1966).

Siegfried Giedion, *Mechanization Takes Command* (New York: Oxford University Press, 1948).

Hans Jenny, *Cymatics. Wave phenomena, vibrational effects, harmonic oscillations with their structure, kinetics and dynamics*, English translation by D. Q. Stephenson (Basel: Basilius Press, 1974).

R. Buckminster Fuller, *Ideas and Integrities: A Spontaneous Autobiographical Disclosure* (New York: Prentice-Hall, 1963).

Gyorgy Kepes, *Language of Vision* (Chicago: Paul Theobald, 1949).

Gyorgy Kepes, *The New Landscape in Art and Science* (Chicago: Paul Theobald, 1956).

Also by the same author, it's worth mentioning this series published by the New York publisher George Braziller: *Education of Vision* (New York, 1965); *Structure in Art and in Science*, (New York, 1965); *The Nature and Art of Motion* (New York, 1965); *Module, Proportion, Symmetry, Rhythm*, (New York, 1966); and *Sign, Image, Symbol* (New York, 1966).

Umberto Eco, *The Open Work* (Cambridge: Harvard University Press, 1968).

Gillo Dorfles, *Simbolo, comunicazione, consumo* (Turin: Einaudi, 1962).

Roland Barthes, *Elements of Semiology* (New York: Hill and Wang, 1967).

Morris Asimow, *Introduction to Design* (Englewood Cliffs: Prentice-Hall, 1962).

Notes (2025)

Jeffrey Schnapp

1   In the Italian original, the phrase
    is *principio formatore*: a formal/
    forming/shaping principle. As
    is the case with Munari's use of
    the word *forma*, the original text
    moves back and forth between
    the notion of form as structure
    (sometimes in the abstract sense
    of logical structure) and form as
    shape (sometimes in the sense
    of volumetric body).

2   This lead chapter of the book also
    served as the first of Munari's
    dispatches from Harvard
    University published under the
    title of "Munari da Harvard. Come
    nasce un artista elettronico"
    (Munari from Harvard: How an
    Electronic Artist is Born), *Il giorno*
    March 9, 1967. Munari eliminated
    two subtitles in the transition
    from newspaper article to book:
    "My Students" and "The Compass
    and the Circle."

3   Integral to Munari's critique of
    the myth of the fine artist is his
    adoption of the phrase *operatore*

visuale which I have translated as
"visual practitioner." The Italian
word *operatore* is closely related
to the word for "worker" (*operaio*)
but distinct. It connotes labor and
activity in the sense of real-world
operations and deliverables.

4   The show took place between
    January 17 and February 12, 1967,
    which is to say at the start of
    Munari's visiting professorship
    at Harvard. *The Projected Image*
    included works by Herbert
    Gesner, Les Levine, USCO, Stan
    Vanderbeek, and Robert Whitman.

5   Harvard is, of course, anything
    but a vocational school. What
    Munari is seeking to convey
    to Italian audiences is an
    alternative approach to arts
    education that is hands-on,
    experimental, learner-centered,
    and studio-based. As is the case
    throughout *Design and Visual
    Communication*, his principal
    targets of criticism are Italian
    art schools and academies.

This concluding sentence replaces the coda to the original newspaper article in *Il giorno* which, in keeping with its subtitle "Come nasce un artista elettronico" (How an Electronic Artist is Born) went on to describe the course: "We will begin these studies of visual communication with experiments involving the use of light: incandescent, mercury vapor, xenon, neon light, and the like. An expert will join us to explain their differing characteristics. Students will then experiment with the different usages to which this medium can be put." The final paragraph concerns the topic to which he returns on page 28 of the book: electrical signage and the need to train designers with domain expertise in the field of urban electrical signage.

Here begins the second of Munari's letters from Harvard, entitled "Qui sono gli allievi a dettare il programma" (Here It's the Students Who Determine the Study Plan), *Il giorno*, March 15, 1967. In the transition from article to book he eliminated the following subtitles: "A Revealing Collage" and "No Private Codes."

In the Italian original, Munari mistakenly refers to the building as Hemerson Hall. The actual name of the building is Emerson Hall, a brick neoclassical edifice built in 1905 to house Harvard's Social Ethics Department and the Social Museum. The Social Ethics Department was later absorbed into the Department of Sociology and the Department of Social Relations, and conjoined with Psychology. Munari's classes were held across the street at Le Corbusier's Carpenter Center for the Arts, completed in 1963.

9   As becomes explicit later in the volume and is explained in the Appendix to the present volume, Munari taught two courses during his visiting professorship within the setting of Mirko Basaldella's Design Workshop: a foundations course in visual studies entitled Basic Design and Advanced Explorations in Visual Communication. The book's emphasis is on the second, though anecdotes regarding the two are sometimes woven together without a clear distinction.

10 In the original newspaper article from *Il giorno* (March 15, 1967), Munari added a parenthetical: "A scattering of clouds has departed and sun returned, so I can now turn off the lights."

11 Here begins the next letter from Harvard: "Munari da Harvard. Ognuno vede ciò che sa" (Munari from Harvard": You See What You Know), *Il giorno*, March 25, 1967, into which Munari inserted two

elements that weren't carried over into the book: a description of the Harvard Faculty Club, where he resided, and an illustration of his blackboard drawings with a descriptive paragraph (see below).

The text reads: "It's not a given that shape alone can visually communicate the nature of a thing. So, to make this point self-evident, a limit case needs to be formulated in which a minimal shape is shared by multiple objects and materials alone become the expressive element. I drew six identical circles on the blackboard and told the students that they were an orange, an apple, a rubber ball, a wooden ball, a skein of yarn, and the moon. How could you tell them apart without knowing their material composition? The lower row of circles provides a response. In the field of the visual arts, Morandi's etchings, Seurat's paintings, Dubuffet's thick impastos, Dorazio's 'weaves'… are all salient examples of this mode of expressivity. Other famous artists, many of them painters, manage to infuse structures and textures into their works with such subtlety that they go unnoticed; others favor paint surfaces as smooth as air-brushed metal, painting with photographic precision."

12 I have translated the Italian noun sensibilizzazione—literally the act of rendering something an object of the senses, as "sensitized" or "sensible"—in various ways depending upon context. Here it is translated as "awareness of the expressive power of surfaces" whereas elsewhere it is translated as "rendering expressive," "rendering communicative," or endowing with "sensitivity" or "awareness."

13 This chapter corresponds to "Munari da Harvard. Dalla polvere nasce l'immagine" (Munari from Harvard: Images Made of Dust), Il giorno, March 29, 1967.

14 Associated with such artists as Giovanni Segantini and Giuseppe Pelizza da Volpedo, Divisionism was a turn-of-the-twentieth-century-Italian offshoot of Neo-impressionism that combined an interest in observation with scientific premises. It was characterized by the technique of separating colors into individual dots or strokes of pure color, rather than blending them on the palette or canvas.

371

The extended opening paragraph of this section of *Design and Visual Communication*, describing his living quarters, was not included in Munari's dispatches to *Il giorno*.

The rest of this chapter is carried over from "Munari da Harvard. Il fondo può diventare figura" (Munari from Harvard: The Ground Can Become a Figure), *Il giorno*, April 4, 1967, with the exception of the last two sentences, once again, reflecting on his everyday life as a tenant at the Harvard Faculty Club.

Munari added the following illustration to the original published in *Il giorno*, April 4, 1967:

L'effetto figura-fondo, noto in tutti i testi di psicologia della visione, dimostra che, osservando, bene, il fondo può essere quello bianco e allora si vedono due profili di fronte, oppure quello grigio e allora si vede una coppa bianca.

The text reads: "the figure-ground effect that one encounters in every psychology of vision textbook which shows that, when you look hard at the image, the ground can be white, in which case one sees two human profiles, or it can be gray, in which case one sees a white vase."

18 Into this portion of the argument in its original version as published in *Il giorno*, Munari inserted the following illustration (that was replaced by an image of one of his own *Negativo-Positivo* (Negative-Positive) paintings in the book.

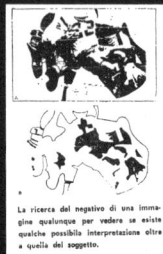

La ricerca del negativo di una immagine qualunque per vedere se esiste qualche possibile interpretazione oltre a quella del soggetto.

The legend reads: "The examination of a random image's negative to see if a secondary interpretation of its content is available."

19 Munari is clearly thinking of his own *Negativo-positivo* (Negative-Positive) abstract paintings from this period, where figure-ground effects are integral to his approach to geometrical abstraction.

20 Until this chapter, Munari had followed the sequence of his dispatches to *Il giorno*. Here he jumps forward a month. The chapter is based on "Munari da Harvard. Viaggio attraverso la luce artificiale" (Munari from Harvard: A Journey Through Artificial Light), *Il giorno*, May 5, 1967, but the entire discussion of avant-gardes, the Cineteca of

Monte Olimpino, and programmed art which follows the first sentence is found only in the book. In the newspaper original, it is the two illustrations, both of which have been modified with respect to the book, that make Munari's argument regarding avant-gardes and rear guards.

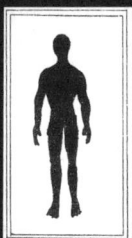

RETROGUARDIA - Se esiste una avanguardia dobbiamo ammettere una retroguardia la quale, ovviamente, riproduce solamente ciò che vede senza « cervellotiche » interpretazioni.

AVANGUARDIA - L'avanguardia nasce come rivolta e dice: l'uomo non è quello che ci hanno sempre mostrato, esso non è altro che un pezzo di macchina nel mondo moderno, eccetera.

Instead of simply "Man" and then "Rear Guard," the first text reads: "Rear Guards: If avantgardes exist, then rear guards exist as well that, of course, reproduce only what they see without tortuous forms of reasoning." Instead of "Man" and then "Avantgarde," the second reads: "Avantgardes: Avantgardes are born in the spirit of revolt and argue 'humanity doesn't correspond to what we have been told; humans are nothing but a piece of machinery in the modern world, etc.'"

21   Due to the belatedness of Mirko Basaldella's invitation to come to Harvard and the last-minute addition of two sections of Basic Design, Munari's courses were not listed in the official print version of the Harvard course catalog. See the Appendix on this subject.

22   The Monte Olimpino studio was established by Munari and Marcello Piccardo (1914–1999) in 1962. During its subsequent ten years of activity, it produced well over a dozen experimental 16 mm and 35 mm films including: *Arte programmata* (1962), *I colori della luce* (1963), *Moire* (1964), *Inox* (1964), *Tempo nel tempo* (1964), *Sulle scale mobili* (1964), *Lettere* (1965), *Scacco matto* (1965), *Omega ricerca n. 2* (1966), *Il mimo e l'oggetto* (1966), *I fratelli Castiglioni* (1967), *Fiat ricerca n. 1* (1968–69), and *After Effects* (1969). For more information, see Marcello Piccardo, *La collina del cinema* (Como: Nodo libri, 1992).

23   *Arte programmata* (programmed art) was the label first applied to a body of works by a group of 1960s Italian artists by Bruno Munari and Umberto Eco on the occasion of an exhibition inaugurated on May 15, 1962, at the Olivetti showroom in Milan. The show featured kinetic, combinatory, and Op art works by Munari and Enzo Mari, as well as members of Gruppo T (Giovanni Anceschi, Davide Boriani, Gianni Colombo, and Grazia Varisco) and Gruppo N collectives (Alberto Biasi, Ennio

Chiggio, Toni Costa, Edoardo
Landi, and Manfredo Massironi).

24 From this section to the end of
the chapter, the text is the same
as "Munari da Harvard. Viaggio
attraverso la luce artificiale"
(Munari from Harvard: A Journey
Through Artificial Light), *Il giorno*,
May 5, 1967.

25 As in the preceding chapters,
here Munari adds some anecdotal
material in the first paragraph
and then inserts the text from
"Munari da Harvard. L'architettura
invisibile della materia" (Munari
from Harvard: The Invisible
Architecture of Matter), *Il giorno*,
May 12, 1967, the article immediately subsequent to "Viaggio
attraverso la luce artificiale,"
which appeared on May 5.

26 Often attributed to Einstein,
the quotation is consistent with
his views but doesn't appear
in his writings.

27 Rather than a quotation or para-
phrase, the statement reflects
the Daoist views found in texts
such as the *Tao Te Ching* by
Laozi which emphasize balance,
harmony, and the natural order
of the universe.

28 The original newspaper article
included the following illustration
of this principle.

Il massimo numero di dischi
su di un piano prende la forma
di un triangolo, ossia la come
base il triangolo equilatero che è
la minima distanza fra tre cerchi
uguali che si toccano. Una struttura di cerchi rientra quindi nelle
strutture triangolari, o esagonali,
vedi l'alveare, il quale nasce dalla
compressione di celle rotonde.

The text reads: "the maximum
accumulation of disks on a
single plane assumes the form
of a triangle, which is to say an
equilateral triangle, which is the
minimum distance between three
tangent identical circles. A structure composed of circles is thus
part of the family of triangular,
hexagonal, hive-like structures
generated by means of the
compression of round cells."

29 In the original article in *Il giorno*
which appeared on May 12, 1967,
Munari added in: "This is my
own personal observation that
is as of yet unconfirmed and
I'd be more than happy if one of
my readers were to rectify
my error. Knowledge of mistakes
is much more important than pre-
sumptuousness." Any technical
limitations of Munari's text have
been intentionally (or unintention-
ally) preserved in translation.

30 Aside from some minor editing,
this chapter repeats "Ogni matita
ha il suo linguaggio," *Il giorno*, May
19, 1967. Several subtitles were
eliminated: "The Signs We Use"
and "Image Blocks." The original

featured the following illustration which is absent from the book.

MUNARI DA HARVARD

Ogni matita ha il suo linguaggio

di BRUNO MUNARI

The explanatory text reads: "Some examples of image blocks structured on the basis of a core sign."

31 Munari is alluding to the Out of Town News kiosk in Harvard Square, built in 1955 and frequented over the years by the likes of the poet Robert Frost, chef Julia Child, and Microsoft founders Paul Allen and Bill Gates.

32 The parenthetical regarding the use of charcoal was added to the book version of the text.

33 The Italian word *segni* denotes both signs in the semiotic sense and marks in the graphic sense. I have mostly translated the word as "signs" to emphasize the connection to the Italian school of semiotics, associated with such figures as Umberto Eco, with whom Munari maintained regular contacts during the 1960s. Eco's *Opera aperta – forma e indeterminazione nelle poetiche contemporanee* (*The Open Work – Form and Indeterminacy in Contemporary Poetics*) had appeared in 1962 and provided additional grounding for Munari's commitment to kinetic, process-oriented, participatory approaches to art and design.

34 The reference is to Munari's slide projections (the *vetrini*), the *Concavo-convesso* series of hanging sculptures, his polarized projections, and works of kinetic art like the *Ora X* and *Tetracono*: works from the 1940s through the 1980s that combine projected light and mobile/suspended structures.

35 The allusion is presumably to Grant Wood (1891–1942), many of whose prints are in the Harvard Art Museum collections and whose *Death on the Ridge Road* (1935) Munari could have seen at the Williams College Museum of Art in Williamstown, Massachusetts, during his semester at Harvard.

36 One of the founders of Gruppo T, Boriani (1936–) is known for kinetic and environmental artworks in which temporality plays a decisive role, such as *Superfici magnetiche* [Magnetic Surfaces] (1959–66), *Ipercubo* [Hypercube] (1961–65), *PH. Scope* (1963–66), *Pantachrome* (1967–76).

37   Aside from a final sentence on
laziness as the driving force
behind progress (dropped in the
book but later picked up on p. 68
["Laziness drives progress."]),
the entire chapter faithfully
replicates "Munari da Harvard.
In scatola il linguaggio dei colori"
(Munari from Harvard: The
Language of Color in a Box),
Il giorno, May 31, 1967.

38   Munari uses the phrase *materia-
luce* with particle physics in
mind, but echoes of Futurism,
with its cult of the vibrant matter,
are surely present as well.
It is perhaps worth noting that
Munari's emphasis on light as
a *medium* resonates with the
opening of Marshal McLuhan's
influential *Understanding Media*,
in which McLuhan underscores
the point that: "the electric light
escapes attention as a communication medium just because it
has no 'content.' And this makes
it an invaluable instance of how
people fail to study media at
all. For it is not till the electric
light is used to spell out some
brand name that it is noticed as
a medium. Then it is not the light
but the content (or what is really
another medium) that is noticed.
The message of the electric light
is like the message of electric
power in industry, totally radical,
pervasive, and decentralized.
For electric light and power are
separate from their uses, yet they
eliminate time and space factors
in human association exactly as
do radio, telegraph, telephone,
and TV, creating involvement in
depth." *Understanding Media:
The Extensions of Man* (New York:
Harcourt Brace, 1962), 9.

39   The reference is to Milan's Museo
Nazionale della Scienza e della
Tecnologia Leonardo da Vinci.

40   The slides that Munari is referring
to throughout this text—the Italian
word is *vetrino* or "vitrine"—are
composed of two thin glass panes
mounted in a hinged metal frame
which allows for the insertion
of thin materials of various kinds
between the panes. Many of the
exercises described thus involve
experimentation with the creation
of such "slides" as composites or
assemblages, whether static
or dynamic.

41   Recipient of the 2003 Edwin Land
Medal, John McCann directed
the Vision Research Laboratory
at Polaroid from 1961–96.

42   Munari's interest in polarized
light extended back to the
mid-1950s but came to head
around the time of his visiting
professorship at Harvard. His
first major exhibition in the
United States, entitled *The
Bruno Munari Exhibition*, was
held only six months earlier,
between September 20 and

October 8, 1966, at the Howard Wise Gallery in New York, and featured versions 3, 10, 12, and 13 of the *Polariscop* alongside the *Tetracono*, *Ora-X*, and *Concave-Convex* projections.

43 The newspaper version contained the following illustration.

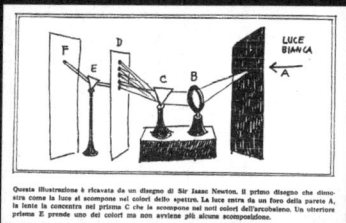

Questa illustrazione è ricavata da un disegno di Sir Isaac Newton. Il primo disegno che dimostra come la luce si scompone nei colori dello spettro. La luce entra da un foro della parete A, la lente la concentra nel prisma C che la scompone nei sette colori dell'arcobaleno. Un ulteriore prisma E prende uno dei colori ma non avviene più alcuna scomposizione.

The text reads, "this illustration is taken from a drawing by Sir Isaac Newton and is the first drawing to demonstrate how light can be broken down into the colors of the spectrum. Light comes in through a perforation in wall A, a lens concentrates it on prism C which separates out the colors of the rainbow. An additional prism (E) captures one of the colors which can't be further broken down."

44 Invented by William Nichols in the nineteenth century, a Nichols prism is an optical device used to produce and analyze polarized light. The prism was made from a birefringent material, in most cases calcite, which has different refractive indices for different polarizations of light.

45 Aside from the book's preface, this is the first chapter inserted into *Design and Visual Communication* that doesn't correspond to one of Munari's contributions to *Il giorno*, perhaps because it largely consists of his reflections on his students' sartorial choices.

46 The 1964 single by the Milanese singer-songwriter Enzo Jannacci "wouldn't make sense" because it treats tennis shoes as a differentiating, uncommon feature, and mark of individualism, rather than a commonplace choice.

47 This chapter corresponds to "Munari da Harvard. Pellicole impazzite rovesciano immagini su tutte le pareti" (Munari from Harvard: Crazed Filmstrips Spread Moving Images Across Every Wall), *Il giorno*, June 15, 1967. The original article contains an element lacking in the book: the poster for an early concert at the Boston Tea Party.

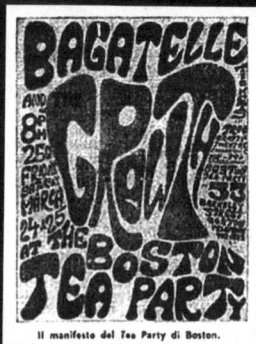

Il manifesto del Tea Party di Boston.

377

48 Munari is referring to Boston's
legendary concert venue, the
Boston Tea Party, founded by
counterculture businessman
Ray Riepen (a former MIT student)
and David Hahn (a student at
Harvard Law School) on January
20, 1967. Riepen and Hahn were
the two "uninvited visitors" to
his classroom at Harvard's
Carpenter Center. Remembered
for hosting some of the most
noted acts of the period, including the Grateful Dead, The Who,
The Stooges, and The Velvet
Underground, the Boston
Tea Party's light shows were
among the most innovative
of the era. For the benefit of his
readers, Munari compares
the Boston Tea Party to the
celebrated Italian discotheque
Piper Club, located in Rome's
quartiere Coppedè, a pop
rather than a psychedelic venue
frequented by Roman elites.

49 The actual location was 53
Berkeley Street in Boston's
South End, at the time somewhat
"peripheral" but today considered one of the city's core
neighborhoods.

50 Around the time of the venue's
opening, the *Harvard Crimson*
wrote: "The founders are still
experimenting with unusual
lighting effects. If you dance near
one of the high frequency stroboscopic lights, your partner's

smooth motion becomes a
panorama of frozen positions
superimposed on each other.
Soon an IBM computer will be
moved in to help control the blink-
ing red and blue lights. And if you
take your date over to a corner,
about all you can see in the ultraviolet light is her glowing blouse
and nail polish." Quoted from
Roger W. Sinnott, "Psychedelic
Discotheque," *Harvard Crimson*
(Jan. 30, 1967).

51 Rho is a town and municipality
located nine miles northwest of
Milan. Throughout this passage,
Munari treats psychedelic light
shows as a kinetic décor solution,
seemingly unaware of their
intimate association with 1960s
drug subcultures.

52 This chapter faithfully repro-
duces "Munari da Harvard. È
nata dal triangolo la cupola di
Montreal" (Munari from Harvard:
The Montreal Dome is Made of
Triangles), *Il giorno*, June 3, 1967.

53 Italy's leading milk producer,
Parmalat, embraced Ruben
Rausing's TetraPak packaging
system during the 1960s,
so tetrahedral containers
became the standard form for
milk cartons.

54 The original article in *Il giorno*
included the following illustration
which was omitted from the book:

Il tetraedro fatto con un tubo: il tubo 1 viene schiacciato da una parte dove è aperto e saldato 2, poi viene schiacciato e saldato anche dall'altra parte 3, ma le due saldature se si guardano come sovrapposte devono risultare incrociate.

The text reads: "A tetrahedron made out of a tube. Tube 1 is compressed on one of its open ends and sealed shut (2); it is then compressed and sealed tight on its other end in such a way as the two seams crisscross one another."

55 Munari is referring to the Montreal Expo 67 geodesic dome, currently known as the Montreal Biosphere. The structure, devised by R. Buckminster Fuller (1895–1983), consists of a double-layer 32-frequency dome in which the inner and outer layers are joined by means of a lattice of struts. It is 249 feet in diameter and 203 feet tall.

56 For the 1954 Triennale, two cardboard Fuller domes were erected in the park surrounding Milan's Palazzo dell'Arte. Each was 36 feet in diameter, 18 feet in height, circa 100 square meters in surface area, and weighed 600 pounds. Munari himself contributed to this Triennale with fabric designs as well the interior décor for Ico Parisi's *Padiglione per il soggiorno* ("Living Pavillion").

57 Until the 1970 FIFA World Cup, the standard soccer ball was composed of eighteen sewn-together strips: a design akin to today's volleyballs. This changed when Adidas took over the manufacture of official game balls, adopting a Fuller-inspired design that consisted in twenty hexagons and twelve pentagons.

58 This chapter and the next do not appear on the pages of *Il giorno*.

59 Munari is referring to what are sometimes called "turning pictures" or Agamographs (after the Israeli Op artist Yaacov Agam): a lenticular variety of anamorphic images, popular in the seventeenth century, whose raised ridges jut out in such a way as to provide the viewer with two different images via a single support: a left and a right view.

60 The British polymath, Thomas Young (1773–1829) contributed to overturning the claim in Isaac Newton's *Opticks* that light is a particle. On the contrary, Young argued for a wave theory of light. He was also central to physiological optics and color theory, arguing that the human eye contains three types of receptors, each sensitive to one of the three primary colors: red, green, and blue.

61 Munari employs the term "modulation" (*modulazione*) to describe the structuring of 2D or 3D works around the interplay of regular structures (such as a grids) and variations in form, spacing, density, scale, volume, and color within those regular structures. He derives these concepts from the writings of the Ulm School, in particular those of Tomás Maldonado and Gui Bonsiepe, as published in the school's journal, *Ulm: Zeitschrift der Hochschule für Gestaltung* (1958–68). Modules (*moduli*) are understood as structural units that can be deployed both serially and in systems; they sometimes contain submodules (*sottomoduli*) which can be deployed serially as well within a given module. Modules are the foundation stones for a consistent, systematic, logic-based practice of visual communication, rather than an impressionistic or subjective one. Modulation involves adjusting and varying design elements to forge visually cohesive, functional, and effective outcomes. This entire chapter repeats: "Ancora misterioso il 'modulo' che dá forma a un fiume, a una nuvola, a un continente, a un nervo ottico, a una vena. Il mondo nell'occhio di una mosca" (The Still Mysterious "Module" that Shapes a River, a Cloud, a Continent, an Optical Nerve, a Vein: The World in a Fly's Eye) *Il giorno*, July 7, 1967. Two subtitles were removed: "The Edges of Shapes" and "Teamwork."

62 This and the successive two chapters were not published on the pages of *Il giorno*.

63 As Munari's introduction to the *Arte programmata* exhibition catalogue suggests, this is a naïve question. The point is, rather, that "a static image, unique and final, does not contain that quantity of information sufficient to interest the contemporary viewer, who is accustomed to life in an environment subject to simultaneous and multifarious stimuli from the most varied sources. This situation gives birth to programmed art, which has as its ultimate aim the production not of a single definitive and subjective image but of a multitude of images in continual variation. The 'programming' of these works, which necessarily because of technical reasons and limits are neither paintings nor sculptures, is to be understood in the sense that each artist choses a particular material and the structural, kinetic, and optical combinations that he considers most suitable for the embodiment of his artistic intuition." Bruno Munari and Riccardo Musatti, *Arte programmata. Kinetic Art*, organized and sponsored by the Olivetti Company of Italy (Milan: Officina d'Arte Grafica A. Lucini & C, 1964), 4.

64 The earliest usages of the phrase "computer art," date back to the mid-1950s when the alternative phrase "computer graphics" wasn't yet in widespread use. The situation changed in the 1960s and 1970s as the two diverged with "computer art" referring to computer-aided art creation and "computer graphics" denoting practical applications of computing in the production of visual materials such as technical drawings and advertising.

65 The reference is to A. Michael Noll's pioneering stereoscopic computer-animated movies of four-dimensional hyperobjects at the Bell Telephone Laboratories in Murray Hill, New Jersey.

66 The model Munari has in mind is informed by his contacts with Max Bill and the Hochschule für Gestaltung (School of Design), known as the School of Ulm, examples of whose work abound in the second half of the book. A Department of Visual Communication was established there in 1956 and served as the model for the subsequent creation of analogous programs at the Politecnico di Milano.

67 Munari's enthusiasm for space travel was genuine even if the lunar reference is playful. As early as 1955 he created a cover for a publication by the illustrated magazine *Tempo* (where he had once served as art director) in which a rocket ship was pointed toward a moon on which photographs of Dwight Eisenhower and Sophia Loren, among others, have been overlaid (*Tempo* (special documentary issue) "Dalla luna alla terra – il 1955 nel mondo").

68 This chapter is mostly based on "Ogni oggetto ha un codice" (Every Object Has Its Own Code), *Il giorno* June 29, 1967. It appears out of chronological sequence. From this date forward, none of Munari's articles in *Il giorno* bear the label "Munari from Harvard," so it is safe to say that he returned to Italy in mid-June 1967.

69 Munari's phrase is "una conoscenza strumentale del fenomeno" which appears to be an echo of standard communications theory textbooks from the period. *Strumentale* means both "instrumental" and tool-based or technical.

70 This entire paragraph is unique to the book, added for purposes of clarification.

71 The final two sentences were added to the book version and are absent from the *Il giorno* article.

72 This chapter corresponds to "Munari da Harvard. La confusione delle lingue" (Munari

from Harvard: The Confusion of Tongues), *Il giorno*, April 8, 1967. Out of chronological sequence, it was moved to the end of Part I of *Design and Visual Communication* during the editorial process. The visuals are mostly the same, even if the original ones were reshuffled for the book.

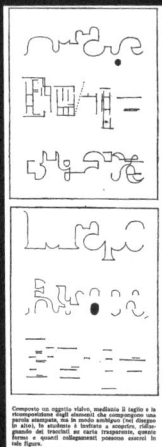

The text reads: "Once a visual object has been composed by means of cuts and the recomposition of the elements that constitute a printed word (however ambiguous they might be, as in the case of the uppermost image), the student is invited to explore the wide range of forms and associations that are present in such a figure by making marks on tracing paper."

73 The second portion of the book was written subsequent to Munari's spring 1967 stint at

Harvard and, accordingly, doesn't include any portions that were pre-published in *Il giorno*.

74 Ugo Mulas (1928–1973) was one of the most influential Italian photographers of the postwar era, noted for his portraits of street life, his cultural reportage, and collaborations with artists like Lucio Fontana.

75 Rino Albertarelli (1908–1974) was a noted Italian illustrator and comics artist who is remembered for creating the *Kit Carson - Cavalliere del West* series, as well as for his cartooning work on Emilio Salgari's *Il corsaro nero*.

76 In the Italian original, the words are *grana*, *zigrinatura*, and *tessitura*.

77 Though it shares the same roots as the English *texture* and is a synonym, the Italian word *testura* has literary connotations. It is more commonly associated with the crafting of a discursive product or weaving together of the strings of a plot.

78 The Italian word for "design" is *disegno* which refers, first and foremost, to drawing, even though its uses include notions of structure, scheme, and plan.

79 Renata Bonfanti (1929–2018) was the most important Italian textile

artist of her generation, remembered for having elevated the perception of textiles and rugs to the status of works of art.

80 An influential graphic designer and artist, Franco Grignani (1908–1999) created the Woolmark logo. He was one of the pioneers of Op art in Italy.

81 Founded by Max Bill, Inge Aicher-Scholl, and Otl Aicher in 1953, the *Hochschule für Gestaltung Ulm* was built on the legacies of the Bauhaus and became one of the most influential postwar centers for innovative design education. Munari was well acquainted with some of its key faculty including Max Bill and Max Huber.

82 The mention of Preusser indicates Munari's contacts during this period with the circle of György Kepes at MIT.

83 The Italian word *forma* means both form and shape, while referring broadly to the notion of structures (of government, discourse, sound, and the like).

84 Apollonio (1940–) is an op art artist close to some the 1960s experimental art groups in which Munari also participated such as the Gruppo N and Gruppo T.

85 Lanfranco Bombelli Tiravanti (1921–2008) was a founding

member of the MAC (Movimento Arte Concreta) in which Munari participated actively during the late 1940s and early 1950s. He also served as the principal organizer of the international exhibition, *Arte astratta e concreta*, at the Palazzo Reale in Milan in 1947 where Munari's works were exhibited in the company of Hans Arp, Wassily Kandinsky, Paul Klee, and Sophie Tauber-Arp.

86 Munari is citing the so-called Kanizsa triangle, named for the Italian psychologist who first published his findings on this optical illusion in his 1955 article "Margini quasi-percettivi in campi con stimolazione omogenea," *Rivista di psicologia* 49.1 (Jan.-March 1955): 7-30.

87 Angiolo Giuseppe Fronzoni (1923–2002) was an Italian graphic designer, designer, and architect, associated with the review *Casabella* (where he served as art director).

88 Krampen (1928–2015) was a noted pioneer in the field of visual semiotics and environmental perception; he is considered the founder of the field of phytose-miotics (which studies processes that occurs at cellular and tissue level). Trained at the School of Ulm, he went on to teach visual communication at Hochschule der

Künste in Berlin from 1977 until 1993. He worked as both a semiotician and artist.

89 Morandini (1940–) is a sculptor/ graphic designer whose work is built around the repetition of simple geometric elements, often in black and white.

90 This work is not a classroom exercise but rather one of Munari's *Useless Machines* (*macchine inutili*). Worth noting is the fact that these early kinetic sculptures served as a stepping-stone to the later motorized works of programmed art. Munari not only worked from gridded modules but also meticulously mapped and choreographed the combinatory movement patterns of his "machines."

91 The illustration features Munari's patented *Esagonale* pendant lights, developed in 1959 for Danese Milano.

92 A long-time acquaintance of Munari's from his art director days, De Biasi was an Italian photojournalist whose collaboration with the magazine *Epoca* endured for over three decades. Numerous of his photographs are also present in *Fantasy*, where he is described as "known for his experiments with new ways of creating images that employ simple procedures"

(*Fantasy–Invention, Creativity, and Imagination in Visual Communication* [Los Angeles: Inventory Press, 2024], 138).

93 Castellano (1932–2015) was a noted graphic designer who designed pavilions for RAI, Italsider, and INA at the Fiera del Levante in Bari during the 1950s and 1960s. He is remembered, among other things, for his work for the Italian publishers Laterza and Vallecchi.

94 Munari's experimentation with xerographic techniques extends back to the early 1960s and established him as one of the pioneers of "copy art." In his "original xerographies" he combines attention to every facet of photocopier's operation: its potential as a generator of image sequences; the distinctive temporality of the scanning process and its openness to the manipulation of image inputs; the simplifying power of high contrast toner printing, whether in black-and-white or color; the photocopy machine's capacity to transform printing into a live and even participatory public event. On this subject, see *Xerografia. Documentazione sull'uso creativo delle macchine Rank Xerox* (Milan: Rank Xerox, 1970) and *Arte e xerografia,* ed. Bruno Munari (Milan: Rank Xerox, 1972).

95   The Venezuelan abstractionist and kineticist Rafael Martinez (1940–2021) began frequenting Milanese circles in the early 1970s, having been based in Paris during the late 1960s. A collaborator of Jesús Soto, he sought to investigate "geometric shapes, developing a changeable structure. I tighten spaces and question angles. My purpose is to reveal what is hidden in geometry. To see beyond the smooth surface whether fabric, metal, wood or anything else. I show lines and play tricks on the wonderful visual system." From https://www.rafaelmartinezart.com/about.

96   The object in question is Ugo La Pietra's (1938–) celebrated *Globo tissurato* lamp, which launched his career as an experimental artist, architect, filmmaker, and designer. The design was executed by drilling a grid of perforations into methacrylate sheets that were then shaped into half spheres (working in collaboration with the plastics technician Michele Moro).

97   The bowl in question is Munari's own *Maldive* bowl, produced in Nickel silver (otherwise known as "alpaca metal") by Danese Milano starting in 1960.

98   Majoli (1929–) is an artist-designer and was a participant in the Italian abstract and Op art movements who directed the Il Grafico design school in Bari.

99   The Olivetti CMC7-7004 was the first of architect Mario Bellini's (1935–) designs for Olivetti to earn the Golden Compass award of the Associazione per il Disegno Industriale (ADI).

100 Noted for his cutouts, hanging mobiles, and designs for children's toys, Zalewski taught architecture at Harvard's Graduate School of Design. During the 1940s he had worked in Le Corbusier's atelier alongside his future colleague Josep Lluís Sert. He was the "associate" referred to in the title of Sert's Cambridge-based firm Sert, Jackson, and Associate, which was renamed in 1963 to include Zalewski.

101 In line with standard Italian mathematical terminology, Munari is employing the word *traslazione* (translation) in the etymological sense also captured in the phrase *translatio imperii* (transfer of rule from empire to empire). The word thus evokes spatial relocation rather than translation across languages.

102 Thea Vallé (1934–1978) was an Italian minimalist sculptor, known for her exploration of architectural forms.

103 Perry (1929–2011) was a trained architect, though he is mostly remembered today for his large scale geometrical public sculptures, the most notable of which is *Continuum*: the sixteen-foot-tall bronze Moebius strip that stands in front of the National Air and Space Museum, in Washington, DC.

104 Vieira (1927–2001) was a Brazilian sculptor remembered for her experiments with the complex geometries of what she referred to as "polyvolumes." Her collaborations with Max Bill, dating back to her presence at the Ulm School in 1953–54, are associated with her work as a faculty member at the Kunstgewerbeschule Basel between 1966 and 1993.

105 A sometime member of Gruppo V and associate of the University of Milan's cybernetic research group, Scarpa (1938–2012) was a designer/artist who worked in the fields of topology and rotational geometry. He was the author of two books: *Modelli di geometria rotatoria* (Bologna: Zanichelli, 1978) and *Modelli di bionica* (Bologna: Zanichelli, 1985).

106 Though a lifelong politician affiliated with Italian Communist Party, Petrocelli (1940–2013) maintained close ties to the Laterza and Zanichelli publishing houses; he played an editorial role in Munari's own "Quaderni di Design" publication series with Zanichelli.

107 Trained as an architect and artist, Crippa (1946–) worked as an experimental filmmaker and educational game designer during much of his career.

108 The vases in question are Enzo Mari's *Camicia* (Shirt) series from the early 1960's. The "shirt" is a bottomless anodized aluminum cylinder which serves as a sleeve to the clear glass container that it supports. Various perforations and window cutouts from the metal sleeve make it possible to peer inside the container, revealing its contents. A frequent Munari collaborator (thanks to their close ties to Bruno Danese) and a powerful influence on his thought, Mari was one of the most significant industrial designers of the second half of the twentieth century, renowned for his egalitarian, politically engaged, anti-consumerist design ethos. Together, in 1956, they had designed an espresso machine for La Pavoni.

109 The object in question is known as the *Kerguelen*. Named after the Kerguelen Islands in the sub-Antarctic, it's a multifunctional aluminum and iron totem that includes storage spaces that can be used in a variety of ways.

110 Known for his innovative metalwork, Lino Sabattini (1925–) was a
craftsman and longtime collaborator of Giò Ponti. After a period
working for Christofle in Paris, he
founded the noted silversmithing
workshop Sabattini in Bregnano,
on the outskirts of Milan.

111 Internationally celebrated for
his work as a furniture designer,
Bellini (1935–) played a key role in
the design of some of Olivetti's
most memorable calculators,
typewriters, and computers from
the 1960s through the 1980s.
The numerical keypad displayed
in Munari's photograph is that
from the Olivetti Programma
101, among the very first pro-
grammable desktop calculators.
Launched in 1964 at the New York
World's Fair, the P101 entered
production in 1965.

112 Working initially with their older
brother Livio, Achille (1918–2002)
and Pier Giacomo Castiglioni
(1913–1968) established one of the
most influential industrial design
practices of the twentieth century. They are remembered for
everything from their exhibition
and lighting designs to the design
of audio equipment for Brionvega.

113 Robert Preusser (1919–1992) was a
painter and art educator remembered in particular for his work
and leadership of the art department at MIT, where he worked

closely with Gyorgy Kepes and the
photographer Minor White.

114 Giuseppe Tovaglia (1923–1977)
was a leading Milanese graphic
artist who cultivated strong affini-
ties with contemporary Swiss
graphics as associated with
figures like Max Bill. In 1972, with
Munari, Bob Noorda, and Roberto
Sambonet, he designed the logo
for the region of Lombardy, still
in use today.

115 Gianni Colombo (1933–1993) was
an artist associated with the
Gruppo T (T = time), a collective
devoted to exploring the use
of new industrial materials
and objects in works of kinetic,
participatory sculpture.

116 Bruno Ezio Caraceni (1927–1986)
was a Rome-based painter and
sculptor, whose works engaged
Munari's attention in the early
1960s due to their use of layering.

117 Not much is known regarding the
Japanese designer Hiromitsu
Kawai, though his teaching
methods at the Milan Polytechnic
appear to mirror Munari's interest
in exercises that work across the
2D/3D divide. His designs include
a motorcycle saddle (executed
by the well-known craftsman
Giovanni Sacchi in 1971) in the
collection of the Triennale di
Milano and a collaboration with
Hans von Klier on an exhibition of

Mexican masks at Milan's Castello Sforzesco in the summer of 1981.

118 The architect and designer, William Graatsma (1925-2017) and his colleague Jan Slothouber (1918-2007) dedicated their lifetimes to exploring applications of the cube in all its possible forms: from modular furniture kits to artworks and toys. They were the creators of the Slothouber-Graatsma puzzle: a packing problem that calls for packing three 1 × 1 × 1 blocks and six 1 × 2 × 2 blocks into a 3 × 3 × 3 box.

119 Richard Filipowski (1923-2007) devoted much of his career to bringing Bauhaus-inspired methods to the teaching of art and design in MIT's School of Architecture and Planning.

120 The Milanese architect Angelo Mangiarotti (1921-2012) was one of the leading industrial designers of his generation. Munari is here referring to Mangiarotti's *Giogali* and *Minigiogali* modular lighting fixtures that earned the designer an honorable mention in the 1969 Compasso d'Oro competition.

121 Between 1952 and the late 1960s, Mari pursued research into perception through the programmatic aggregation of prefabricated modular elements. Much as Munari is theorizing in *Design and Visual Communication*, he approached modularity as a means to uncover unforeseen and expressive relationships implicit in a structure. The resulting works bore the title *Struttura* followed by a number to emphasize their seriality.

122 *Lavori in corso* (Work in Progress) was the Swiss Television Network's (Televisione Svizzera Italiana) most prestigious educational television program of the late 1960s and early 1970s. Hosted by Grytzko Mascioni, it covered topics in the areas of literature, art, philosophy, and science.

123 A self-taught artist and graphic designer, Mimmo Castellano (1932-2015) collaborated with Achille, Pier Giacomo, and Livio Castiglioni on the design of the Italian Radio and TV pavilions in 1956 in Bari and 1967 in Milan, before his work on the Osaka Expo '70 pavilion.

124 The painter Vittorio Mascalchi (1935-2010) was the director of the Academia delle Belle Arti in Bologna.

125 Alberto Seassaro (1939-2020) was the founder of the School of Design at the Milan Polytechnic, Italy's first. In 1964, he opened a design studio with the experimentalist Ugo La Pietra.

126 Munari is referring to the orna-
mental plant species sometimes
dubbed the wandering Jew
or inch plant, known for its
trailing vines and silver- or white-
striped leaves.

127 Although he makes no mention of
it, the images illustrate Munari's
own *Continuous Structures*,
issued in editions of one hundred
by Bruno Danese between 1961
and 1967. As the text indicates,
they were made up of folded,
right-angled metallic plates with
cuts that allowed for interlocking.

128 Bozzola (1921–2010) was a painter
and sculptor active in the kinetic
art movement. He was co-author,
with the art historian Caroline
Tisdall of one of the first English
language books on Italian
Futurism: *Futurism* (London:
Thames and Hudson, 1977).

129 A close friend of Munari's, Donzelli
(1921–1984) was a longtime graphic
and industrial designer associated with such mobility brands as
Gilera, Bianchi, and Moto Guzzi.

130 The raum-technik-system
received the coveted iF design
award in building technology in
1973; it has been widely used (and
copied) in subsequent modular
structures and furnishings.

131 The CUB 8 system was developed and marketed in a period

advertising campaign as a "modular wall system that subdivides
rooms, creating usable spaces
and opportunities for interior programming. It is more neutral than
an ordinary partition wall." "Walls
are lost space, CUB8 is functional
space," the ads insisted.

132 The German engineer Max
Mengeringhausen (1903–1988)
was a pioneering figure in the
field of structures and statics and
the winner of numerous awards
for his work with Mero structures.
The Mero System has been used
to create flat structures, domes,
barrel vaults, pyramids, towers,
and paraboloid structures in
some sixty countries for purposes that vary from shopping
centers to sports halls.

133 Munari is referring to Interbau
1957, officially known as the
International Building Exhibition.
Held in West Berlin's Hansaviertel
district, it showcased the
integration of modern living
with green spaces and the
cultural and democratic values
of West Germany. The *city of
tomorrow* exhibition was sited in
a space frame pavilion designed
by Karl Otto (1904–1975) with
Frei Otto and Günther Günschel.

134 The references are to R.
Buckminster Fuller (creator of
the 1967 Montreal Expo dome), the
German industrial conglomerate

Mannesmann, skeletal space structures pioneer Zygmunt Stanislaw Makowski (1922–2005), and Arthur. E. Fentiman, the inventor of triodetic connectors (1918–1983).

135　Frey Egger Peterhans was an architectural studio based in Bern, Switzerland, active between 1960 and 1982. Its founding partners were Willy Frey (1911–2004), Werner Peterhnas (1927–2015), and Alois Egger (1922–).

136　The reference is to one of Kenneth Snelson's so-called tensegrity sculptures from the 1960s.

137　This point becomes integral to Munari's later treatise *Fantasy*: "The most fundamental expressions of fantasy are usually the result of situations that have been turned on their head: the play of contraries, opposites, complementarities. If he says 'green,' then I say 'red.' A well-known vintage print, entitled *The World Upside Down*, displays a horse straddling a rider, a landscape floating above the clouds, sheep herding a flock of humans, and other similar niceties.) Children chuckle when we tell them that sugar is bitter and are tickled pink when we read them the story of a turtle who moves as quickly as a bolt of lightning." (Munari, *Fantasy*, 38).

138　Munari is referring to a number of key interventions in the field of design and engineering processes that were being tracked by members of the Ulm School: Leonard Bruce Archer (1922–2005), Professor of Design Research at the Royal College of Art (RCA) and author of *Systematic Method for Designers* (London: The Design Council, 1964); James N. Sidall (whose name Munari has misspelled), the author of "A Survey of a Modern Theory of Engineering Design," *Product Design and Value Engineering* 11, no. 9 (Sept. 1966); H. Carlos Fallon, creator of the Combinex decision matrix system at RCA (Radio Corporation of America) and author of *Value Analysis to Improve Productivity* (Hoboken, NJ: John Wiley & Sons, 1971) and contributor of several major chapters to *Value Analysis, Value Engineering—The Implications for Managers*, ed. William D. Falcon (New York: American Management Association, 1964); and Morris Asimow (1906–1982), the author of *Introduction to Design* (Englewood Cliffs, NJ: Prentice-Hall, 1962), a pioneering study of morphology in engineering design.

Postface:
Bruno Munari Goes to Harvard

Jeffrey Schnapp

The year 1967 marked a watershed in Bruno Munari's career.

Munari had consolidated his reputation as one of the most original, prolific, and polymorphous visual artists of his generation. Surrounded by younger acolytes, he was increasingly prominent on the international scene, recognized for pioneering forays into mobiles, projection art, geometrical abstractionism, xerographic copy art, artist's books, experimental filmmaking, and kinetic sculpture. Building on his passage through the second Futurism and leadership of the Concrete art movement (Movimento arte concreta = MAC), he had emerged as the senior figurehead of the more recent Programmed art (*Arte programmata*) movement, whose commitment to combinatorics was embodied in kinetic objects like the *Tetracono* (1965).[i] Munari's career as an industrial designer was, likewise, nearing its zenith thanks to flourishing collaborations with Danese Milano and Olivetti (who hosted the first *Programmed Art* exhibition in their Milan showroom in 1962). The exhibition subsequently toured Europe and North America, in the latter case with Smithsonian Institution sponsorship.

Despite this international prominence on the art and design fronts, the Italian publishing industry remained Munari's enduring base of operations. During the World War II period he had authored some of the twentieth century's most imaginative children's books, many of which were now being published in translation. He was hard at work crafting the graphic identity of some of Italy's most influential book series: among them the Nuova Universale Einaudi selection of literary classics; Nuovo Politecnico (dedicated to political theory); the Piccola Biblioteca Einaudi (essays); and Italo Calvino's Centopagine series (short literary works). He was likewise responsible for the design of hundreds of book covers for publishing houses such as Bompiani, Club degli Editori, Rizzoli, Ricordi, and Editori Riuniti, not to mention founding and directing six book series of his own.[ii] It's fair to say that no major Italian publisher eluded

Munari's influence during the second half of the twentieth century and that this influence was panoramic in character. It encompassed everything from limited edition artist's books to mass market paperbacks to magazines and the popular press.

Though an insider in the publishing world, Munari never authored a conventional book before *Design and Visual Communication* (*Design e comunicazione visiva*; 1968). The sole exception was *Design as Art* (*Arte come mestiere*; 1966), less a treatise than an assortment of practical and theoretical ruminations.[iii] Like its successor, *Design as Art* dances back and forth between arguing that design is the defining artform of the second half of the twentieth century ("The designer of today reestablishes the long-lost contact between art and the public, between living people and art as a living thing") and reflections on his own art-design practice, from his *Useless Machines* (1935–80) to the Falklands ceiling light (1964) to his *Theoretical Reconstructions of Imaginary Objects* and *Waterslide Fountain* (from the Venice Biennale, 1954)—the examples with which the book concludes.[iv]

Design and Visual Communication follows a similar template. But its scope and ambitions are more sweeping and its core argument more systematic. As Munari states in his prefatory remarks, it aspires less to becoming "the definitive treatise on the teaching of visual design" than "a field-tested contribution to the development of a comprehensive course."[v] Part One thus consists in twenty chapters that, anecdotal digressions aside, elaborate a then-state-of-the-art model of design pedagogy built around the skilled use of today's tools (including computers) to tackle today's visual communication challenges. Part Two consists in fifty supplementary chapters on topics ranging from optical illusions to space frame structures in which visual documentation and examples of practice abound. Some chapters fill in gaps in the "comprehensive course" like those dedicated to Textures, Forms, Structures, Color Use for Designers, and Design Methods. Other chapters are more idiosyncratic and resemble the sections of *Design as Art* that reflect upon Munari's own work or that of peers like Enzo Mari, Mario Bellini, Angelo Mangiarotti, and Achille, Pier Giacomo, and Livio Castiglioni. The titles of most are listed in the table of contents but don't appear within the text. Munari describes Part Two as "a structured and annotated corpus of illustrative materials that constitute a relatively complete course on visual design."[vi] The book is subtitled "Contribution to an Educational Method," which clearly positions it in what, for Munari, was a new domain.

The shift in emphasis from *design as art* to *design education* marked by *Design and Visual Communication* is consequential. It would reshape the concluding decades of Munari's existence: decades during which he dedicated himself to running workshops that hinged on the principle of participatory, hands-on experiences with processes of making, often with unconventional tools such as photocopy machines and staplers, as an alternative to conventional forms of art education. Starting with the 1977 Pinacoteca di Brera "Laboratory for Children," in which participants were invited to "play with art" in conversation with masterpieces from the past, extending through the time of his death in 1998 (and well beyond, thanks to the work of his son Alberto, Donata Fabbri, and their collaborators), the "Munari method laboratories" (*laboratori metodo Munari*) would come to sum up a career devoted to desacralizing art, professionalizing design practice, and promoting an ethos of playful experimentalism. Their work is documented in the book series *Playing with Art—Notebooks on Visual Communication* (*Giocare con l'arte—Quaderni per l'educazione alla comunicazione visive*) published by Zanichelli Editore in Bologna.

The occasion for this pivot was an invitation to teach at Harvard University during the spring semester of 1967 extended by Mirko Basaldella, the Sardinian painter-sculptor who had succeeded Costantino Nivola as chair of Harvard's Design Workshop. The Design Workshop was founded in 1954 on the heels of an initiative, supported by the likes of Sigfried Giedion and Josep Lluís Sert, to transform the nature of design and arts training in North America.[vii]

The endeavor unfolded in a broader institutional setting within which, under Sert's leadership, the Graduate School of Design was branching out into Urban Design and bold ventures like the Harvard Laboratory for Computer Graphics and Spatial Analysis were opening up new frontiers in computational cartography. All the while, since the late 1950s, efforts had been underway to carve out an institutional home for the visual arts at Harvard that went beyond the standard "Studio Art" liberal arts school paradigm: efforts that began with the creation of the Committee on the Practice of the Visual Arts in 1957 and matured with the opening of Le Corbusier's Carpenter Center for the Arts in spring 1963. Along with Architectural Sciences (an undergraduate architecture program) and Visual Studies (Harvard's expanded studio art program), the Design Workshop was integral to the programming of the Carpenter Center. It was also the incubator for the ongoing merger of Architectural Sciences and Visual Studies into an innovative new academic unit known as the Department of Visual and Environmental Studies (VES), launched in the fall of 1968.

The Harvard Munari set about exploring during the winter of 1967 remained much the same genteel institution that it had been for the past century where male students, mostly trained in New England's elite prep schools, were wont to don ties and female students, mostly prep school trained as well, were assigned their own college. But even beyond the subtly sculpted cement confines of the Carpenter Center, change was in the air: dramatic shifts in student demography, the region's economics, and the cultural-political climate. Boston was fast on the way to becoming one of the world's leading tech hubs as indicated by the presence of the corporate headquarters of Wang Laboratories, Polaroid, Raytheon, Data General, and Digital Equipment Corporation: the Hub was becoming a hub of the Information Age. The presence of figures like Walter Gropius at Harvard and György Kepes at MIT had energized the regional design and architecture community, giving rise to a plethora of new studios like the Architects Collaborative and retail establishments like the Design Research lifestyle store. Boston was also emerging as hotbed of antiwar activism and political radicalism, thanks to the presence of some fifty universities and colleges in the greater Boston area. All these developments leave a dense filigree of traces on the pages of *Design and Visual Communication*.

Shunned by the Italian academic establishment (of which he was fiercely critical), Munari had never taught before coming to Harvard. But, immersed in the Milanese design community, he was close to recent developments in design education, in particular the visionary work Max Bill and Tomás Maldonado had carried out at the Ulm School (Hochschule für Gestaltung Ulm),

and friendly with leading figures in Italian semiotics and structuralism such as Umberto Eco. He was also familiar with the lineage of radical educational thinking extending from Maria Montessori to contemporaries like Gianni Rodari and Mario Lodi, that sought to promote experiential, hands-on, democratized models of learning in Italian schools, particularly at the elementary and middle school levels. Basaldella's invitation foresaw the teaching of a single course: Advanced Explorations in Visual Communication. But, upon his arrival at the beginning of February, Munari was offered an additional two sections of Basic Design (which he accepted).

Munari joined the Harvard Design Workshop without the intent of authoring a book, not to mention helping VES to shape a new curriculum. Before leaving Milan, he had committed to serving as a freelance correspondent to the Milanese daily *Il giorno*, an alternative to the mainstream, establishment newspaper *Corriere della sera*. The genesis of the book was the dispatches that appeared in *Il giorno* mostly published under the rubric "Munari da Harvard" (Munari from Harvard) . Some were abridged by the newspaper's editors; others appear to have gone unpublished: six chapters out of the twenty that make up Part One aren't present on the pages of *Il giorno*. Passages were added or amended here and there as part of the transition from dispatches to book. The book entirely omits one article which I have added as an appendix to the present volume.

Design as Art sold relatively well and has remained in continuous print with Editori Laterza since its publication in 1966. So, upon Munari's return to Italy in June 1967, Laterza suggested that he transform his "Munari from Harvard" columns into a full-length second book. Ten months of subsequent expansion and editing ensued, mostly involving the assemblage of visual materials for Part Two. The volume saw the light of day in Laterza's Modern Culture Library (Biblioteca di Cultura Moderna) series in October 1968. Reflecting the bipartite structure of its genesis, Part One was now designated "Letters from Harvard" ("Lettere da Harvard"); Part Two as "Visual Communication" ("Comunicazione visiva"). An acknowledgements page and bibliography were appended later; the visual materials in Part Two were also expanded at the time of the fourth Laterza edition (1972).

The present volume is the first English translation of *Design and Visual Communication*. It corrects numerous errors present in the Laterza original and all translations into other languages, as well as providing an apparatus of notes to facilitate reading and provide background information. An Appendix features the text of "Munari da Harvard. Fanno scuola dietro la vetrina" (Munari from Harvard. Teaching in a Vitrine), from *Il giorno* Feb. 26, 1967. The student slides from the Advanced Explorations in Visual Communication course, some of which are featured on the pages of *Design and Visual Communication*, are preserved in the Harvard University Archives, Pusey Library, UAV 869.5295 (Carpenter Center Teaching Collection—Slides of Student Work and Exhibitions).

i   On the Programmed art move-
    ment see Lindsay Caplan, *Arte
    programmata: Freedom, Control,
    and the Computer in 1960s
    Italy* (Minneapolis: University of
    Minnesota Press, 2022); Marco
    Meneguzzo, *Arte programmata
    cinquant'anni dopo* (Monza: Johan
    & Levi, 2012); and *Programmare
    l'arte: Olivetti e le neoavanguardie
    cinetiche*, eds. Marco Meneguzzo,
    Enrico Morteo, and Alberto
    Saibene (Monza: Johan & Levi,
    2012). On the *Tetracone* see David
    Reinfurt's https://tetracono.net/.

ii The series founded and directed
    by Munari were: *Tantibambini*
    (1972–78, 66 volumes, Einaudi);
    Quaderni del Design (1976–86, 14
    volumes, Zanichelli), *Disegnare
    Colorare Costruire* (1978–88, 10
    volumes, Zanichelli); *Giocare con
    l'arte - Quaderni per l'educazi-
    one alla comunicazione visiva*
    (1979–92, 11 volumes, Zanichelli);
    and *Block Notes* (1992–97, 14
    volumes, Corraini).

iii *Design as Art*, trans. Patrick
    Creagh (Harmondsworth:
    Penguin, 1971). It's perhaps worth
    noting that the Italian title
    reads "art as a profession"; the
    phrase is polemical and implies
    that when art becomes a true
    profession (and not the preserve
    of elites), it is transformed into
    design practice.

iv Ibid., 25.

v   *Design and Visual
    Communication*, 6.

vi Ibid., 6.

vii In a letter dated May 13, 1957,
    Sert wrote to Basaldella: "This is
    an extremely important position
    for this country, and the
    University is now starting a
    new program on the visual arts
    that will grow and develop in
    the coming years..." Quoted
    in Kevin McManus, *Italiani a
    Harvard. Costantino Nivola, Mirko
    Basaldella e il Design Workshop
    (1954–1970)* (Milan: Franco Angeli,
    2015), 104. McManus provides
    a fine archivally based recon-
    struction of the larger setting
    within which Munari's visit to
    Harvard transpired; see in partic-
    ular pp. 151–57.

Appendix:
Munari from Harvard.
Teaching in a Vitrine

Il giorno Feb. 26, 1967

While a small subset of the chapters that make up Part One of *Design and Visual Communication* appear to have gone unpublished in *Il giorno*, one contribution to the newspaper's "Munari from Harvard" rubric was excluded from the book. Translated below, that article describes the circumstances of Munari's arrival, his initial impressions of Harvard campus, and his admiration for Le Corbusier's Carpenter Center for the Arts.
Two photographs accompanied the article: one of the Carpenter Center's exterior, another of the studios filled with student work.
    —JS

Once the Good Lord enabled us to safely reach the shores of New England, once we had built homes, secured essential provisions, erected places of worship worthy of our Maker, and established a civil government, our principal concern was to promote knowledge and its future transmission, thereby ensuring the literacy of the successor generation to our present ministry. As we set about this noble endeavor, it pleased God to plant in the heart of Mister Harvard, a pious gentleman who treasured study and the pursuit of knowledge, the urge to donate half of his estate and his library as well, to the establishment of a college. Other donations came in due course and the State took care of the rest. It was agreed by all that said college should be built in Cambridge and that it should be named "Harvard College," after its founding donor. This from a document published in London in 1643.
    Harvard College is the United States's most venerable college: the only such institution that has been in existence during the entire span of

the nation's history. Founded in 1636, it has grown into a world university with around one hundred buildings, thirteen thousand students from all over the world, five thousand professors, sixty-three specialized libraries, fourteen School libraries with collections totaling more than eight million volumes. In addition to the core Schools, there are ten professional Schools, each with its own faculty, endowment, and academic programs. More than five hundred of the faculty, scientists, and technicians are foreigners, invited to Harvard to share their experiences with students. I am one of those five hundred.

Cambridge is five miles from the ocean. It's a city of about one hundred thousand inhabitants. Massachusetts is beautiful with lots of trees. It snows here, but the temperatures aren't especially cold. A river divides Boston from Cambridge.

The building in which I will be holding my two courses, Basic Design (on the fundamentals of design) and Advanced Explorations in Visual Communication (exploration of advanced techniques of visual communication), was built by Le Corbusier in 1963. It's a vast and luminous building intersected by a walkway from which one can peer into its studios. Every aspect of visual communication has a dedicated, fully equipped studio space here that comprehends all the elements of visual communication and extends to filmmaking.

I'm afraid that I was a bit imprudent when I accepted an invitation to come to Cambridge to teach only one course: Advanced Explorations in Visual Communication. When I learned that the course in question involved only two two-hour sessions per week, I worried that I wouldn't know what to do with all my free time. So, they kindly offered me the opportunity to teach Basic Design as well. I accepted and now I have no free time at all.

Eighty students applied to enroll in my classes. But we are currently trying to get the group down to around sixty while dividing Basic Design into two sections. Classes ordinarily involve some fifteen to twenty students, but it seems that mine elicited a surfeit of student interest.

Students come from all over the world and are highly diverse here. They are unencumbered and open to new experiences. Freedom is a fundamental Harvard value: the university is free from external influence and control, whether political or other. It is independent and self-governing. Academic freedom is a second expression of this commitment: the freedom to pursue the truth in every field. "Veritas" is Harvard's watchword. A third aspect of this commitment to freedom is student freedom. Harvard isn't a paternalistic institution. It imposes a minimum of rules and offers a maximum of freedom to both students and faculty.

The weather has changed constantly during my initial days here. There was a snowstorm that slowed traffic and led to school closures yet the day after was lovely. The weather can vary in a matter of hours. This morning the sky was gray and it was snowing; now the sun is out and the wind is dry. White clouds stream across the sky projecting their moving shadows across the cityscape. The light is everchanging.

Designed by Le Corbusier, the Carpenter Center for Arts takes local climate conditions into consideration. Various structural solutions give rise to an architecture that keeps the sun from shining directly into workspaces (note the slanted walls in the photo) while other luminous zones arise in the pursuit of an ideal balance between exterior and interior illumination. The building as a whole is like a series of panels that protect but don't partition, allowing for flexible laboratory spaces—there are no traditional classrooms—and large windows exposed only to indirect sunlight.

An elevated walkway, a sort of shortcut joining together the streets that extend in front of and behind the building, allows the public to traverse the building and gaze into the studios through windows that are no less spacious than the walls.

Few people stroll by. But when one does and peers in, students can be seen at work. Their objects, constructions made with the widest possible range of materials, appear suspended in the air or hanging from a wire. These constructions are usually simple, made with wood laths, aluminum plates, and plastic. They are structures generated by means of modulation and the rotation or conjoining of components that have been multiplied.

—BM

Bruno Munari:
Design and Visual Communication
is published by
Inventory Press
2305 Hyperion Ave
Los Angeles, CA 90027
inventorypress.com

ISBN: 978-1-941753-71-2
LCCN: 2024945799

Distributed by
ARTBOOK | D.A.P.
75 Broad St, Suite 630
New York, NY 10004
artbook.com

Translation
Jeffrey Schnapp

Copyediting and Proofreading
Eugenia Bell

Technical Review
Philip Ording

Design and Facsimile Production
IN-FO.CO (Adam Michaels,
Shannon Harvey, Diellza Veliqi,
Clara Chirila-Rus, James Blue)

Color Separations
Echelon

Printed and bound in China through
Asia Pacific Offset